EXPLORATIONS ·IN·CANADIAN· ·FOLKLORE·

EDITH FOWKE
CAROLE H. CARPENTER

EXPLORATIONS ·IN·CANADIAN· ·FOLKLORE·

McClelland and Stewart

The Canadian Publishers
McClelland and Stewart Limited
25 Hollinger Road, Toronto M4B 3G2

Canadian Cataloguing in Publication Data
Main entry under title:
Explorations in Canadian folklore
Includes index.
Bibliography: p.
ISBN 0-7710-1909-2

1. Folklore — Canada — Addresses, essays, lectures.
2. Canada — Social life and customs — Addresses,
essays, lectures. 3. Folk music — Canada —
Addresses, essays, lectures. I. Carpenter,
Carole Henderson, 1944— II. Fowke, Edith, 1913—

GR113.E96 1985 398'0971 C85-098336-3

*The publisher gratefully acknowledges the financial
assistance of Multiculturalism Canada. The views
expressed in this book do not necessarily reflect the
position or policy of the Government of Canada.*

Typography and assembly by The Literary Service,
Toronto, Ontario

Printed and bound in Canada by Webcom Limited

Acknowledgements

"String Figures of the Eskimo" by Diamond Jenness, from *Report of the Canadian Arctic Expedition 1913-1918*, Volume 13, Part B. Reproduced by permission of the Minister of Supply and Services Canada.

"Ballads from Devil's Island" by Helen Creighton, reproduced by permission of *Dalhousie Review*.

"Cruising for Ballads in Nova Scotia" by W. M. Doerflinger, from *Canadian Geographical Journal*. Reproduced by permission of the Royal Canadian Geographical Society.

Excerpt from *The Music Hunter* by Laura C. Boulton. Copyright © 1969 by Laura C. Boulton. Reprinted by permission of Doubleday & Co., Inc.

"D'Sonoqua," from *Klee Wyck* by Emily Carr © 1941, Clarke, Irwin & Company Limited. Used by permission of Clarke, Irwin (1983) Inc.

"The Man Who Plucked the Gorbey" by Edward D. Ives. Reproduced by permission of the American Folklore Society from the *Journal of American Folklore* 74(291): 1-8, 1961.

"The Cut-Off Head Frozen On: Some International Versions of a Tall Tale" by Herbert Halpert. Reproduced by permission of Herbert Halpert and *Canadian Folklore canadien*.

Contents

Introduction

There is at present no book that deals with English-language folklore studies in Canada in any comprehensive way. In an attempt to fill that gap, we offer a variety of articles by many of our major folklore scholars and by some interested amateurs, collectors, and informants. The items range in time over a century or more, and they deal with various types of oral traditions drawn from many sub-cultural groups, including Canadians of English, Scottish, Irish, French, German, Jewish, Mennonite, Ukrainian, Amerindian, and Inuit ancestry. Introductory notes on each item tell something about the author and suggest the reasons why the article has been chosen.

The material has been arranged in four groups, beginning with early descriptions of contacts with Indians and Inuit and a pioneer article on Newfoundland dialect. The second section, dealing with personal experiences, presents first-hand descriptions of old-time customs among Scots in Nova Scotia and Mennonites in Ontario, plus a traditional singer's account of her family background and the part songs played in her childhood. In the third section, collectors describe their experiences with their informants: three accounts by major Maritime collectors convey a wealth of information about the backgrounds of the people who have preserved our songs along with comments on the songs themselves, and a fourth collector, Laura Boulton, gives a colourful account of her recording of Inuit songs. The final article in this section comes from a woman who, though best known as an artist, was also a sensitive writer and an ardent observer of Indian life.

Our fourth section moves into more straightforward folkloristic pieces: comprehensive surveys of folktales, folk dancing, old-time fiddling, and folk medicine. The last section proceeds to the final stage of folklore studies: analysis. Here the authors move beyond description and comparison to discuss the operation and functions of various types of folklore within their communities. They tell us how threats of bogeymen figures help to control children in Newfoundland, how French-Canadian story-tellers use the theory of a soul separated from the body, how parables are used to influence conduct in a Jewish family, why ethnic jokes continue to be a popular form of folklore, and why Anglo Canadians have neglected their folklore.

As far as possible we have selected material that is not easily available. Some of the items come from out-of-print volumes; others appeared originally in rather obscure journals or in early issues of better-known journals. The sources of the items are listed on pages 387-90, and they are followed by a brief bibliography. Footnotes for all articles are given in the endmatter, beginning on page 361.

By bringing together articles from many diverse sources, we have tried to give a general perspective on the different types of folklore studies in Canada. Subjects covered include folksongs, folktales, folk fiddling, folk language, folk dances, folk medicine, and folk customs. However, a glance at the table of contents will indicate that a high proportion of the articles deal with folksong. This is deliberate and almost unavoidable, for until recently Canadian collectors have concentrated on folksong. We have a great many fine collections of traditional songs but comparatively few dealing with folktales or other forms of folklore. That disparity is being corrected by modern folklore students, and in the future it will be possible to present a more balanced picture. In the meantime, we believe that our selection is fairly representative of what has been done up to the present.

We hope that this book will show the reader the various ways in which folklore material can be studied, and will suggest how such study can improve our understanding of different peoples. Many Canadians, especially those of the majority Anglophone group, are not sufficiently aware of folklore and its meaning. We feel that to appreciate folklore is the key to cultural maturity. In our multicultural environment we need to understand the role of folk traditions in each person's life so that distinctive cultural heritages may not be divisive. If all Canadians could come to realize that everyone has these traditions, it would help to unify people of various ancestries. The differences among them are relatively superficial: the important thing is that all peoples have traditions and consider them significant at some level. We hope that the articles in this book will help our readers to appreciate this common heritage.

— Edith Fowke and
Carole H. Carpenter

I. EARLY ACCOUNTS

Life Among the Haida
W. H. Collison

*Of all the available early accounts of contact with Amer-
indians, some of the most interesting are those of missionaries. These documents — diaries and journals, reports to
superiors, and memoirs alike — contain not only records of
actual traditions but also clear evidence of the Europeans'
critical opinions of and reactions to the North American
native cultures.*

*During the latter half of the nineteenth century, mission-
aries of various persuasions travelled the rugged coastline
of British Columbia ministering to the spiritual and,
frequently, physical needs of the Northwest Coast tribes.
The entrenched attitudes and principles of Victorian times
surface in the writings of these men: most importantly
their sense of superiority to the "savages" they were
bringing to God; their dedication to the Protestant Work
Ethic; their acceptance of progress, technology, and the
consequent inevitable destruction of the native way of life.
Few indeed were those servants of a foreign God who
sympathized with the confusion of the Indians: pre-
contact, their cultural traditions were highly developed
and exceptionally elaborate; post-contact, they straddled
two cultural worlds, unable to dwell at peace in either.*

William Henry Collison was an unusually sensitive missionary. He spent some twenty-one years (1873-1894) in service with the Church Missionary Society on the Northwest Coast. The first missionary to work among the Haida on the Queen Charlotte Islands, Collison was in a unique position to witness the transformation of a people through contact with the white man's church. The two excerpts from his memoirs that follow represent his attempts to record and comment upon native customs on the one hand, and to document the adaptation of the Indians to Euro-American ways on the other. The first segment concerns the potlatch, the central ceremony of the Northwest Coast people and a prime target of many missionaries and government officials; while the other concerns the natives' interpretation of and reaction to a key Christian festivity, Christmas.

A. The Potlatch

A large fleet of Haida arrived from several other villages to attend a great potlatch by special invitation, and a great reception had been prepared for them. As their large canoes approached the shore, each propelled by from twelve to twenty rowers arranged in equal numbers on either side of the canoes, a skilful display of paddling was given. Now they made the stroke as one man, without causing the slightest sound or raising a ripple on the water, indicating the stealthy manner in which they approached their foes in a night attack. At a given signal, with a loud war whoop they dashed their paddles deep into the water, causing the foam to fly, while the canoes were almost lifted by the stroke as they made a united dash upon their supposed enemy. Instantly this was changed to a paean of triumph, while they kept in perfect time to the chant with their paddles. They swept shorewards, imitating the flight of the weary eagle by two strokes and a rest between, alternated with three strokes and a pause. This exhibition was ended by every two oarsmen crossing their paddles in mid-air over the centre of their canoes as they touched the shore.

The chiefs and leading men occupied the seats between the rowers, the women and children, with their provisions and bedding, were accommodated on the bottom of the canoes, thus ballasting their light craft. Several of the leading canoes had small cannon mounted on the bows. From these a salute was fired on nearing the shore; but the concussion was too strong for one of the canoes. It split almost from bow to stern, and this would have proved serious had it not been so close to land. The occupants remained quite composed although the water was rushing in, and they succeeded in beaching the canoe just as she was sinking. But as the chanting and dancing were well sustained by the occupants of the other canoes, this accident passed almost unperceived by the others.

Many of the dancers wore headdresses and wooden masks of various patterns; in every case the mask or head-dress indicates the crest to which the bearer belongs. Thus the masks and headdresses worn by the members of the eagle crest bear a resemblance to the eagle either by the likeness of the nose to the eagle's hook-shaped beak, or by the white eagle feathers surmounting the mask. The members of the finback whale crest wear masks surmounted by a large fin; while the wolf, the bear, and the frog were all well represented by the members of the crests of which these are the signs.

It is not a little significant, however, to find how very

closely the use of the ermine skin by the Indians of all the tribes on the Northwest Coast approaches the use of it in the state dresses of royalty and nobility in England. The higher the rank of an Indian chief, the greater the number of ermine skins he was entitled to wear attached to his *shikeed*, or dancing dress, and hanging from it down his back, in rows of three to six in width. The Master of the Robes in the English court is careful that neither duke, earl, or knight may adorn himself with more ermine skins than is permitted by court etiquette. And, as it cannot be said that the Indians have adopted the custom from the whites, we hesitate to admit that the whites have acquired it from the Indians. We can only recognize in it the similarity of human nature, and admit that here, indeed, the extremes meet in the tastes and adornments of the highest civilization and the gay trappings of the untutored Indian chief.

A great feast had been prepared for the visitors in the houses of the leading chiefs, and to this they were led, preceded by the dancers. On entering, great fires of logs, piled several feet in height, diffused a glow of heat around, and the blaze was intensified by slaves pouring seal oil and eulachon grease in large quantities upon the fires. The visitors having been seated according to rank, entertainers entered arrayed in their dancing costume, of which the most attractive objects were the *dadjung*, or dancing headdress, and the *shikeed*, or dancing robe. The crown-shaped receptacle on the top of each of the dancing headdresses was well filled with the swan and eagle's down. As they danced in and around before their guests, they bowed before each, causing a shower of down to fall on each guest, a most significant mark of both peace and honour. The dance was accompanied by the music of the chant and drum, while the words of the chant expressed their pleasure and the rank and record of their guests. When the *ithdanua,* or down, had thus been scattered, their feasting began.

It was not uncommon to place a small canoe filled with berries, preserved in grease and mixed with snow, before a number of their guests. The chief dishes were served up in wooden bowls and trenchers, skilfully carved, and inlaid with mother-of-pearl. Dried salmon and halibut with eulachon grease followed, with boiled seaweed (dulse), also mixed with fish and grease, and, lastly, as dessert, a bitter-tasting berry (*hugutlite*), beaten up with water until it became a mass of froth. This was eaten in a peculiar manner, with long, narrow wooden spoons (shaped like miniature oars or paddles), being pressed out of the mouth and quickly drawn in again in order to expel part of the air with which it is mixed. This is attended with an unusual sound. In endeavouring to imitate and execute this native custom, the white man, if a guest, is seldom successful, and must be prepared to be greeted with salvos of laughter at his failure.

The first item in the program of this potlatch to which these visitors had been invited was the erection of a great totem or crest pole. Among all the tribes on the coast, none surpassed the Haida in the carving and erection of these totems. In this, and in the designing and finishing of their large war canoes, the Haida excelled all the coast tribes, whether in British Columbia or on the Alaskan coast. They had one natural advantage: the very fine cedar trees which were to be found in their islands.

A tree, proportionate to the dimensions of the totem required, and free from large knots or blemishes, was first selected, roughly prepared, and conveyed to the camp. Then the chief of a crest differing from that of the chief for whom the totem was to be carved was invited to enter upon the work. If he was not sufficiently skilful himself, he called one or more of the most skilful of his own crest to assist him in the undertaking. Having received instructions as to the various figures to be represented, their number and order, proceeding from base to top, the workmen commenced operations.

In the carving of a totem pole very often a legend or tradition in which the ancestors of the chief and his crest were the chief actors is selected, and thus the totem is but an illustration of the legend. In some villages may be seen totems surmounted by figures resembling men wearing tall hats. This indicates that the owner's ancestor or ancestors first saw the white men who are here represented. Standing by a skilled carver on one occasion who had been engaged to carve a very elaborate totem, I was surprised at the apparently reckless manner in which he cut and hewed away with a large axe as though regardless of consequences. "Where is your plan?" I inquired. "Are you not afraid to spoil your tree?" "No," he replied, "the white man, when about to make anything, first traces it on paper, but the Indian has all his plans here," as he significantly pointed to his forehead.

Having cut out the outline roughly with the axe, he then proceeded to fine workmanship with an adze. On my last visit I found him polishing off a perfect pattern with the dried skin of the dogfish, which is much more effective for this purpose than sandpaper.

When it is remembered that formerly all such work as the preparation and carving of their totem poles, the construction of their well-proportioned canoes, and the building and decoration of their dwellings were executed with stone tools, it will appear less surprising that they can accomplish such work now with the improved tools and implements. The chief or chiefs who are engaged to carve the totem or crest pole are not paid until the potlatch takes place. They are then rewarded, not according to their time and labour, but rather according to their rank and the amount of property at the disposal of the chief for distribution to those who have been invited.

But there were yet other customs among the Haida connected with the potlatch. One of these was tattooing. I had occasion to enter a lodge one morning shortly before a potlatch took place, and was not a little surprised to see all around the lodge men in every attitude undergoing this painful operation, some on the chest, some on the back, and others on the arms, all being tattooed with the figures peculiar to their own crest. In this instance the figures were the eagle and beaver, as they belonged to the eagle crest.

The operators were evidently quite expert in their work. Each of them had a number of thin strips of wood of various widths, in which needles were firmly fixed as teeth in a comb. Some of these sticks had but two or three needles, others more, according to the width of the pattern or device to be marked. The peculiar sound caused by such a number all pricking the skin of their subjects caused quite a nervous sensation in the bystander. Blood was flowing freely from many of them, and that it was rather a painful process was evidenced by their faces. Many were smoking, thus seeking to conceal their misery and console their feelings with the pipe. Others had their lips firmly compressed, but not one by either sign or sound indicated the painfulness of the process. That the subsequent suffering when inflammation had set in was severe I discovered by a number of them coming to me for some application to subdue the swelling and soothe the irritation. This was caused by the poisonous colours which had been rubbed in.

Not a few of the Haida had their faces tattooed when I first went among them, and these reminded me strongly of the Maori of New Zealand. The few of these who now remain are ashamed of the disfigurement, especially on embracing Christianity. When the potlatch took place, these men who had been thus tattooed were rewarded by receiving blankets or other property proportionate to the honour which they had thus rendered to the chief. Even worse practices were sometimes resorted to in the erection of the totem at a potlatch. It was not uncommon formerly, when the opening had been dug out in which the totem was to be erected, to bind one or more slaves, either male or female, and cast them alive into the opening. Then, amidst shouting and clamour which drowned the cries of the victims, the great totem was hoisted up into position by hundreds of helpers and the opening around it filled in with stones and earth firmly beaten down.

On one occasion a young woman, a slave, fled over one hundred miles to our mission in order to escape such a terrible fate. The night before the day fixed for her destruction she succeeded in launching a small canoe, unaided and unperceived, and fled. The punishments and privations which she had passed through had prostrated her, and although we used every means to restore her to health, she succumbed three weeks after her arrival. There was hope in her death, as we had with the assistance of another freed slave endeavoured to lead her to a saving knowledge of the Truth.

When the day for the great event has arrived, all the property is brought forth and exhibited in heaps within and without the lodge. The guests are then arranged around according to the rank, their first or inner row being formed of the leading chiefs. Behind them sit the sub-chiefs or those of the second rank. Next appear the *haade*, or free men. These are the counsellors of the chiefs. The next rows are arranged according to the social position in the tribe. On the outside are assembled the slaves. The presiding chief then delivers an introductory speech, recounting the rank and deeds of his ancestors and his own exploits and position among them. Not infrequently this opportunity is used to resent an insult either actual or supposed, or to inflict one. The chief's assistants, being sub-chiefs of his own crest, then call out the name of each recipient and the amount and description of property given.

Often large numbers of slaves were first given away, then copper shields, furs, blankets either in bale or numbered, guns, rifles, canoes, and latterly, as currency has become more common among them, both gold and silver is distributed; also whole pieces of print, white calico, and flannel. These latter are generally torn up in pieces and strips, and given away to the rank and file, as also blankets, &c. At one of the latest potlatches, where I was permitted to enter and conduct a short service, I observed near to where I stood a washbasin nearly full of silver, in one-dollar and half-dollar pieces. Much has been said and written, both for and against this custom, principally by outsiders who are unacquainted with the social life of the Indians. Having resided among them for three decades, and learned their languages, Tsimshian, Haida and Nishga, I can testify from knowledge and experience that the potlatch of today is not what it was in the past. The same may be said of the heathenism of the present as compared with that of a quarter of a century ago. Both have been reformed by the influence of Christianity. The tearing and devouring of dogs and human flesh was then almost a nightly practice in every heathen camp. Now it is unknown. Slavery has been abolished. Sorcery is ashamed to declare itself, and the medicine man has been denuded of all his terrors.

B. A Haida Christmas

On my return to Masset, my first object was to select a suitable site for our proposed Mission House. . . . We selected a site on a raised plateau on the edge of the forest behind the village, and succeeded in inducing a number of the young men to assist us in clearing it.

But the Haida were not familiar with regular work, and we had to be content with an occasional spurt. I succeeded, however, in persuading some of them to procure me a raft of cedar logs. Having provided myself with a ship saw, I constructed a sawpit, and taught them how to saw every log just down the centre, having first hewn off two sides. In building I erected these, all being made equal in length, with the sawn sides turned inwards, thus giving me a smooth surface on the interior. By first placing the wall-plate in position, each upright was spiked to this, and thus my walls stood firm.

I was unfortunate, however, in my sawyers. One after another they began haemorrhaging, caused probably by the continual up-and-down motion of the arms acting upon the lungs. The medicine men were not slow in making use of this to my disadvantage, by assuring them that it was owing to my sorcery, as I was endeavouring to kill them.

With the aid of my Tsimshian, who was a good workman and a faithful Christian, I encouraged them to resume work. I had some difficulty in persuading them to rest on Sunday. Hitherto every day had been alike to them, and as my Dance House had now been transformed and prepared for our services, I was anxious to assemble as many as I could for instruction. Accordingly I had a flagstaff erected, and, having provided myself with two flags, one small and one large, I publicly announced that the smaller ensign would be displayed on the Saturday, while the large flag would be hauled up on the day of rest.

From this, Saturday became known as *Sunday ga hwitzoo*, or little Sunday, while the Sunday proper became known as *Shantlan shanzotang*, or the rest day. It is interesting to note in this connection that the Tsimshian had learned to designate Sunday as *hali kanootk*, or the dress day, prior to the advent of the missionaries. Under Christian teaching, Sunday is known by a term similar in meaning to the Haida, *hali squait-ka-sha*, the day of rest. In the same way the Tsimshians had acquired from the employees of the H.B.C. the idea that Christmas was the great dress day, *Welaixim hali kanootk*, and from the Tsimshian the Haida had learned of this. Consequently my congregation at the first Christmas service on the islands was the most singular I have ever ministered to.

As the Dance House had been fully prepared for service, I sent out messengers to announce the service, and informed them of the occasion. I had induced two fine young chiefs, who had evinced their desire to help me, to act as stewards or sidesmen, and to preserve order.

As the Haida began to crowd in, I was surprised at the strange garments in which many of them were clothed. A sub-chief entered arrayed in a dressing gown with a large old-style pattern on it, reminding one of the garbs worn by the victims of the Inquisition when proceeding to an *auto-da-fé*. He was followed by his wife, with a bright counterpane fastened around her by a girdle of rope. Next my attention was attracted by musical sounds approaching and a young lad, the son of a leading chief, entered in a harlequin's dress of many colours, trimmed around with many small bells, which jingled and tinkled with his every movement, and which attracted the attention of all. The next most striking figure was that of an old chief, gaunt and of great stature, dressed in an admiral's uniform, which was much too small for him. The sleeves of the coat extended below his elbows, while the epaulettes stood out from his neck somewhat like a horse collar, and the trousers only reached a little below his knees. On the back of his head a tall beaver hat was fastened, to prevent it from falling off, as it was also too small. He evidently considered himself a most important personage, as he waited until one of the attendants approached and conducted him to a seat.

All shapes and colours of garbs were in evidence, especially naval and military uniforms of England and the United States. I was reminded rather of a fancy dress ball than of a congregation gathered for a religious service. But the most striking figure was yet to come. The building was crowded, and I had just stood up to commence the service, when the door was thrown open and a leading medicine man appeared, arrayed in a white surplice. His long hair was rolled around a pair of horns, which extended out from either side of his head at the back, giving him a demoniacal appearance. He advanced steadily, without looking to either side, and made his way towards the platform on which I stood. Suddenly it flashed upon me that he considered it his right to occupy a place beside me, because of his robe of office. To my great relief, however, he stopped short and took his seat just beside the platform.

With some difficulty I collected my thoughts and proceeded with the service, which was indeed unique, whether as regarding the building, the congregation, or the occasion. They had obtained these dresses and uniforms by barter with the southern tribes during their annual expeditions. The surplice which the medicine man appeared in had probably been stolen and then sold to the Indians. But these showed that they were beginning to realize the necessity of something more suitable in which to array themselves than a bearskin or a blanket. And I never saw these again. Before the next Christmas came around, the Haida had become more enlightened in regard at least to dress.

One of their objections to the reception of the truths of Christianity was that it had impoverished the people who had abandoned the potlatch and the old heathen customs, and had accepted it. "Formerly," I was told, "the Tsimshian lodges were well furnished with boxes all filled with blankets and other property, but now their chests are empty. Our chests are well filled now, but, if we become Christians, we too shall be poor." "Yes," I replied, "but the Tsimshian have all good clothing now, both for Sundays and dress days, and also for working in, and their houses are more comfortable and better furnished. This is better than heaping up blankets for the potlatch. And after a potlatch you are really poor, for you have given away all you had."

W. H. Collison, 1915

The Buffalo Hunt
John Macoun
Paul Kane

Folklorists find much of value in journals, diaries, reports, and letters from yesteryear. When most people were illiterate and the mass culture was largely oral, contemporary written records were scarce, and those available are valuable as documents of otherwise unrecorded cultural traditions. Further, if careful observers objectively recorded what they saw or experienced, their accounts are more important than the removed judgements of later writers.

Pioneer Canada was blessed with numerous documentors — amateur and unconscious ethnographers. In the early seventeenth century the Jesuit priests recorded their missionary activities among the Indians and so produced accounts of native traditions from the time of early contact. Explorers such as Henry Kelsey and John Franklin meticulously recounted what they saw and experienced in new lands and among different peoples. Travellers like Alexis de Toqueville and Isabel Lucy Bird sometimes provided accounts and interpretations of considerable value.

The records of visitors and literate settlers are particularly significant to Canadian folklorists where virtually no contemporary accounts by members of cultural groups themselves exist, as of the Métis traditions. The Métis were

migratory people of mixed culture who recorded excep-
tionally few of their traditions, and by the end of the
nineteenth century little remained of their culture, even in
memory. Consequently, their traditional life must be
reconstructed from the available documents of outsiders.

Two particularly good accounts of the famed Métis
buffalo hunt follow. Paul Kane (1810-1871) travelled
across the Hudson's Bay territories from Ontario to the
west coast and recorded his impressions both visually and
in writing. The paintings he produced are an important
ethnographic document of native traditions. His descrip-
tions are, like this one, personal and impressionistic, yet
replete with information. For comparison, John Macoun,
a historian, gives a more impersonal account, although he
also includes an eye-witness story.

THE BUFFALO HUNT I

The Bison or Buffalo, in former times, covered the great
plains, both in summer and winter, and, today, their bones
lie bleaching on the prairies from Pembina to the Rocky
Mountains, and from the International Boundary to Peace
River. It is doubtful whether the great herds passed constantly from the Saskatchewan to Peace River, but this, at
any rate, is certain: their bones lie on those northern
prairies, and their paths yet seam the foothills of the Rocky
Mountains. In the winter of 1870, the last buffalo were
killed north of Peace River, but in 1875, about 1,000 head
were still in existence between the Athabasca and Peace

rivers, north of Little Slave Lake. These are called Wood Buffalo by the hunters, but differ only in size from those of the plain. During the last three years, the great herds have been kept south of our boundary, and as the result of this, our Indians have been on the verge of starvation. Where the hills were covered with countless thousands in 1877, the Blackfeet were dying of starvation in 1879. A few returned last fall, but they are only the remnants of the former myriads, and soon these will disappear, never to return. While on the plains with the Halfbreeds, many a spot has been pointed out where they had a splendid "run." As they related the incidents of *conflict*, their eyes would glow and their whole demeanour would change, so that they appeared different beings from what they were a few minutes before.

Buffalo hunting in former days was peculiarly exciting and gave a zest to prairie life that was most bewitching to the young and adventurous. Twice a year, hundreds of families would assemble on the Red River plains, and placing themselves under the leadership of tried hunters and fearless Indian traders, start for the buffalo plains. When they entered the Indian country, they coralled their animals every night, and set regular watches like soldiers in an enemy's country. Often five or six hundred carts would be in the train, and every evening when they stopped for the night, these carts would be formed in a circle with their shafts inwards. After the horses had fed, they were brought within the circle and the watch was set. All men in the party were amenable to the same laws and assisted at the making of them, so that a Halfbreed encampment was a small military republic.

When the party struck buffalo, a permanent camp was pitched, and the "buffalo runners" (horses trained to hunt buffalo) were caught and examined. Scouts were sent out to locate a herd, and on their return, all the men intending to take part in the "run" presented themselves mounted, with gun on arm and whip in hand, or rather hung by a thong to the wrist. Under direction of their captain, they quietly separate in skirmishing order, and advancing under cover of the swells, almost if not altogether surround the herd. At a given signal, all dash forward; as they charge, the light of battle shines in their faces, and their very steeds quiver with excitement.

Hurrying to the top of a hill, a *non-combatant* sees a wide and almost circular plain filled with horsemen and wild terror-stricken animals dashing hither and thither, and over all the confused tumult, the bellowing of bulls and the sharp crack of the rifles are heard. Apparently, the horses are moving without guidance. See that beautiful black dash up to a fat cow and almost halt, while his rider sends the death-dealing bullet. Like a flash, the buffalo turns and charges the horse, but a slight pressure of the knee causes him likewise to swerve, and the buffalo dashes past. In another instant, the horse is again alongside, and another shot rolls her over dead. While we have been watching this episode, a number of old bulls have led the way over the rise, and a few minutes elapse before the grassy plain is left untenanted, except by the dead and dying. The women now come on the scene and set to work, each apparently knowing those killed by her friends. On the return of the hunters, it is found that over two hundred animals have fallen, and by the camp fires that night enough anecdotes of former "runs" and reminiscences of Indian fights are told to fill a volume. After witnessing one buffalo hunt, I cannot blame the Halfbreed and the Indian for leaving the farm and wildly making for the plains when it is reported that buffalo have crossed "the border."

Doctor Hector gives the following account of what he saw on the morning of the 26th December, 1857, about sixty miles to the west of Fort Pitt, in the valley of the Vermilion River: "This morning we were off by 4.30 a.m., and had gone a considerable distance when we saw fresh traces of Indians, and soon heard the bawling and screaming of an immense camp, all in a high state of excitement. Diverging from our path to pay them a visit, we found that they had succeeded in driving a large band of buffaloes into their 'pound' during the night, and were now engaged in slaughtering them. The scene was more repulsive than pleasant or exciting. The pound is a circular strong fencing about fifty yards in diameter, made of stakes with boughs interlaced, and into this place were crammed more than 100 buffaloes, bulls, cows, and calves. A great number were already killed, and the live ones were tumbling about furiously over the dead bodies of their companions, and I hardly think the space would have held them all alive without some being on the top of the others, and, in addition, the bottom of the pound was strewn with fragments of carcasses left from former slaughters in the same place. It was on a slope, and the upper part of the fencing was increased in height by skins stretched on poles, for the purpose of frightening the buffaloes from jumping out. This is not needed at the lower part of the enclosure, as the animals always endeavour to jump uphill. The entrance to the enclosure is by an inclined plane made of rough logs leading to a gap, through which the buffaloes suddenly jump about six feet into the ring, and then they cannot return. To this entrance converge lines of little heaps of buffaloes' dung or brush for several miles into the prairie which surrounds the clump of wood in which the pound is concealed. These lines serve to lead the buffalo in the required direction when they have been driven into the neighbourhood. When first captured and driven into the pound, which difficult matter is effected by strategy, the buffaloes run round and round violently, and the Indians affirm, always with the sun. Crouching on the fencing were the Indians, even mere boys and young girls, all busy plying bows and arrows, guns and spears, and even knives to accomplish the destruction of the buffaloes. After firing their arrows, they generally succeeded in extracting them again by a noose on the end of a pole, and some had even the pluck to jump into the area and pull them out with their hands; but if an old bull or a cow happened to observe them, they had to be very active in getting out again. The scene was a busy but a bloody one, and had to be carried on until every animal was killed, to enable them to get the meat. I helped by trying the penetrating power of rifle balls on the shaggy skulls of the animals with invariable success; and it is the least cruel way of killing them, as they drop at once. There are many superstitions connected with the whole business, and the Indians always consider their success in procuring buffaloes in this manner depends on the pleasure of the Manito, to whom they always make offerings, which they place under the entrance of the pound where I saw a collection of Indian valuables, among which were bridles, powder horns, tobacco, beads, and the like, placed there by the believing Indian, only to be stolen by the first scamp in the camp who could manage the theft adroitly. In the centre of the pound, also, there is a tall pole on which they hang offerings, to which pieces of idolatry I was in a manner an accessory by giving them my pocket handkerchief to convert into a flag."

John Macoun, 1883

33

THE BUFFALO HUNT II

The following afternoon we arrived at the margin of a small lake, where we encamped rather earlier than usual, for the sake of the water. Next day I was gratified with the sight of a band of about forty buffalo cows in the distance, and our hunters in full chase; they were the first I had seen, but were too far off for me to join in the sport. They succeeded in killing twenty-five, which were distributed through the camp, and proved most welcome to all of us, as our provisions were getting rather short, and I was abundantly tired of pemmican and dried meat. The fires being lighted with the wood we had brought with us in the carts, the whole party commenced feasting with a voracity which appeared perfectly astonishing to me, until I tried myself, and found by experience how much hunting on the plains stimulates the appetite.

The upper part of the hunch of the buffalo, weighing four or five pounds, is called by the Indians the little hunch. This is of a harder and more compact nature than the rest, though very tender, and is usually put aside for keeping. The lower and larger part is streaked with fat and is very juicy and delicious. These, with the tongues, are considered the delicacies of the buffalo. After the party had gorged themselves with as much as they could devour, they passed the evening in roasting the marrow bones and regaling themselves with their contents.

For the next two or three days we fell in with only a single buffalo, or small herds of them; but as we proceeded, they became more frequent. At last our scouts brought in word of an immense herd of buffalo bulls about two miles in advance of us. They are known in the distance from the cows by their feeding singly and being scattered wider over the plain, whereas the cows keep together for the protection of the calves, which are always kept in the centre of the herd. A Halfbreed, of the name of Hallett, who was exceedingly attentive to me, woke me in the morning, to accompany him in advance of the party, that I might have the opportunity of examining the buffalo whilst feeding, before the commencement of the hunt. Six hours' hard riding brought us within a quarter of a mile of the nearest of the herd. The main body stretched over the plains as far as the eye could reach. Fortunately the wind blew in our faces: had it blown towards the buffaloes, they would have scented us miles off. I wished to have attacked them at once, but my companion would not allow me until the rest of the party came up, as it was contrary to the law of the tribe. We, therefore, sheltered ourselves from the observation of the herd behind a mound, relieving our horses of their saddles to cool them. In about an hour the hunters came up to us, numbering about one hundred and thirty, and immediate preparations were made for the chase. Every man loaded his gun, looked to his priming, and examined the efficiency of his saddle-girths.

The elder men strongly cautioned the less experienced not to shoot each other; a caution by no means unnecessary, as such accidents frequently occur. Each hunter then filled his mouth with balls, which he drops into the gun without wadding; by this means loading much quicker and being enabled to do so whilst his horse is at full speed. It is true that the gun is more liable to burst but that they do not seem to mind. Nor does the gun carry so far or so true; but that is of less consequence, as they always fire quite close to the animal.

Everything being adjusted, we all walked our horses towards the herd. By the time we had gone about two hundred yards, the herd perceived us and started off in the opposite direction at the top of their speed. We now put our horses to the full gallop, and in twenty minutes were in their midst. There could not have been less than four or five thousand in our immediate vicinity, all bulls, not a single cow amongst them.

The scene now became one of intense excitement; the huge bulls thundering over the plain in headlong confusion, whilst the fearless hunters rode recklessly in their midst, keeping up an incessant fire at but a few yards' distance from their victims. Upon the fall of each buffalo, the successful hunter merely threw some article of his apparel — often carried by him solely for that purpose — to denote his own prey, and then rushed on to another. These marks are scarcely ever disputed, but should a doubt arise as to the ownership, the carcass is equally divided among the claimants.

The chase continued only about one hour, and extended over an area of from five to six square miles, where might be seen the dead and dying buffaloes, to the number of five hundred. In the meantime, my horse, which had started at a good run, was suddenly confronted by a large bull that made his appearance from behind a knoll, within a few yards of him, and being thus taken by surprise, he sprung to one side, and getting his foot into one of the innumerable badger holes with which the plains abound, he fell at once, and I was thrown over his head with such violence that I was completely stunned, but soon recovered my recollection. Some of the men caught my horse, and I was speedily remounted, and soon saw reason to congratulate myself on my good fortune, for I found a man who had been thrown in a similar way lying a short distance from me, quite senseless, in which state he was carried back to the camp.

I again joined in the pursuit; and coming up with a large bull, I had the satisfaction of bringing him down at the first fire. Excited by my success, I threw down my cap and galloping on, soon put a bullet through another enormous animal. He did not, however, fall, but stopped and faced me, pawing the earth, bellowing and glaring savagely at me. The blood was streaming profusely from his mouth and I thought he would soon drop. The position in which he stood was so fine that I could not resist the desire of making a sketch. I accordingly dismounted, and had just commenced when he suddenly made a dash at me. I had hardly time to spring on my horse and get away from him, leaving my gun and everything else behind.

When he came up to where I had been standing, he turned over the articles I had dropped, pawing fiercely as he tossed them about, and then retreated towards the herd. I immediately recovered my gun, and having reloaded, again pursued him, and soon planted another shot in him; and this time he remained on his legs long enough for me to make a sketch. This done I returned with it to the camp, carrying the tongues of the animals I had killed, according to custom, as trophies of my success as a hunter.

I have often witnessed an Indian buffalo hunt since, but never one on so large a scale. In returning to the camp, I fell in with one of the hunters coolly driving a wounded buffalo before him. In answer to my inquiry why he did not shoot him, he said he would not do so until he got him close to the lodges, as it would save the trouble of bringing a cart for the meat. He had already driven him seven miles, and afterwards killed him within two hundred yards of the tents. That evening, while the hunters were still absent, a buffalo, bewildered by the hunt, got amongst the tents, and at last got into one, after having terrified all the women and children, who precipitately took to flight. When the men returned, they found him there still, and being unable to dislodge him, they shot him down from the opening in the top.

Paul Kane, 1859

Notes on the Dialect of the People of Newfoundland
George Patterson

Scholars frequently note that the primary means of identifying a folk group is a distinctive speech. It clearly separates insiders from outsiders and facilitates communication within the group while inhibiting it without.

No other Canadian dialect is more unusual and readily recognized than the folk speech of Newfoundlanders. Popular writers and scholars alike have recorded the characteristic sayings, meanings and usages of Newfoundlanders for years. Tourism literature and other works designed for external consumption, such as The Book of Newfoundland *edited by Joey Smallwood, have typically carried sections devoted to this distinctive way of talking that, in its archaisms, vocabulary, syntax, and other technical characteristics, reflects the predominantly West English and Irish heritage of the Newfoundland people.*

A concern for language is often connected with folklife studies, especially when nationalist or regional sentiments are also present. French-Canadian scholars have, for instance, seriously studied the distinctive speech of their heritage since the early years of the nineteenth century. That language and culture are inextricably linked explains this concern as well as the union of studies of language and popular traditions in the primary Francophone folklore centre in North America, CÉLAT at Université Laval in Quebec City.

In Newfoundland the academic study of folk speech developed hand-in-hand with folklore work so that the depository of traditional material at the Memorial University of Newfoundland in St. John's is the Folklore and Language Archive. Recently the research on Newfoundland speech bore fruit in the form of The Dictionary of Newfoundland English *(compiled by G. Story, W. Kirwin & J.D.A. Widdowson), an especially well-received and valuable book.*

The following article is the earliest important discussion of Newfoundland speech. George Patterson (1824-1897) was a minister from Nova Scotia who visited in Newfoundland in the late 1800s. Because the language of the persons he encountered fascinated him, he undertook to study it seriously. This work is his major publication on the subject.

In recently visiting Newfoundland, I had not more than begun to associate with her people till I observed them using English words in a sense different from what I had ever heard elsewhere. This was the case, to some extent, in the speech of the educated, in their law proceedings, and in the public press, but of course was more marked among the uneducated. Among them, particularly, I found, in addition, words in use which were entirely new to me. Further intercourse convinced me that these peculiarities presented an interesting subject of study, and during the short time at my disposal, with the assistance of kind friends, among whom I must specially mention Judge

Bennett of Harbour Grace, I made as full a collection as circumstances would permit of words in use strange to me or used in peculiar senses.

In explanation of the origin of these peculiarities, I may mention that most of the original settlers of Newfoundland came either from Ireland or the West of England. In consequence, the present generation very generally speak with an Irish accent. But they seem to have adopted few words from this source. From a very early period the coasts were frequented by fishermen of all nations, and thus may have been introduced words whose genesis we find difficult to trace. This influence, however, has been very limited, and their language is almost entirely English. Even the peculiarities which we are to consider will, I think, be seen by the following collection to be survivals of older forms of the language in many cases.

I. We find English words which are either obsolete or used only in some limited sense. We note the following:

Barvel, sometimes pronounced *barbel*, a tanned sheepskin used by fishermen, and also by splitters, as an apron to keep the legs dry, but since oilskin clothes have come into use, not now generally employed. Wright, in his *Dictionary of Obsolete and Provincial English*, marks it as Kentish, denoting "a short leather apron worn by washerwomen, or a slabbering bib."

Barm has now generally given way to the word yeast, but it is still commonly, if not exclusively, used in Newfoundland. So *billets*, for small sticks of wood, has now, with most English-speaking people, gone out of use. But it is quite usual in Newfoundland to hear of buying or selling billets, putting in billets, etc. The word, however, seems to have come from the French.

Brews. This is a dish which occupies almost the same place at a Newfoundlander's breakfast table that baked beans are supposed to do on that of a Bostonian. It consists of pieces of hard biscuit soaked overnight, warmed in the morning, and then eaten with boiled codfish and butter. This is plainly the old English word usually written *brewis*, variously explained. Johnson defines it as "a piece of bread soaked in boiling fat pottage made of salted meat." Worcester derives it from Gaelic *brathas*, W. *briw*, a fragment or morsel, and represents it as denoting small pieces of bread in broth. But Webster properly, we think, gives it as from the Anglo-Saxon *briw*, broth, and represents it as obsolete in the sense of broth or pottage ("What an ocean of *brewis* shall I swim in," Beaumont and Fletcher), but as still used to denote "bread soaked in gravy, or prepared in water and butter." This is the relative New England dish. Wright gives it in various forms, *brewet, brewis*, etc., as denoting pottage, but says that in the north of England they still have "a *brewis* made of slices of bread with fat broth poured over them."

Child is used to denote a female child. This is probably going out of use, as gentlemen who have resided for some time on the island say they have never heard it, but I am assured by others that on the occasion of a birth they have heard at once the inquiry, "Is it a boy or a child?" Wright gives it as Devonshire, and it was in use in Shakespeare's time, *Winter's Tale*, iii. 3, "A boy or a childe, I wonder."

Dresh, to go round visiting. A man said of a minister, "He's na'ar a bit of good for dreshing round." In old English the word is the same with the modern threshing or thrashing. This peculiar use of the word may have originated in the practice before threshing mills were in use, of men going round among farmers threshing their grain.

Drung, a narrow lane. Wright gives it under the form of

drun, as Wiltshire, with the same signification.

Dwoll, a state between sleeping and waking, a dozing. A man will say, "I got no sleep last night, I had only a dwoll." This seems kindred to the Scotch word *dwam*, which means a swoon. "He is no deid, he is only in a dwam." Wright gives a similar, if not the same word, as *dwale*, originally meaning the plant nightshade, and then a lethargic disease, or a sleeping potion.

Flaw, a strong and sudden gust of wind. Norwegian, *flage* or *flaag*. The word is used by Shakespeare and Milton:

Should patch a wall, to expel the winter's *flaw*.

— *Hamlet*.

And snow and hail and stormy gust and *flaw*.

— *Paradise Lost*.

It is still used by English seamen, and Tennyson also uses it:

Like *flaws* in summer laying lusty corn.

Frore, for froze or frozen. This is used by Milton:

The parching air

Burns *frore* and cold performs the effect of fire.

Glutch, to swallow. "My throat is so sore that I cannot *glutch* anything." Wright gives it as old English in the same sense, and adds the word *glutcher*, as meaning the throat.

Gulch. The dictionaries give the similar word *gulch* as an obsolete word, which meant to swallow ravenously, and Wright gives it as Westmoreland for to swallow. In this sense I do not hear of its being used in Newfoundland. As a noun it is used as in other parts of America, as denoting a ravine or small hollow. It is also applied to those hollows made by vehicles in snow roads, known in Canada as *pitches*. But as a verb it has come, on the Labrador coast, to have a meaning peculiar to that region and to those who frequent it. In summer, men, women, and children from Newfoundland spend some weeks there at the fishing, living in a very promiscuous way. As there is no tree for shelter for hundreds of miles of islands and shores, parties resort to the hollows for secret indulgence. Hence gulching has, among them, become a synonym for living a wanton life.

Hat, a quantity, a bunch, or a heap. A hat of trees means a clump of trees. According to Jamieson's *Scottish Dictionary*, in some parts of Scotland the word means a small heap of any kind, carelessly thrown together.

Heft, as a verb, to raise up, but especially to prove or try the weight of a thing by raising it, is marked in dictionaries as Provincial English and Colloquial United States, but it is still used in the same sense in Newfoundland. Thus one returning home with a good basket of fish may say to a friend, "heft that," feel the weight of it. And so, as a noun, it is used with the relative meaning of weight.

House place, the kitchen. In old English, according to Wright, it meant the hall, the first large room after entering the house. It is still in common use in Scotland.

Jonnick, in Newfoundland, means honest, but according to Wright, in the Northamptonshire dialect it means "kind or hospitable."

Kilter, regular order or condition; "out of kilter," dis-ordered or disarranged. It is common in old English, but generally spelled *kelter*. Thus Barrow says, "If the organs of prayer be *out of kelter*, or out of tune, how can we pray?" Under the spelling "kilter" it is common in New England.

Knap, a knoll or protuberance above surrounding land. It appears in Anglo-Saxon as *knappe*, and in kindred languages as denoting a knob or button, but in old English it denotes "the top of a hill or a rising ground" (Wright).

Linney, a small building built against a bank or another building. In New England it is generally *linter* or *lenter*. This is commonly regarded as a corruption of *lean-to*. But

Eggleston, in an article in the *Century Magazine* for April, 1894, doubts this. At all events, Wright gives *linhay* as, in the Westmoreland dialect, denoting an open shed. In this form, also, it appears in *Lorna Doone*, a novel written in the Devonshire dialect.

Mare-browed. The word *mare*, in Anglo-Saxon, means a demon or goblin, and we have a remnant of this in the word "nightmare." But there is in Newfoundland a curious survival of it in the term *mare*-browed, applied to a man whose eyebrows extend across his forehead, and who is dreaded as possessed of supernatural powers.

Mouch, to play truant, and also applied to one shirking work or duty. This is the same old English word, variously spelled *meech, meach,* and *miche*, to lie hid or to skulk, hence to cower or to be servilely humble or mean. The form *mouch* is still retained in the North of Ireland, and is also common in Scotland. I lately observed this used by the tramps in New York to denote concealing or disguising one's self. I find it also used by schoolboys in some places in Nova Scotia.

Nunch, the refreshment men take with them on going to the woods. It is an old form of the word "lunch," as "nuncheon" for "luncheon" (Wright). It is said, in old English, to denote a thick lump of bread or other edible. But by others it is regarded, we think not so probably, as referring to noon, and meaning the refreshment that the labourers partook of at that hour.

Then a Newfoundlander speaks of his head as his *poll*. Elsewhere the word is only used in reference to numbering persons, as for poll tax, or holding a poll. Shakespeare, however, uses it in its original signification — "All flaxen was his poll."

Peek, to peep, common in New England. Thus we have in Lowell's poems:

Zekle crep' up, quite unbeknown,
An' *peeked* in thru the winder.

Pook, a haycock. Wright gives it as having the same meaning in the Westmoreland dialect.

Prong, a hay or fish fork. This is the meaning given by Johnson, who does not mention it as denoting one tine of a fork. So Wright gives it as an old English word denoting a hayfork.

Putter along, an old English form, still in use in New England, for "potter," to walk languidly, or labour inefficiently.

Rampike, a dead spruce or pine tree still standing. It is used in the same sense by the lumbermen of the Maritime Provinces, and probably of New England. It is probably the same as the old English word *rampick*, an adjective "applied to the bough of a tree which has lesser branches standing out at its extremity" (Wright).

Ram's horn, a wooden pound for washing fish in. But Wright gives it as a Somerset word, denoting a sort of net to enclose fish that come in with the tide.

Randy is used, both as a noun and a verb, of the amusement of coasting. "Give us a randy," or "The boys are randying." In Anglo-Saxon it means boisterous, and "on the randy" meant living in debauchery. The word is retained in Scotland, where it means a romp or frolic, but generally in an unfavourable sense. The dictionaries, however, give *randon*, both as a noun and a verb, in old English and old French, as denoting rapid and violent motion, or going at random.

Robustious is an old English word used by Milton, the same in meaning as "robust," originally used in a favourable sense, but coming to mean violent and unruly. Hence it became a term of reproach, and finally fell out of use. But the Newfoundlanders still use it, or the similar word *robustic*, in its original favourable signification.

Scred, a piece or fragment, seems the same as "shred," the Anglo-Saxon *screade*. Webster gives Provincial English *screed*.

Seeming, judgement or opinion. Given by Johnson and Webster as obsolete, but used by the best writers of the past. Thus Milton has:

The persuasive words impregnd
With reason to her *seeming*.

And Hooker says:

Nothing more clear to their *seeming*.

In Newfoundland the sled or sleigh of the Continent, the sledge of the English, is called a *slide*, but according to Wright this is the original form in old English. *Shard* is used, as in Shakespeare's time, to denote broken pieces of pottery.

Spancel, a noun, denoting "a rope to tie a cow's hind legs," and a verb, "to tie with a rope." By Webster it is given as Provincial English, and an English gentleman informs me that the word is still common in Yorkshire.

Strouters, the outside piles of a wharf, which are larger and stronger than the inner ones, which are called *shores*. According to Wright, in Somerset dialect it denotes "anything that projects."

Starve, viz., with cold or frost. I have heard the same in Nova Scotia. Johnson gives it as a verb neuter, with one of its meanings, "to be killed with cold," and as active, with the meaning "to kill with cold," and quotes Milton's line:

From beds of raging fire to *starve* in ice.

Webster gives this meaning as common in England, but not in the United States, though he quotes W. Irving as writing "*starving* with cold as well as hunger."

Tilt, a long-house such as lumberers use; a rough, temporary shelter, like a shanty in Canada, only, instead of being built of logs laid horizontally one on the other, it is usually composed of spruce or fir sticks placed vertically and covered with bark. In Anglo-Saxon it appears as *telt* and *telde*, from *telden*, to cover. According to dictionaries, from Johnson onward, it is used to denote a tent, an awning or canopy, as over a boat.

Troth plight, one espoused or affianced. So Shakespeare:

This your son-in-law

Is *troth plight* to your daughter.

— *Winter's Tale.*

Tussock, a bunch or tuft of grass, is marked in the dictionaries as obsolete, but it is still in use in Newfoundland to denote the matted tufts of grass found on the bogs.

It is well known that the word *girl* is not found in the Anglo-Saxon or other languages of the North of Europe, and that it only occurs in two places in the authorized English [King James, 1611] version of the Bible, showing that it was then only beginning to be introduced into English. In Newfoundland it is only where the people have been intermixed with persons from other quarters that it has been used, and in more remote places it is perhaps not used yet, the word "maid," pronounced m'y-id, being almost universally employed instead.

A number of words are pronounced so differently as to seem to be almost different words. Thus "seal" is pronounced as if written *swile*, a sealer is a *swiler*, and seal hunting is *swile* hunting. A hoe is a *how*, the fir is *var*, snuffing is *snoffing*, and "never" is *naar*, which is equivalent to "not," "naar a bit" being a favourite expression to denote a strong negative.

There are also remains of old English usage in their use of the pronouns. Thus every object is spoken of as either masculine or feminine, and has either "he" or "she" applied to it. "It" seems only to be used where it has been acquired by intercourse with others. A man speaking of his head will say "he aches." Entering the court-house, I heard a witness asked to describe a cod-trap that was in dispute. He immediately replied, *"He* was about seventy-five fathoms long," etc. Other objects are spoken of as "she," not only boats and vessels, but a locomotive. I see no principle upon which the distinction is made. But of this old usage we have a remnant in the universal use of the feminine for ships.

Another old form still common is the use of the singular *thee* and *thou* instead of the plural *you.* With this is joined what is still common in parts of England — the use of the nominative for the objective, and to some extent the reverse.

Some peculiarities may be noticed also in the formation of the past tense of verbs. Thus the present *save* has the past *sove,* and *dive* is *dove.* But the very general usage is to follow the old English practice of adding "ed." Thus they say *runned* for ran, *sid* for saw, *hurted* for hurt, *falled* for fell, *comed* for came, even *sen'd* for sent, and *goed* for went. This last, however, is true English, retained in Scotland in *gaed,* while *went* does not belong to the verb at all but is the past of another verb to wend. More curious still is the use of *doned* for did or done.

The use of the letter *a,* as a prefix to participles or participial nouns, to express an action still going on, is still retained; as, a-walking, a-hunting, etc.

Again, in some places there is retained in some words the sound of *e* at the end where it is now omitted in English. Thus "hand" and "hands" are pronounced as if written "hande" and "handes." This is old English. We find it in Coverdale's version of the Bible, Tyndale's New Testament, which, however, sometimes has "honde" and "hondes," and Cranmer's. The same usage appears in some other words, but I do not know to what extent it prevails.

The word or syllable *am* is affixed seemingly only as an expletive, perhaps for the purpose of emphasis. My conjecture is that it is a corruption of the word *same*. Thus *"thisam"* and *"thesam"* were probably originally "this same" and "these same."

A number of words written with *ay*, and with most English-speaking people having the long sound of *a*, are in Newfoundland sounded as if written with a *y*. Thus they say w'y, aw'y, pr'y, pr'yer, b'y for way, away, pray, prayer, bay. So n'yebor for neighbour. This pronunciation is still retained in Scotland, and R. Lowell refers to it as in Chaucer, and quotes it as an example of the *lastingness* of linguistic peculiarities.

In their names of objects of natural history, we find the retention of a number of old English words. Thus whortleberries or blueberries are called *hurts*, nearly the same as the old English whurts or whorts, marked in the dictionaries as obsolete. Then they call a flea a *lop*, the Anglo-Saxon *loppe*, from *lope*, to leap; and wasps they call *waps*, which is the same with the Anglo-Saxon *waps* and the Low German *wepsk*. A large vicious fly is called *stout*, but according to Wright this is the Westmoreland name for the gadfly. Then the snipe is called a *snite*, which is the old English form: "The witless woodcock and his neighbour *snite*." (Drayton's "Owl.") Earthworms are termed *yesses*, which Wright gives as Dorsetshire, and which is found in dictionaries as late as Walker's.

Some names are retained, but altered in form or differently applied. Thus *grepe* seems unquestionably the same word as *grebe*; but it is used in Newfoundland to denote the sea eagle, while the original word is used to denote certain kinds of waterfowl. Then *stoat* is used for *shoat*, a young pig, and the American brown thrush or robin is called the *blackbird*.

They have a number of other names whose origin I cannot trace, some of which may have originated among themselves, but most of which were probably brought with them. Thus the medusae, or sea-nettles, are called *squidsquads*, sometimes *squidsqualls*; the echinus or sea-urchin, *ox eggs*; freshwater clams, *cocks and hens*; and to the westward smelts are known as *ministers*. The black fly is known as the *mosquito*, and the mosquito as the *nipper*.

II. A number of English words are used in peculiar senses, and it is often interesting to trace the process of the change. Perhaps in this respect the stranger is most frequently struck by the use of the words *plant* and *planter*. He reads of administration of the estate of A.B., planter, or sees the name of C.D., planter, as a candidate for the legislature, and he hears the words in connection with all their fishing operations. A planter is a man who undertakes fishing on his own account, a sort of middleman between the merchants and the fishermen. He owns or charters a vessel, obtains all supplies from the merchants, hires the men, deals with them, superintends the fishing, and on his return deals with the merchants for the fruits of the adventure. A man will speak of going on a plant, that is, going fishing on his own account. On the West Coast, a man who owns a boat and hires another man is called a small planter.

It is easy to see the origin of this. When England began to plant colonies, they were called plantations, and those who formed them were called planters. In general they were really engaged in cultivating the soil, as the planters of Jamaica, the planters of Virginia, etc. But in Newfoundland the settlers or planters had, indeed, land assigned them, but for a length of time only for carrying on their fishing, but they still retained the name of planter.

The word *clever*, it is well known, is used in different senses in England and New England. In the former it expresses mental power, and means talented or skilful; in the latter it describes the disposition, and means generous or good-natured. In Newfoundland it is used in quite a distinct sense. There it means large and handsome. It is applied not only to men but to animals and inanimate things. A fisherman will speak of a "clever-built boat," meaning that it is large and shapely. The dictionaries, from Johnson onward, give, as one meaning of the word, "well-shaped or handsome." But he describes it as "a low word, scarcely ever used but in burlesque or in conversation, and applied to anything a man likes, without a settled meaning." But Wright gives it as in the East of England meaning good-looking, and in Lancashire as denoting lusty, which is nearly the Newfoundland idea, and probably the nearest to the old English.

Sign, in the phrase "a sign of," is used to denote a small quantity. One at table, being asked if he would have any more of a dish, replied, "Just a sign." This I have no doubt originated in the use of the term on the fishing grounds in something of its proper meaning. When, on reaching them and seeking spots where the fish were to be found, they first caught some, it afforded a sign of their presence, just as a gold-miner speaks of a "show" of gold. When they caught them in greater abundance, they spoke of it as "a *good* sign of fish." Hence the term came to express the quantity, without reference to what it indicated, and in this sense to be applied to any object.

Atert, or *atort*, is the same as athwart, but it is used as equivalent to across. Thus they say "atert the road," or "atort the harbour." *Tert* is also used for thwart.

Bread, with a Newfoundlander, means hard biscuit, and

soft-baked bread is called *loaf*. The origin of this is easily understood. For a length of time the coast was frequented by fishermen, who made no permanent settlement on shore, and whose only bread was hard biscuit. In a similar way fish came to mean codfish.

"Going into the country" is used to express going into the woods. A man going for an outing, taking a tent to encamp in the woods, will be said to have gone into the country. We can easily understand how this could have arisen. In Newfoundland there are really no settlers or settlements away from the shore. Therefore to go into the country is in reality to go into the woods. On the other hand, the people of St. John's speak of persons coming in from the outposts as "coming *out of* the country." We find the same form in the authorized version of the English Bible (Mark XV. 21), where the Revised has simply "coming *from* the country."

The word *fodder* is not used to denote cattle-feed in general, but is limited to oats cut green to be used for that purpose. This use of the word, I am informed, is found in New England. So the words *funnel* and *funnelling* are used in Newfoundland, and also in some parts of the United States, for stove-pipe. It is common in both to hear such expressions as, "The funnels are wrong," or "He bought so many feet of funnelling." This sense of the word has gone out of use elsewhere, except as regards a steamer's funnel.

Hatchet is used for an axe. This is a little singular, as the word was not originally English but is the French *hachette*, the diminutive of *hache*, and really meaning a small axe or hatchet.

A Newfoundlander cannot pass you a higher compliment than to say you are a *knowledgeable* man. This word, however, I understand is common in Ireland, and I suppose was brought here by the Irish settlers.

Liveyers, a name applied by the Newfoundland fishermen to those who permanently reside on the Labrador coast, in contrast with those who come there during summer. It seems simply the word *livers*, but curiously altered in the pronunciation.

Lodge is used in an active transitive sense, as equivalent to place or put, as "I lodged the book on the shelf," "She lodged the dish in the closet." This was the original meaning of the word, but this use of it in common life has almost entirely ceased. We have, however, a survival of it in such expressions as, "lodging money in the bank."

Marsh, often pronounced *mesh* or *mish*, is the usual name for a bog, of which there are many throughout the island. So *pond* is the name for a lake. Even the largest on the island (fifty-six miles long) is known as Grand Pond. This usage prevails to some extent in New England, where, however, both terms are used without any clear distinction between them, but in Newfoundland "pond" alone is used. In this connection it may be also noted that a rapid in a river is usually known as a *rattle*. I do not find this elsewhere, but I regard it as very expressive.

Model, sometimes pronounced *morel*, is used in general for a pattern. Thus a person entering a shop asked for "cloth of that model," exhibiting a small piece.

Ralls, a word applied to riots that took place some years ago. Robert Lowell, in his work, *The New Priest of Conception Bay*, supposes that the word means "*rallies*," but Judge Bennett informs me that it is a corruption of "radicals," and was applied to those engaged in these disturbances as enemies to civil and ecclesiastical authorities.

Rind, as a noun, is invariably used to denote the bark of a tree, and, as a verb, to strip it off. The word *bark*, on the other hand, is only used as a noun to denote the tan which the fisherman applies to his net and sails, and as a verb to denote such an application of it. Thus he will say, "I have been getting some juniper or black spruce *rind* to make tan *bark*," or "I have been *barking* my net or sails," meaning that he has been applying the tannin extract to them.

One of the most singular peculiarities, however, of the dialect of Newfoundlanders is the use of the word *room* to denote the whole premises of a merchant, planter, or fisherman. On the principal harbours, the land on the shore was granted in small sections, measuring so many yards in front, and running back two or three hundred yards, with a lane between. Each of these allotments was called a *room*, and, according to the way in which it was employed, was known as a merchant's room, a planter's room, or a fisherman's room. Thus we will hear of Mr. M.'s upper room, his lower room, and his beach room; or we have Mr. H.'s room, the place where he does business, at Labrador. One of these places, descending from father to son, will be called a family room.

Shall, probably the same as *shell*, but we find it as *shale* used by older writers. Johnson defines it as "a husk, the case of seeds in siliquous plants," quoting Shakespeare's line, "Leaving them but the *shales* and husks of men," and later writers use it as a verb to denote the stripping off this husk. In Newfoundland it is used in both ways, and in addition to denote the hulling of strawberries and such fruit.

The word *skipper* is in universal use, and so commonly applied as almost to have lost its original meaning of the master of a small vessel. It is used toward every person whom one wishes to address with respect, and is almost as common as "Mr." elsewhere. Generally the Christian name is used after it, as Skipper Jan, Skipper Kish. In like manner the word *uncle* is used without regard to relationship. In a community every respectable man of, say, sixty years of age will be so called by all the other people in it.

Spurt, meaning a short time. "Excuse me for a spurt." "How long did you stay?" "A short spurt."

Having much to do with the weather, as might be expected, they have peculiar words and expressions regarding it. Thus a calm day is *civil*, and a stormy one is *coarse*. This last I think I have heard among Scotch people. A very sharp, cutting wind driving small particles of ice, which strike the face in a painful manner, is expressively called a *barber*. A Newfoundlander will also speak of the wind being *scant* when it may be blowing something of a gale. He means that it is too nearly ahead for him to make the course which he wishes. I find, however, the same use of the word among seamen in Nova Scotia. This I think must be a corruption of the word *askant*. From this perhaps comes the word *scantalize* or *scandalize*. A gentleman heard a captain, on bringing a vessel to anchor, give an order to "scantalize the mainsail." The command was obeyed by letting the peak drop and gathering up the sail as far as was necessary to take the wind out of it. The word, however, does not appear to be in common use.

It will be seen that several of the old English words in use in Newfoundland are also found in New England. The question has been raised whether each derived them from their common English parentage, or whether the New-foundlanders received them by intercourse with New England fishermen visiting their coast. I am decidedly of opinion that most, if not all, the old English words used in Newfoundland were an original importation from the mother country. The intercourse of New England fisher-men was too limited and too transient to have so generally affected their language. Still there are a few words in use which seem to have come in that way. For example, *callibogus*, a mixture of spruce beer and rum; a *scalawag*, a scamp; *tomahawk*, the name by which the American shingling hatchet is known; *catamaran*, a word originally denoting a raft of three logs lashed together, used first in the East and afterward in the West Indies, but in New-foundland used to denote a wood-sled, and when side sleighs were first introduced, applied to them; and *scrod*, in New England *escrod*, a fresh young codfish broiled.

III. There are a large number of words the origin of which is to me unknown or uncertain. Thus a species of white bean is advertised commonly and sold under the name of *callivances*. Eggleston, in an article in the *Century Magazine* for 1894, mentions "*gallivances* and potatoes" as given in 1782 among the products of Pennsylvania; and in the same year, in "A Complete Discovery of the State of Carolina," a list is made of several sorts of pulse grown in the colony, to wit, "beans, pease, *callavances*," etc. He is puzzled about the word, and supposes it to mean pumpkins, and to be from the Spanish *calabaza* (gourd). But this would not be pulse. Probably it meant there, as it does now in New-foundland, the small white bean, in contrast with the broad English bean. But what is the origin of the word, and how did it come to be found in places so distant, and circumstances so different, as in Carolina and Newfound-land? And is it not singular to find it surviving in the latter place, when it has so entirely disappeared elsewhere that the learned are unable to ascertain its meaning?

Of other words of unknown origin to me, I may mention *chronic*, an old stump; *cockeying* at Harbour Grace, *copying* in St. John's, describing an amusement of boys in spring, when the ice is breaking up, jumping from cake to cake, in supposed imitation of the sealers; *cracky*, a little dog; *dido*, a bitch; *gandy*, the fisherman's name for a pancake; *mucksy*, muddy, doubtless from muck, but I do not find it in any dictionary within my reach; *scrape*, a rough road down the face of a bank or steep hill, used specially in regard to such as are formed by sliding or hauling logs down; *shimmick*, used on the west coast as a term of contempt for one who, born of English parents, attempts to conceal or deny his birth in Newfoundland; *sprayed*, describing chapped hands or arms; *tolt*, a solitary hill, usually somewhat conical, rising by itself above the surrounding country; *trucklymuck*, a small two-handed car for dogs, with a handle for a man to keep it straight; and *tuckamore*, in some places *tuckamil*, a clump of spruce growing almost flat on the ground and matted together, found on the barrens and bleak, exposed places.

To these may be added the following words: *droke*, e.g., of wood, denoting a wood extending from one side of a valley to the other. In old English the word denotes a filmy weed on the surface of stagnant waters, but I cannot trace any connection of this with the use of it in Newfoundland.

Dwy, a mist or slight shower. "Is it going to rain today?" "No, it is only a dwy," a Newfoundlander may reply.

Starrigan, a young fir tree, which is neither good for firewood nor large enough to be used for timber, hence applied with contempt to anything constructed of unsuitable materials. The word sounds as if it were from the Irish.

Sprawls of snow, heavy drifts; the origin and proper meaning of the word I am unable to trace.

Under this head we may also notice a number of technical terms connected with their fishing, which may be used by fishermen elsewhere, but of most of which I am unable to trace the origin. Thus we have *collar*, a mooring laid down for the purpose of fastening the fishing punt or skiff to it: the rope has a loop at the end for pulling over the stern of the boat, and this rope gives its name to the mooring; *faggots*, small piles of fish on the flakes; *high rat*, a boat with a board along the edge to prevent the water coming over, called a *washboard*, a term applied to objects which have a similar arrangement; thus a man boarding in town complained that he had to sleep in a bed without any washboard; *pew*, an instrument consisting of a shaft with a sharp piece of iron, like one prong of a fork, at the end of it, used for throwing fish from the boats on to the stages, hence the verb *to pew*, to cast them up in this manner, but this seems to be the French word *pieu*, which is defined as meaning a stake or pale, but which I am informed is used by the French Canadians to denote a fork; *rode*, the hemp cable by which the vessel, boat, or punt rides on the fishing ground; *swatching*, watching open holes in the ice for seals to come up to shoot them; and *waterhorse*, a pile of fish after being washed, usually three or four feet wide about the same height, and as long as may be.

The hunting of seals on the ice has produced a number of technical words which seem peculiar to that employment. Thus a cake of ice is uniformly known as a *pan* of ice, and *to pan* is to gather at one place a quantity, say, of seals. This last, however, seems a survival of an obsolete English word meaning to join or close together. Ice ground fine is known as *swish ice*, but broken into larger pieces it is called *slob ice*. Large cakes of ice like small icebergs floating about are called *growlers*; and when, by the pressure of sea and storm, the ice is piled in layers one upon the other, it is said to be *rafted*. The process of separating the skin with the fat adhering to it from the rest of the carcass is called *sculping*, and the part thus separated is called the *sculp*.

Like all uneducated people, Newfoundlanders have phrases, or sort of proverbial expressions, based on the circumstances of their daily life, which are frequently very telling. Thus they will describe a simpleton or greenhorn as "not well-baked" or only "half-baked." They will also describe a man as having "a slate off," indicating the same as is meant by a man having something wrong in his upper story. This saying was doubtless brought with them from the old country, but as slates are not used among them for the covering of houses, they have adapted the saying to the country by speaking of such a man as having "a shingle loose." An increase of cold may be described as the weather being "a jacket colder," and when feeling its severity they will speak of being "nipped with cold." Again, a man describing his poverty said he had had nothing to eat but "a bare-legged herring," meaning a herring without anything to eat with it. But one of the most amusing uses of a word is that of "miscrable" simply as intensive. Thus a person will speak of "a miserable fine day." I believe that similar words are used in a similar manner, and that one may be described as "terrible good."

George Patterson, 1895

Eskimo Superstitions
Concerning String Figures
Diamond Jenness

Diamond Jenness (1886-1969), a native of New Zealand, first came to Canada in 1913 to join the Canadian Arctic Expedition led by Vilhjamur Stefansson. As part of the many volumes issued as Report of the Canadian Arctic Expedition, 1913-18, *he produced* The Life of the Copper Eskimo *(Vol. 12),* Eskimo Folk-Lore *(Vol. 13),* Eskimo Songs *(with Helen Roberts) (Vol. 14), and* Eskimo Language and Technology *(Vol. 15).*

In 1926 Dr. Jenness became director of the anthropological section of the National Museum of Canada, a post he held until his retirement in 1953. His major work, The Indians of Canada, *first published in 1932 and revised through five later editions, continues to be a standard text. He also produced National Museum Bulletins on the Ojibway, the Sarcee, and the Sekani Indians, along with many extensive articles. In 1970 he was posthumously awarded Canada's highest honour, the Companion of the Order of Canada, "for his services in the field of anthropology, particularly in connection with the Indian and Eskimo population of Canada."*

The following article formed part B of Eskimo Folk-Lore. *String figures in which a string is passed around and*

*between the fingers to form different patterns are known
throughout the world. Today the form is known as cat's
cradle and is a popular children's game. Among primitive
peoples the string figures had magical overtones and were
often related to myths. The same figures are found in
different parts of the world but their names are drawn
from the environment: thus there are palms from the
tropics, coyotes from the American west, and seals and
polar bears from the north. Dr. Jenness' study provides
detailed information on the patterns of string figures in
various regions across the northern coast of Canada and
Alaska. Most of the figures had descriptive names such as
"brown bears," "two caves," "two men hauling on a sled,"
"two dogs feeding out of one bowl," "a man carrying a
kayak," and "a woman pulling another by the hair." In
this introduction he describes some of the beliefs and
legends associated with the string figures.*

Among nearly all Eskimo tribes there were various superstitions concerning string figures, although for the most part
they have disappeared under the influence of Europeans.
From Kotzebue Sound, in Alaska, to Kent peninsula, at
the eastern end of Coronation Gulf, there was a taboo
against playing the game except in the winter, when the
sun no longer rose above the horizon. The Eskimos of
Alaska and the Mackenzie delta have long since abandoned
this taboo, and the game has become a pastime for every
season of the year; but in Coronation Gulf it was observed,
though not very rigidly, down to the year 1916. Thus a
woman showed me some new figures in the summer of
1915, but remarked that we ought to postpone playing the

game until the winter. In the same summer a girl who was showing me some figures carefully closed the door of the tent in order that the sun might not shine in on us; for the Eskimos of this region base their taboo on a legend that the sun once beheld a man playing cat's cradles and tickled him. In the autumn of 1915 my halfbreed interpreter was making some figures before the sun had disappeared, and an old man accused him of causing all the blizzards that were raging at the time. Dr. R. M. Anderson informs me that while some Coppermine River natives were making string figures in his tent during the spring of 1910, a curious noise was heard outside. His Alaskan interpreter then told him they thought an evil spirit had come amongst them because they were violating the taboo.

This last superstition resembles the Alaskan belief that there is a definite spirit associated with string figures. The same superstition was evident again in a shamanistic seance that took place in Dolphin and Union strait during the winter of 1915. It was not at all prominent among the Copper Eskimos, however, and there is a strong probability that it was introduced by some western natives within comparatively recent times. In Alaska, on the other hand, many stories are told about this spirit of string figures, which could even become the guardian spirit of a shaman. It was thought to reveal its presence by a peculiar sound like the crackling of dry skins, and it made string figures with its own intestines or with an invisible cord. At Cape Prince of Wales the Eskimos believed that Opening A would drive it away, if the proper words were uttered; but in other parts of Alaska there was a special figure for the purpose. A mere pretence at making the figure was enough, if no string were available; but if the movements were not made, every inmate of the house would be paralyzed and die.

The following story about this spirit was narrated by a woman of Cape Prince of Wales:

On the site of Tin City (a deserted tin mine near Cape Prince of Wales) there once lived a boy who spent all his evenings in making string figures. One evening, as he was amusing himself with his usual pastime, the spirit of cat's cradles entered the house, drew forth its own intestine, and began to make the figures also. The mother of the boy snatched the string from her son's hands, exclaiming, "I told you not to be always playing that game." Sitting down on the floor opposite the spirit, she made Opening A, unmade it, made it again, again unmade it, then, with the exclamation "I've raced you," quickly made the figure for the third time and flourished it in the intruder's face. The spirit shuffled nearer the door, and the woman shuffled after it, each striving to outdo the other in manipulating the string. At last the spirit vanished through the door — the woman's presence of mind had saved both her son and herself.

From Alak, a North Alaskan Eskimo who lived on the Noatak river during his youth, came these two stories:

The Noatak river Eskimos once constructed a dance-house and gathered inside to practise their dances before sending out runners to invite their neighbours to the festival. Another boy and myself were sent to bring in more food, and while we were absent, some of the children created a great uproar, despite the warnings of the older people. Everything seemed normal when I returned, but suddenly there was a sharp report outside the house, and a noise like the crackling of dry skins. The sound travelled around the house until it reached the door, which was merely an opening covered by a curtain of skin. Presently a stream of mist began to pour in, and behind it, concealed by the mist, the spirit of string figures entered the room. The lamps at first flared brightly, then slowly grew dimmer and dimmer. We sat motionless, paralyzed with fear. One by one the lamps expired and no one stirred, although now and then an old man would cry, "Will no one go out?" The house grew darker and darker, and my grandfather, who was sitting on one of the benches, called me over to his side. I ran quickly, for I was very frightened, and my grandfather placed me on his knee. Nearly all the lamps had expired when an old man suddenly rushed outside with one of them and raced around the house. The air outside extinguished his lamp, but the people re-lit it, and then lit all the other lamps that had expired. The spirit disappeared, and everything seemed normal again; but presently the old man's hands grew very cold and he sat dumb and motionless. His brother asked him what was the matter, but he could not answer. Then some shamans who were present invoked their magic powers, and in the morning the old man was able to move about again, although his speech did not return to him until some time afterwards. Had he not carried out one of the lamps before they were all extinguished, every one of us would have been paralyzed and died.

I knew also of two men who lived in another settlement on the Noatak river. They did not believe in a spirit of string figures, but said they originated from two stars, *ayyuk*, which are visible only when the sun has returned after the winter night. Onc of these men was inside a dance-house when a flood of mist poured in through the curtain door. His two companions rapidly made and unmade the figure "Two Labrets," uttering the usual formula that goes with it; but the mist kept pouring in. Presently it cleared a little, and between the door and themselves they discerned the form of an old man who was moving his hands as though he were making string figures; nor could the men drive him away, despite the persistency with which they made "Two Labrets." The lamp was slowly expiring when the sceptic caught it up, raced around the house with it and returned inside again. The figure vanished as soon as he rushed towards the door. Both the sceptic's companions were shamans, and by their magic they saved the man from any evil consequences.

From Aqsiataq, a Colville river Eskimo, comes the following account:

I was a young boy at the time, and staying inside the house with my mother. We heard a loud crackling sound outside as though a number of dried skins were shaking in the wind. My mother immediately ran outside and raced around the house. When she came in again, she told me that the sound had been made by the spirit of string figures. We listened again for a time, but the noise was not repeated.

Certain shamans can control this spirit. I once saw a shaman extend his hands as though he were holding out a string figure, yet no cord could be seen on his fingers. Some of the men laid their belts over the invisible cord, and their belts remained suspended in the air.

The Eskimos of Hudson Bay have a slightly different belief from their kinsmen in Alaska. According to Captain

Comer, the natives of Iglulik play cat's cradles in the fall when the sun is going south, to catch it in the meshes of the string and so prevent its disappearance. Again, the same authority states that on the west coast of Hudson Bay "boys must not play cat's cradle because in later life their fingers might become entangled in the harpoon-line. They are allowed to play this game when they become adults. Two cases were told of hunters who lost their fingers in which the cause was believed to be their having played cat's cradle when young. Such youths are thought to be particularly liable to lose their fingers in hunting ground-seal." Among the Copper Eskimos, as well as farther west, young and old play alike; indeed the parents take a special delight in teaching their young children.

Diamond Jenness, 1924

II. PERSONAL EXPERIENCE ACCOUNTS

Old-Time Customs
John B. Calkin

The entire way of life of a folk group is of interest to a folklorist. Many are the material articles, customary practices, patterns, and formulae that pass from person to person by oral means and that are old enough to be considered traditional among the people who possess them. These artifacts — behavioural or material — are used by the group members as a means of expressing their identity and by others as a means of identifying the group. Such cultural elements constitute the folklife of the group.

Folk groups were formerly thought to be limited to peasant societies, for in Europe, where academic folklore studies developed in the nineteenth century, folklorists studied peasants. In North America, however, especially after World War I, there were almost no true peasants north of the Rio Grande. But folklorists found that other groups had much in common with peasant societies, so scholars came to define as their subjects small groups sharing one or more factors such as geography, language, age, religion, education, sex, occupation, race, economic status and similar traits. These groups, then, were little traditions within larger societies, not the dominant or mainstream tradition.

It is, therefore, not necessary to search Canada's past to find folk and their lore. Yet accounts of days gone by often provide us with little-known information about how our predecessors actually lived — the traditional ways they had, the recurring patterns in their lives.

The following account of traditional practices is particularly interesting for its discussion of the means of lighting fires in mid-nineteenth-century Nova Scotia. John B. Calkin was an erudite man with rustic roots who, in his later years, recounted his memories of the way of life in his youth, thereby providing Canadians with a documentary account of Nova Scotian folklife in the last century.

It may be fancied that some people, ill-taught in the ways of the olden time, will be saying — "Tell us about the making of brooms out of ash and birch trees. Were they like our corn brooms?" Not very much. But they did the sweeping just as well, though, on account of narrower reach, they took longer time to do the job. Ash made the better broom, though it cost more labour in the making of it. The stick chosen was straight, free from knots, about three inches in diameter and about five feet in length. The bark was removed from about ten inches of the larger end. Here a ring of bark an inch and a half wide was left, and above this ring the bark was removed to the end of the stick. We now make a pencil line around the stick eleven and a half inches above the ring of bark and run a saw around this line evenly to the depth of about three-fourths of an inch, leaving the heart wood an inch and a half in diameter intact. We may now make a rough handle for our broom by dressing off the wood above the pencil line and to the depth of the cutting by the saw.

We are now ready to make the brush which will consist

of two parts — an outer and an inner brush, making the inner brush first from the ten inches below the ring of bark. The sap wood is now peeled up, each year's growth being separated from that of the preceding year, and turned back over the ring of bark. Birch wood may be easily stripped up, but the grains of ash adhere so closely that they require to be carefully pounded to loosen them up. This may be done by one person holding the end of the stick on a block and turning it slowly around, while another pounds it with the head of an axe. The pounding will need to be followed up separately for each year's growth. The process is thus continued to the heart wood which is then sawed off. The strips or ribbons are then divided into narrow threads and turned down, forming the inner part of the brush. The part above the ring of bark is then treated in the same manner and turned down, forming the outer part of the brush. The whole brush is now firmly bound by twine around its upper part next to the handle. Finally the handle is dressed to the proper size and made smooth. The broom is finished.

In no way, perhaps, is a people's progress in home comforts more clearly indicated than in its means of lighting the house in the evening. Nature's simple provision, often adopted in the early days, was the resinous pine knot. It was often split into several pieces and some sort of stand was used to hold the lighted section in erect position. Contemporary with it was the feeble *rush light*, consisting of the spongy pith of the leafless tapering rush which we see so commonly growing in tufts in wet land. The pith, with a strip of rind on one side left to hold it together, was dipped in hot grease, forming a sort of candle, giving a good light, but short-lived. Different kinds of stands were used for its support, similar to the candlestick. In early times, before carpets became common, rushes were strewn on the floors of houses as a covering which was sometimes allowed to remain so long as to be filthy as well as a lodging place for disease germs. A new layer of rushes was thus an important part of house cleaning.

From the pine knot and the rush light to the electric light is a long stride, and there were various intermediate steps between them. A strip of cotton cloth saturated with grease was one of the rudest appliances. In some parts of the country a lamp fed by whale oil or some sort of fish oil was in common use. The tallow candle, made chiefly of beef fat with a wick of soft cotton yarn — rarely of tow — held a long time almost undisputed and brilliant reign as an illuminant. The time came, however, with "the widening of man's thoughts," when the tallow candle was compelled to share its empire with ambitious rivals — *coal gas* and *kerosene* — now holding a wide field in the lighting of our homes. And yet the tallow candle with its attendant, the snuffers, is by no means extinguished; and it still holds honourable recognition as the standard in estimating the brilliancy of illuminators of higher power. In many a home, too, where the candle has been superseded by "modern improvements," the brass candlesticks, clean and bright, adorn the parlour mantel as memorials of "ye olden time." For the information of those by whom the making of this old-time light is considered a lost art, some details of the process may be given.

It may be stated that tallow candles, at least in the olden days, were divided into three classes or ranks according to the service for which they were intended. First were the "moulds" made by pouring melted tallow into a tin mould — larger and smoother than the other kinds — a *tony* light for company occasions; those of the second class were the cotton-wick dips, made for ordinary use; the third and lowest class were the two-wicks, dipped last, when the tallow was nearly used up. They gave a very uncertain sort of light and sputtered and spat like an angry cat. They were often called "sluts," probably on account of the menial service they were made for, being intended for work in the cellar for which little light was needed.

The material required for making the "dips" comprised good clean tallow, a ball or two of soft cotton yarn for the wicks, several dozens of stiff, smooth rods about twenty inches long and three-eighths of an inch in diameter, two poles eight or ten feet long with benches about two feet high to rest on — kitchen chairs often served the purpose — and a large iron pot or kettle about half full of hot water.

The wicking was cut into pieces about twenty inches in length; six or seven wicks were strung on each rod, so that the middle of the wick would rest on the rod and the parts hung down on each side. The two parts were then twisted together six or seven wicks being thus strung on each rod about an inch and a half apart. When a rod was filled and the wicks were straightened out by pulling them down with the thumb and finger, it was placed across the poles. The pot containing the water and melted tallow was placed beside the suspended rods. It scarcely needs to be stated that tallow, having less specific gravity than water, must rest on the top of the water. It may be observed, too, that the pot must be kept filled to the top — otherwise the upper part of the candle would not profit by the dipping. For this purpose, a supply of hot water and melted tallow must be kept on hand.

Everything made ready, the dipping began. Beginning at one end, the dipper lifted the rods one after another consecutively and plunged them into the pot, took them out quickly, straightened out the wick where necessary, and replaced them on the poles. Thus the process went on through the whole row, and was repeated until the candles had grown to the full size. It will be understood that the growth was effected on the same principle as is that of the icicle suspended from the eaves of a building, only in the case of the icicle there is no wick to begin on and it grows vertically as well as horizontally, and is smallest at the lower end.

It is difficult to fully estimate the convenience and economic value of the friction match now universally used in making a new fire. The common way three-fourths of a century ago, when some of us were boys, was in the first place to follow the custom of the vestal virgins of ancient Rome in their precaution for the maintenance of the sacred fire. In his boyhood days the present writer observed the care with which his father kept the fire alive overnight. A partially burned stick — a hemlock knot suited best — its face glowing with fire, was covered with a deep layer of ashes for the exclusion of air, thus arresting combustion. In the morning, when the covering was removed, there remained a fine bed of coals for starting the fire. The last spark, however, may have fled! Then what to do? First, the small boy was sent to the nearest neighbour's "to borrow fire." Seizing the brand between two sticks, he hastened on his homeward way. The faster he ran, the more fruitless appeared the outcome of his errand. Sometimes, indeed, fanned by the opposing current of air, the inflammable tongs lost their grip, and the remains of the brand fell to the ground. It was seldom, however, that these laudable efforts were thus luckless, and never did he give up without resort to new expedient for overcoming the difficulty. The old flint lock musket, now hanging on the kitchen wall, which perhaps had seen service in the hands of a Loyalist in the American Revolution and had since proved its worth in the pursuit of a bear which had done mischief in the farmer's barnyard or sheep pasture, came to the rescue. The spark generated by the sharp blow of the hammer on the flint fell on the powder, passed on to the tinder, and the morning fire was soon ablaze.

Other expedients were used for obtaining fire, most of them of a chemical nature. We were often told that it could be done by briskly rubbing two pieces of wood together. The Indians had done it from time immemorial, it was said. But no responsible person claimed to have done it, or to have seen it done. The chemical match — a splinter of wood tipped with a mixture of chlorate of potash and sugar — when dipped in sulphuric acid was an effective, though rarely adopted, expedient.

In the early years of Queen Victoria's reign, friction matches were sold as a curiosity in the streets of London. It is said that before this match had been perfected, Sir Humphrey Davy, one of the foremost chemists of the day, in writing to a friend, spoke of the newly originated match and wondered if it would ever come into common use!

It was a strenuous as well as a simple life that our pioneer ancestors passed through in clearing away the forests and securing for us the rich heritage they have left us. Being compelled to endure hardship and to rely on their own resources, they were developed into the robust, many-sided and resourceful men and women that they became — never nonplussed, never lacking in expedients. In this there was wonderful compensation for many deficiencies. What they lacked in elegance and in culture, they gained in broadness and grit. The limitations attendant on specialization they escaped.

And here we must not forget that many of the early settlers in this country of ours were of the flower of the British people — among the choicest in manly vigour, in mental ability, independent thinking and moral culture. Above all, they had the will to dare and to do.

John B. Calkin, 1918

The Old-Order Mennonite Wedding and Highlights of Their Social Life
Allan M. Buehler

During and immediately after the American Revolutionary War, many Anabaptists — primarily of German extraction — immigrated with the United Empire Loyalists to the region that became Ontario. They settled on rich farming land granted to them primarily in Waterloo County and elsewhere in southwestern Ontario. Though a prominent group in pioneer days and a highly visible minority even to the present, these religious sectarians are not well-known or understood by the larger society. People may see their black buggies, recognize their old-fashioned dress, and even buy in their inviting and prosperous markets, yet few appreciate their way of life and its rationale. One reason for this situation is the dearth of information available to the public from members of the various groups among the Anabaptists who are commonly termed "Pennsylvania Dutch." Not all were from Pennsylvania, though many were; the others came mostly from New York, and few, if any, were Dutch — outsiders typically misunderstood "Deutsch" (meaning German), as the people called themselves.

The Mennonites are the largest group of Anabaptists in Ontario. Allan M. Buehler was raised an Old-Order Mennonite — that is, amongst the most conservative sub-

division of Mennonites who will not drive any vehicle that moves by itself or have electricity, telephones, radios, televisions, or the like in their homes. Typically, they are farmers; they do not fraternize with the outside world except for commercial purposes, and seek to live unto themselves, worshipping God as Menno Simmons taught their ancestors to do during the Protestant Reformation. Few Old-Order Mennonites write about their culture, for it does not welcome the intrusion of the outside world. Mr. Buehler's account is, then, all the more valuable because there are very few others like it in Canadian literature. Here Mr. Buehler describes a major rite of passage and the highlights of social activities in a Mennonite Community as he remembers them.

In 1922 there was another great change in my life. As an Old-Order Mennonite, I was allowed to have a repair shop and repair car tires, but was not allowed to have a car. I was allowed to have a telephone in my shop, but not in my home. Then in 1922 my girl friend, Lovina Clemmer, and I decided to get married, and set the date for November that year. It may be of interest to those of my readers who do not know how such a wedding is performed to describe my own wedding in detail.

When a girl and a boy decide to get married, they will select a date well in advance. They will notify the bishop and request that the "bans" be read in the church. These bans are then read by the bishop on three Sundays in the church. A list of guests is drawn up by the bride and groom, and invitation is by word of mouth where possible, or by letter to those at some distance. They would first select the bridal party. These would always be single young people; no married couples are in the bridal party. They may be sisters, brothers or good friends, or cousins of the bride or groom. At our wedding we had six couples. One couple would be selected as bridesmaid and best man. Then the list will include married couples, brothers, sisters, parents, uncles, aunts, cousins, and friends of the family. At our wedding there were about twenty couples. Then there were six to eight young girls. These would help to prepare and set the tables, and be waitresses, and seven young boys who would be hostlers, and they would look after the guests' horses as they arrive. Unhitch them and stable them, and when guests wish to leave in the evening, they will hitch the guests' horses to the buggy and drive to the house for the guests to mount the buggy. They also do the usual "chores" that need be done on the farm, so that the family would not leave the wedding to do chores. And then there will be young children. These young children also have a function which I will describe later on. This then constitutes the wedding guests, except for the addition of the bishop and his wife, who are to perform the wedding. They have a place of honour, and will be at the head table.

On the morning of the wedding the bridegroom arrives soon after breakfast, and so do the young girls who help in the kitchen and serve dinner. The wedding is to begin at 9 a.m. in the bride's home. Tables and chairs will have been borrowed from neighbours. The large room, "parlour," is arranged for the wedding. A small table and chair at one end for the bishop, and as many chairs in rows as the room will hold. The front rows, at the bishop's table, are reserved for the bridal party. At our wedding this required fourteen chairs. The rest of the chairs are for the married guests. If there is not sufficient room for all guests, then side rooms are used for the overflow. The rooms upstairs are set aside for the bridal party; young people and married couples will stay downstairs.

When the first guests arrive, the bride and groom will go upstairs and wait for those in the bridal party to arrive. As the guests arrive, those in the bridal party will be ushered upstairs where they are greeted by the bride and groom. The married couples will be ushered into the parlour. Upstairs with the bridal party there is a lot of kidding going on. They will tell the groom, "You still have time to change your mind," or "My, you look nervous. Do you want to call the whole thing off?" They have a lot of fun while waiting for everything to come to order downstairs. The young girls will now come upstairs and serve wine to the bridal party, while other girls will serve all the guests downstairs with wine. The bridal party can hear a lot of talking and laughing from the guests downstairs. Then all of a sudden everything is quiet. The young girls will then come upstairs and tell the bridal party that everything is ready. The bridal party will then line up to go downstairs. The bridesmaid and best man will lead the way, then the bride and groom hand in hand, and the rest of the bridal party following in couples. The bridal party is seated in the two front rows, with the bride and groom in front of the bishop's table. A short period of silence, and then one of the guests who has been invited as song leader will announce a hymn to be sung. All guests join in the singing except the bridal party. The bishop will then read a portion of scripture, after which he will preach a sermon on the responsibility of husband and wife, and will then say "Let us pray" and everyone turns around and kneels, while the bishop prays. After they rise from prayer, the bishop will ask the bride and groom to stand up (there is no giving away of the bride). After a few words of advice on the responsibilities of married life, he will then perform the marriage ceremony, much the same as in other denominations, except it is all in Pennsylvania German. He will then pronounce them husband and wife. The married couple sits down, and the bishop again announces prayer, and everyone will again kneel while the bishop prays for the young couple. After rising from prayer, there is the signing of the marriage certificate. The bishop will sign as the officiating bishop, and the bride's father and the groom's father usually sign as witnesses, but as my father had died, my stepbrother, Sylvester Martin, signed on my behalf. Bishop Ezra Martin was the officiating bishop at our wedding. The marriage certificate is then handed to the groom as the head of the "family." There is then the singing of another hymn, after which the bridal party will again go upstairs. They will be sitting around and having fun, waiting for the wedding dinner to be ready. The young girls are now busy setting the table and arranging the order of seating. This is a long table, and the bishop will sit at the head of the table, then the bridal party and close relatives. There are usually a couple of tables, some in another room, but even then it will require a few sittings to feed everyone. After everyone is seated, there may be a hymn, and the bishop will ask the blessing. The tables are loaded with a variety of food that you will only find at a Pennsylvania German special meal. Everything is on the table and the dishes, which are loaded, are passed around and you help yourself to whatever you want and as much as you want.

While the guests are at the table eating, the girls will gather the young children together and will pick two of them and tell them what to do. They will crawl under the table and will take one of the bride's shoes off. The bride knows what they are doing, but pretends not to notice.

They will take the shoe and hide it. When the meal is over, the bride will announce. "I have lost one shoe," while the children are watching and giggling with delight. The best man and bridesmaid will then ask the children what they have done with the shoe, and they tell them they have hidden it. They pretend to be searching all over for it but cannot find it. The children will say, "If you pay us, we will get it for you." The best man will tell the bridegroom that the children want money for the shoe, and he will pay them each twenty-five cents. The children then bring the shoe. This is always great fun for the children.

When the wedding feast is over, the bridal party will again go upstairs. The groom will now bring out boxes of cigars and offer a cigar to everyone. While the girls do not smoke, they will, however, often take a cigar as a souvenir of the wedding. The boys will start smoking and the room is soon full of smoke. When all the guests have eaten, and the tables are cleared, then the girls may again serve glasses of wine to all the guests. This is real wine, and not grape juice, and the custom stems from John Chapter Two, where Jesus made wine at the marriage in Cana of Galilee.

The bride and groom will now come downstairs and will shake hands and visit with all the guests. Instead of having a reception line, the bride and groom will go to the guests to greet them. The groom will have a box of cigars and will hand them out to all who want one, and again, there are some women who will take one as a souvenir. They will visit for quite some time with the guests, then the whole bridal party will come down and gather around the table and have a singsong. They now sing English hymns, and will sing in parts. Everyone, young and old, will join in and sing. This is a very friendly social time.

Towards evening some guests will want to go home. They are mostly farmers and have chores to do. When they arrived in the morning, the hostlers had numbered tickets. They gave one ticket to the guest, attached one to the buggy and one to the harness. When a guest wanted to go home, he would send his ticket out to the hostlers, who would then get his horse, hitch it to his buggy, and drive to the gate where the guest would get into the buggy and go home. Most of the guests will go home towards evening. Close relatives and the bridal party will remain for the evening meal. The young girls serving and the hostlers will stay, as they will have to serve the evening meal and the hostlers will have to hitch up the horses for those going home later. The evening meal is not so elaborate and is mostly left over from the wedding dinner.

When it gets dark and all the married couples have gone home, the young people of the neighbourhood will gather outside the house to "shivahree." They bring all kinds of noise makers, tin pails, tubs on which they will make a great noise. They will keep this up for some time, then some of the bridal party will go out and they are told: "We want the young married couple." They come in and tell the groom this, and he may say they have not made enough noise yet. So they will make more noise until the young couple go out to speak to them. Most of them will be chums of the couple and belong to the same "gang." The groom may tell them they will have to sing before they will get anything. He will then pass the cigars around for them, and the bride may give them some cookies. This is all in good fun.

When all the married guests have gone home, and the parents of the bride have gone to bed, then the bridal party, together with the young girls and the hostlers, will have a singsong for a while, then have games and fun until late into the night. After everyone has gone home, then the young married couple will go to bed in a room set aside for them. They do not go on a honeymoon. I remember that the day after my marriage, I helped my father-in-law to bring in the turnips. I did not go back to my welding shop to work until the second day after my marriage.

We were now a married couple and would no longer fellowship with the young people and go to the "times." We were now expected to socialize with married people, and in church we would now sit in the section for young married people. This is a sudden change. Before our marriage, we could be somewhat rambunctious and it would be overlooked and they would say: "He is young, he will settle down when he gets a little older." But now the time to settle down has come. You are now expected to be more sober and sedate, taking on the responsibility of a married man.

To an outsider the "way of life" of an Old-Order Mennonite may seem very strange indeed. But if you were raised in such a home, where for many generations this was the "way of life," then this is the only way and the tradition. "We must keep up the old ways of our forefathers and be separated from the world of pleasure and lust" is then not a burden but rather creates the desire to please God rather than man, in a humble and contrite heart. To be obedient to the traditions and ordinances of the church has been instilled into them for many generations and is accepted by them with pleasure rather than it being a burden.

Again, to an outsider it may seem that there would be no pleasure living such a restricted life. Let us examine what their joys and pleasures are:

(1) Children. While children are raised in a strict and disciplined code of ethics, they are, however, shown much love and affection. They are given responsibil-

ities young in life, but are commended for a job well done. Many people have an idea that such a child must have a drab and dull life. Let me assure you that an Old-Order Mennonite child has as much joy and pleasure as any child. And who has ever heard of juvenile delinquency among Old-Order Mennonite children?

(2) Young girls. Girls are taught by their mothers at a young age to cook and bake, to sew and do good housekeeping. What pleasure she gets when she bakes her first pie or makes her first dress. They are commended for this and they get great satisfaction from doing it.

(3) Young boys. Young boys are taught at a young age how to care for animals, and probably given the chore of feeding a calf or chickens. He will be taught all phases of farming, and he is taking his part in it. One thing I remember as a young man is the pride a young man has in ploughing a straight furrow. Everybody watched your ploughing, and you watch everyone else. A straight furrow signifies that he is a good farmer, and he has a great satisfaction on a job well done.

(4) The mother. She gets great satisfaction in being a good housekeeper. A good cook, making her own dresses, quilting, teaching her young daughters, and enjoys looking after her own garden, having rows of shelves filled with preserved fruits and vegetables. I do not know of an Old-Order woman who is not able to make her own dresses, and she is as proud of the new dress she has made as any woman who wears the latest and expensive style, but she is proud of her handiwork rather than the style.

(5) The father. He usually is a farmer, and he gets a great satisfaction in being a good farmer. Well-kept farm

buildings, fences that are kept in good shape. A fine stock of cows and other cattle, and especially fine horses. Making money from his farming operation is important, and he is frugal and cost conscious, but I do not feel that this is his main purpose and satisfaction. Old-Order Mennonites do not have the most modern farming equipment available, yet they are considered amongst the best farmers in the country. You can tell by their crops, the well-kept buildings and fences, the fine horses and livestock that they are good farmers, and they get a great satisfaction from their efforts. As head of the family, he has a great responsibility in being a good example to the family, and teaching them to become good farmers when they grow up.

Highlights of Their Social Life

I have already described the social life of the young people, the conservative and liberal "gangs" and their "times." For the married couples, visiting among themselves is probably their social highlight. They enjoy visiting their friends and relatives on Sundays. They have no telephones and cannot talk to each other, except they make a personal visit. They cannot phone and announce that they will be coming for a visit, but will come unannounced. It is not uncommon for a family with four or five children to come unannounced for a visit on a Sunday. And it may be that two or three others will come at the same time, which means there could be ten to twelve guests coming unannounced on this same Sunday noon. This is not considered rude, but rather this is an honour that they will come to visit you. But this is no big problem for the woman of the house. She is always well prepared for visitors on Sundays. Their larder is always well filled with canned fruit and vegetables they have grown. They will butcher their own pigs, and a young steer, and would have a good supply of home-made smoked sausage, preserved in jars, summer sausage, and ham. Friday was baking day, and it is not uncommon for them to bake ten or twelve pies; and when I was young they baked their own bread and churned their own butter. There were always cakes and cookies on hand. Then they have jams, jellies, apple butter and maple syrup, and a variety of canned fruits. There was "Kuhch Kays" and "Shmeer Kays," and some even made Swiss cheese. The only cooking that had to be done was the sausage or ham and the potatoes. The ham or sausage would be fried, and the potatoes can be made in a variety of ways, boiled or fried. My favourite potatoes were what we called "bahdah groombairah." The potatoes were peeled and sliced into thin slices, then boiled in a small amount of water until soft, and milk and a little flour added. (I think this is the way they do it.) They also have mashed or fried potatoes. Sometimes boiled and then fried. In the fall they would make apple butter. They would sort the culls and these would make cider, and the better ones were peeled and sliced. They would take these to the cider mill and there they would press the culls for cider, boil the cider and add the sliced apples and keep on boiling until it thickens. This is apple butter, and I can still remember that when we made fresh apple butter, my mother would bake bread. We would take this fresh warm bread, put on a layer of butter, then a thick layer of fresh apple butter. This was a treat fit for a king.

It is therefore not such a big problem for the woman of the home to prepare such a large meal for a large number of unannounced visitors on a Sunday. This would indeed

86

be a problem for a city housewife of today. After such a sumptuous meal, they will visit all afternoon. There is always much to talk about, and everybody is enjoying it. As a child going visiting with my parents, I remember that we used to play in the barn. A good place to play hide and seek, or we would swing on the long hay-rack lifter ropes. This made an ideal swing and was a lot of fun.

I will try to describe what a hay-rack lifter was, as the young people of today may never have seen one. To do this, I will go back further and try to describe the method of harvesting in the early days. The first settlers had to cut their grain with a scythe and cradle. One man would cut the grain, and another would follow with a wooden rake. He would rake the grain into bundles, then taking a handful of cut grain and twisting it in a certain way, he would use this to tie the bundle into a sheaf. You had to learn how to twist and tie these sheaves. When I was a young man, we still cut a swath around the field in this way, so that the binder would not trample the grain down. This was not done later on. However, I did learn how to do this and could still do it today. The sheaves were then stacked in rows. Later the reaper was invented, and this was horse-drawn. It cut the grain, and the grain fell onto a platform, then the machine had revolving arms that would push bundles of grain from the platform; a man would follow and tie the bundles, as described. There was still the odd reaper in use when I was young. Then the binder was invented, and this was also a horse-driven machine. It cut the grain, elevated the grain to the tying mechanism, where a bundle was tied and thrown out to the ground. A great improvement over the reaper. Later they invented the sheaf carrier. This would carry a number of sheaves sufficient to make one stook, and was then stripped, and this made it easier for the man following to do the stooking. This last was the method used all the days I was working on the farm. There are still some Old-Order Mennonites who use this method. The combines came much later.

After the grain was all cut and stooked, they would take a team of horses on a wagon with a hay rack and drive along the row of stooks. One man would pitch the sheaves up onto the wagon, while another man or boy would pile them. When they had a big load, they would drive up into the barn. In the barn, up near the roof, were two heavy rounded logs. One was located above the front end of the wagon, and one at the rear. These were resting in wood bearings on the top beams of the barn frame. There were large wooden pulleys about four feet in diameter attached to these rounded logs. These pulleys had "dogs" so that they could not turn backwards. From the round logs there were long ropes with a steel ring at the lower end. These ropes were then hooked to four hooks that were attached to the wagon rack. A long rope from these pulleys ran down through a small pulley near the floor and would reach out to where they would hitch a team of horses; and when the horses pulled away from the barn, it would rotate the logs and the rope would wind up and lift the hay rack up to near the roof. A man would then go on the load and pitch the sheaves into the mow, and another man would pile them in the mow. The grain was all hauled into the barn in this way, and would be threshed in the winter time. This then was a hay-rack lifter.

Old-Order Mennonites have other social activities. They do a lot of co-operative work. Helping one another. To do this, they have a *bee*. They get together for work, but also for a social time. There are the quilting bees, or a shnitsing bee, where they peel and slice apples to prepare them for drying. These would then be dried in the "drying house" and would be eaten in the winter as "shnits dessert" with "gnehb," or as "shnits pie." They also had the threshing bees in the winter. But probably the greatest social event in the Old-Order Mennonite life is to take a trip by train to Pennsylvania, Ohio, or Indiana, to visit Old-Order friends and relatives. When they arrive, they will be picked up at the station by their friends and taken to their home. The following day these friends will drive them in horse and carriage from one Old-Order Mennonite home to another for short visits and meals. Towards evening they will be taken to a home for supper and overnight lodging. The couple that drove them that day will go home, and the couple where they stay overnight will then drive them the next day, visiting home after home. These visits could last for a week.

When these Old-Order Mennonite friends from Pennsylvania come to Canada to visit, they will also be driven around visiting with Old-Order friends in Canada. There are very close ties between the American and Canadian Old-Order Mennonites. When Canadian Old-Order refer to anyone from the United States who is not an Old-Order, they are referred to as Americans, but if they are Old-Order Mennonites, then they are referred to as "shdaytsah," literally meaning "statesers." If Old-Order friends from Pennsylvania are visiting in Waterloo County, the word is passed along that *shdaytsah* are here visiting. It is considered an honour if they will come to your home for a visit.

Allan M. Buehler, 1977

A Heritage of Songs
Carrie Grover

Carrie Grover was born in Nova Scotia in the 1880s and lived there until she was twelve. Then her family moved to the United States where she grew up, married, and settled in Gorham, Maine. She gained a local reputation as a folksinger, and in 1941 Alan Lomax recorded some forty of her songs for the Library of Congress.

In The Ballad Tree *Evelyn Kendrick Wells describes Carrie Grover as a typical traditional singer and quotes her words from a letter:*

> *I was born in a house where someone was singing most of the time, and when song was the only entertainment. The women made their labour sweeter by singing the old songs as they worked at spinning, weaving, knitting, piecing patchwork, and hooking rugs. Father did some work as a cooper, and I remember how he had a special song he always sang when he was finishing an axe handle.*

Mrs. Wells goes on to comment: "She used to hang about the smithy just to hear the blacksmith sing. She tells of a singing match crowded with listeners that went on till night turned into morning."

Prompted by a comment from her mother, "When you and I die, our songs will be forgotten," Mrs. Grover began to write down her songs for her children, and in the 1950s prepared the book A Heritage of Songs, *for which the following piece was the introduction. The book has two sections: 51 "Mother's Songs" and 189 "Father's Songs." It is an amazingly rich collection of child and broadside ballads, sea chanteys, lumbering songs, folk hymns and Negro spirituals, vaudeville ditties, and nineteenth-century popular songs. Quite a few are rare, but many of them are versions of songs Roy Mackenzie and Helen Creighton collected later in Nova Scotia.*

Carrie Grover's introduction and notes on individual songs are particularly significant because they show how the songs were preserved and used in a family where traditional singing is a natural part of life. Other collections compiled by folklorists present a more objective view; in this account we share the attitude of one to whom the songs were, as her title indicates, a precious heritage.

In making this collection of songs, sung by my people and their friends, I have come to realize as I never did before what these old songs must have meant in the everyday lives of the everyday people of long ago.

It would be hard for the young people of the present day to realize what the singing of these old songs meant to these long-ago ancestors of ours. The people who came from the old countries brought their songs with them and many lonely hours must have been cheered by these reminders of the homes they had left. Many of the old songs sung by my parents have been sung by members of my family for four generations, and I have every reason to believe that they were sung by the same old tunes that I use.

My songs come from many sources. About 1811 my great-grandfather, William Hutchinson, was given a grant of land by the government on which he was required to build a public house halfway between the towns of Windsor and Chester in Nova Scotia. Here my grandmother spent her childhood and girlhood and learned many songs from hearing them sung. She could even sing a bit in Indian and dance to her singing. Her mother, who came from England as a child, I believe, died when Grandmother was twelve years old. Grandmother learned several old songs from her. I owe my Scotch blood to my great-grandfather Hutchinson's mother, and the few Scottish songs that we call family songs may have come from her.

My mother's grandfather, William Long, came from Ireland as a boy and to him, no doubt, my grandfather was indebted for the many Irish songs he knew and sang.

Of my father's side of the family I know very little beyond the fact that his grandfather, John Davis, came from Glenmorganshire, Wales, and his mother from England. My great-grandfather Davis brought twenty-three of the Robin Hood ballads from Wales, three of which my grandmother remembered and taught to Father. He could remember only one, the ballad of Robin Hood and the Pedlar. I can only give comparative dates, but as Grandmother Spinney's oldest child was born about 1810, and her youngest in 1839, it was a long time ago.

The singing of songs played a large part in the daily lives of my family as, no doubt, it did in the lives of other families of that time. My grandmother sang at her spinning wheel and at her loom, for she spun and wove both wool and flax. My father's older sister used to spin for my grandmother Long and I have heard my oldest brother say that she would spin and sing all day and never sing the same song twice. He said she knew more songs than anyone he ever knew.

Men used to walk several miles to their work when my father was a young man; and coming through the woods after dark, they would sing songs to make the land seem less lonely. My father always did this.

Another way the songs were used in my family was a sort of signal. We lived at the foot of a pond called Sunken Lane, which was nearly a mile long. The road seemed to wind around this pond, never far from the shore. A voice would carry a long way across the water; and when Father would be on his way home after delivering a load of wood or lumber, he would begin to sing when within a mile of home, and Mother, who would go out and listen when she thought it was about time for him to be coming, would hear him and have his supper ready when he got there.

In my home the singing of songs and ballads seemed a part of our daily lives. Mother always sang at her work, melancholy songs or gay songs according to her mood, or just a humming of the tune without any words. Often in the evening before the lamp was lighted, as Father sat with his elbows on his knees, his pipe held between his hands after his evening smoke, he would start singing; and Mother would join him, the steady click of her knitting needles sounding like a sort of accompaniment. Sometimes they would walk to a neighbour's house to spend an evening, and then we youngsters would play grown-ups and sing the songs we had heard our elders sing, often not knowing in the least what we were singing about and miscalling many of the words. Because I could sing any song I heard before I could talk, my elders found it very amusing to teach me songs and hear me struggle with the pronunciation of the words.

In the little town in Nova Scotia where I was born and

where I lived until I was twelve years old, almost everyone sang or tried to sing these old songs and ballads. Neighbours were few and far between, books and magazines were scarce, and we had to make the best of what we had. In all our little neighbourhood gatherings, paring bees, and old-time dances, the singing of a few songs was a part of every evening's entertainment. Often a singer knew only one song, which he was asked to sing on every occasion. If anyone had learned a new song, he was asked to sing it everywhere he went till everyone had learned it.

If a stranger came to the house or to one of our neighbourhood gatherings, it was considered a breach of good manners not to ask him to sing. The result was not always a happy one for so many people tried to sing who could not even carry a tune, or as one old fellow expressed it, "carried it a ways but dropped it before he got very far." Unfortunately, these singers did not always pick up their tunes where they dropped them, but wandered on and off the tune from beginning to end.

It was rare to find a really good singer of folksongs, one whose voice could adapt itself to all the crooks and turns of the queer old tunes and make his hearers feel the tragedy of his tragic songs or respond to the happy lilt of the gay ones; and needless to say, such a singer was always in demand. When two such singers got together, it meant a fine evening's entertainment for song lovers, for such a singer was always proud of the number of songs he knew and a bit jealous of his reputation. Sometimes when two good singers got together, they would have a friendly contest and first one would sing a song and then the other, till one or the other had run out of songs or they had both sung till they could sing no more. I have heard of these singing matches lasting until two o'clock in the morning. My oldest brother, twenty years older than I, had a fine natural voice and a wonderful fund of songs. In his youth he frequently took part in these endurance contests.

In this introduction, I have tried to tell you what these old songs meant to my people and the reason they meant so much to them. It was a real grief to my parents to realize that the time was fast coming when these old songs would no longer be sung, and with the passing of their generation the songs that had been kept alive through so many generations of singers would pass away with the people who sang them. I once overheard my father say to my mother, "Liza, when we die, our old songs will die with us. There will be no one left to sing them." At different times they would ask me to learn and remember some song that was especially dear to them, and the very first song in my collection is one my mother asked me to learn over forty years ago because it was one her mother had learned from her own mother when she was a child.

As I began to grow old myself, I came to a better realization of what these old songs meant to my parents, and began working on my collection in real earnest, cheered on by the thought of how much happiness it would give them if they could know. Then, too, I hoped that this collection of songs and ballads with the notes that accompany them might give my children and grandchildren an insight into the lives of their ancestors, who lived at a time when the singing of these old songs was almost their only recreation and helped, I believe, more than any one thing to lighten the burden of their hard-working lives.

Carrie Grover

Ballad Singing in Nova Scotia
W. Roy Mackenzie

W. Roy Mackenzie (1883-1957) was the pioneer collector of Anglo-Canadian folksongs. Born in River John, Nova Scotia, he graduated from Dalhousie University in 1902 and took a graduate degree at Harvard under George Lyman Kittredge, of whom he wrote:

> *In my student days he infected me with something of his own broadly human interest in folklore. He showed such generous enthusiasm over my first scanty finds that I was forthwith emboldened to look for more, and he persuaded me to attempt my first brief essays in describing my experiences.*

Mackenzie began serious collecting in 1908 and continued it for a number of years from his summer cottage at River John after he had become an English professor at Washington University in St. Louis. His two books, The Quest of the Ballad *(1919) and* Ballads and Sea Songs from Nova Scotia *(1928), are both important contributions to North American scholarship. Not only was he the first "to carry the study of balladry in America out of the library and into the field," as MacEdward Leach put it, but he was also the first to recognize "the fact that these songs of Nova Scotia were not only important as songs but even more as expressions of the lives of the people who sang them."*

Both his books are still widely used by folklore students. This early article, his first published report of his ballad collecting, which appeared in the Journal of American Folklore *in 1909, is less well-known but still important for an appreciation of his work. As Professor Kittredge notes, "His observations are not only interesting in themselves but they make up an important document as to ballad tradition in general." One item relating to ballad tradition is his account of a "singing match": a custom that Carrie Grover also mentioned.*

While he developed some of his observations at greater length in The Quest of the Ballad, *this article is significant for its more detailed description of how the songs passed from the early Scotch settlers to the Huguenot emigrants. The influence of the Presbyterian Church on folksinging has been noticeable elsewhere in Canada: in Ontario the large Scotch Presbyterian settlements preserved few songs compared to the many found among the Irish and Scotch Catholics.*

[Mr. Mackenzie has noted down the following facts and observations at my request. They are not only interesting in themselves but they make up an important document as to ballad tradition in general. The conditions in Nova Scotia have been such as to render the evidence which he has collected highly typical.

Several processes which we are often obliged to infer or to conjecture with respect to the course of tradition through long periods of time have there gone on with such rapidity that their history may be followed by means of the recollection of living persons. No student of the popular ballad can fail to see the large significance of Mr. Mackenzie's notes. — G. L. Kittredge.]

The north-shore counties of Nova Scotia have been, until recently, a peculiarly rich field for the ballad seeker. Unfortunately, most of my seeking has been done recently, but, even so, I have found a few old men and women who still sing the ballads that were current in their youth, and who, in their attitude of mind as well as in their accurate memories of the old days, still represent the traditions of an elder time.

Summer before last I ran across a Mr. Henderson who, by his own account and by his neighbours, had been a famous ballad singer in his day. Though he has been living for several years in Tatamagouche, Colchester County, he was brought up in the West River district, Pictou County, which was settled, during the latter half of the eighteenth century, by Highland and Lowland Scotch. He is now over eighty years old, and during his youth ballad singing was a well-known and recognized form of entertainment throughout the country districts of Pictou County.

One day, when Mr. Henderson was vainly attempting to recall the words of a song which had been popular in his youth, he apologized to me for his present lack of memory, and, as an offset, explained that he had once had a better memory for ballads than any other man in the West River district. To prove this, he went on to describe a signal victory which he had once gained in a big ballad contest.

Pictou town is placed on the sea coast almost directly

opposite Charlottetown, the capital of Prince Edward Island, and "in the old days" practically all the travelling between the two provinces was by way of Pictou. One winter, when Mr. Henderson was a young man and still living at the West River, he drove to Pictou to take the boat for Charlottetown. A storm came up which made it impossible for the boat to leave at the regular time, so Mr. Henderson spent the night at an inn, along with several other people who had driven in from the country on the same errand. After supper, the company gathered in the big living room and one of them proposed a ballad contest or "singing match." (The word "ballad" was apparently very seldom used.) This was to last all night, if necessary, and if it did, so much the better. Everyone assented eagerly and the contest began, one singer "matching" another until long after midnight, when all were "sung out" except Mr. Henderson and another man whose name he did not know. The unknown held out for some time longer but finally had to admit that he was beaten, whereupon Mr. Henderson exclaimed, with a fine assumption of surprise and disappointment, "What, man? Don't say ye're through already! I hae fifty more on the tip o' me tongue."

This is the story as I received it, though in less picturesque language. And during the narration the old man showed a fire of enthusiasm which made it quite clear to me that the supremacy thus gained was one not to be lightly esteemed. Indeed, I have more than once, in my conversations with old men and women throughout Pictou and Colchester, been assured that the man who, forty or fifty years ago, had the biggest stock of "old songs" in his district was to be regarded with a good deal of veneration.

The West River district, which I have mentioned several times, is one of the Scotch settlements that were opened up during the latter half of the eighteenth century. To this district Mr. Henderson's parents came about 1820. According to his account, they brought from Scotland a collection of broadsides which they prized very highly, and were in constant receipt of newly printed broadsides from the old country. Also, they "kept the office" at the West River (which meant simply that the mails were brought to their house for distribution), and Mr. Henderson remembers that ballad sheets were continually arriving from Scotland, for people throughout the district, and that they were always hailed with joy. I am taking West River as the typical Scotch settlement, which it was; so it may be seen that, what with the ballads brought out in the memories of the emigrants and in broadside form — which were continually added to by newly printed broadsides from Scotland — the north-shore settlers of Nova Scotia, during the early years of the nineteenth century, were fairly familiar with ballad music.

It will seem strange, then, when I go on to say that one may now travel these districts from side to side and find scarcely a man or woman of Scotch blood who has even a speaking acquaintance with the ballad. The usual reason given is, of course, that ballad singing as an active form of entertainment has been shamed out of existence by more up-to-date music and forms of amusement. For my particular field, however, this explanation is not enough. I have visited many sections which have not yet been changed by the uplifting influence of modern songs and latter-day amusements, and even here the most cheering answer I could receive, except in rare instances, would be, "Ach, yes! Me feyther knowed some o' yon songs but he never sung them unless he was feelin' guid." Now, this state of "feelin' guid" is very far removed from the Scotchman's ideal state of ethical goodness. The phrase, in fact, savours unmistakably of alcohol and is about the strongest one employed by these people to denote a state of boisterous hilarity, a very rare condition with the self-respecting Scot.

In short, the explanation I have been leading up to is that the fanatical religious feeling of the Scotch is largely responsible for the decay of ballad singing among them. The first settlers who came out, during the last part of the eighteenth century and the first of the nineteenth, were not deeply religious: on the contrary, they were for the most part — and this applies especially to the Highlanders — an active, roistering class of men who cheerfully travelled miles to congregate for an evening's revelry and drank gallons of Jamaica rum at a barn raising. Later on, when preaching became the regular thing throughout the country districts, they became fanatically religious as a class, and the ballads, now regarded as profane and immoral, gave place to the Psalms of David. William McKay, a resident of Lime Rock, Pictou County, told me that his father, though possessed of a long list of ballads which he had learned in his youth, would neither sing them himself nor allow them to be sung in his house and, furthermore, had warned his children against polluting their mouths with such profane music. Of course, no district was entirely free from unregenerate Scots who, when they combined a distaste for religion with a taste for music, still kept alive a few of the old songs.

What I have just said applies mainly to the purely Scotch districts set back from the sea coast. In the settlements directly on the coast, the history of the ballad is somewhat different and is affected by an influence that I have not mentioned before — namely, that of the French-Swiss emigrants who came to Nova Scotia some few years after the first Scotch settlements were made. These were formerly French Huguenots who went from their own land to Switzerland, and afterwards migrated to Nova Scotia, taking up land along the north shore near the settlements made by the Scotch. A few years later we find communities, along the coast, of Scotch and French-Swiss together. The latter usually refer to themselves as Swiss, so I adopt the rather clumsy term French-Swiss by way of compromise. The language they spoke was a dialect of French. They are notably a music-loving people, and in a great many cases they acquired ballads from their Scotch neighbours and retained them, while the Scotch abandoned them altogether.

Of course, this did not all happen on a summer's day. The French-Swiss had their own language, which was not English, and it was reserved for their children, who acquired the English language, and dropped their own, to set in motion the shifting process that I have mentioned. This race has always been socially inferior to the Scotch element, and it was as servants in the houses and on the farms of the latter that the second generation of the French-Swiss learned many of the ballads which were in vogue with their masters. An old man of this nationality, Edward, or rather "Old Ned" Langille, of River John, Pictou County, told me that his father — who was a son of one of the first settlers — had been a famous ballad singer and had learned most of his songs while in the employ of a Scotch family. Old Ned himself retained many of these ballads and was always very eager to sing them up to the day of his death, which came two summers ago, and was apparently hastened by a resolution which I had made in the spring to get his entire stock of ballads during the summer. He had followed the example of his father in shunning the alphabet, so that the ballads, in this case, were purely a matter of oral tradition. Some few ballads well worth saving have, I fear, gone down to the grave with him.

In these mixed settlements, then, there is an additional reason why ballad singing was dropped by the Scotch. The

French-Swiss learned the ballads so eagerly and sang them so often that they soon had a monopoly of this kind of music, since the Scotch began to regard as beneath their dignity a form of amusement regularly practised by their servants.

Of course, one cannot discuss the decline of ballad singing in any district without taking into account the influence which I mentioned at the beginning of my sketch — that is, the influx of up-to-date songs and of up-to-date amusements in general. I have a very good illustration of this influence in the case of Mr. Henderson himself, who, without despising the ballad either from a religious or a social point of view, has nevertheless allowed his ancient store of ballads to gradually slip away from him. He moved from the West River to Tatamagouche when he was between forty and fifty years old, and since that time, has taken a fairly prominent part in the village life of Tatamagouche. Possessed of a good voice and a fondness for performing at the little social entertainments and local concerts of the village, he soon outgrew such an antiquated practice as ballad singing; and the few ballads that he can still sing he has retained almost by accident. "The Blaeberry Courtship," for instance, a rather long ballad which I got from him last summer, he remembered, as he told me, because an old friend of his — a woman living at the West River — had been very fond of it and had always asked him to sing it for her on his visits to his old home.

Living a mile or so outside of Tatamagouche is an old man of French-Swiss descent, Robert Langille, who has been a ballad singer all his life. Last summer, though he was eighty-six years old, he still sang with unabated energy, and remembered perfectly many of the old songs which had been current in his neighbourhood when he was a boy, and which he had had special opportunities of learning since he was one of the old race of cobblers who went from house to house to do their work. He has taken no active part in the life of the community and has lived for years in a quiet spot outside the village with his two sisters. To these three old people ballad singing is still a live form of entertainment, and "Old Bob" has always had the most appreciative kind of audience in his own household. Here, then, living within two miles of each other, we have two types that are specially interesting in the present history of the ballad — the singer who has outgrown the ballad, and the singer to whom the old songs are forever young.

But the broadsides, where are they? I have asked this question so often that it looks back at me now from the sheet like an old friend. Mr. Henderson must again adorn my tale. In his home there was an unusual collection of broadsides, but today he cannot account for one of them, nor does he regret the fact. Indeed, why should he? I have said that these broadsides were greatly prized by the Henderson family, but that was in the days when it meant something to know more ballads than your neighbour. The housemaids were finding a real and practical use for the Percy Manuscript when it was taken from them, and the old ballad sheets were in at least as convenient a form for household use as the Percy Manuscript.

W. Roy Mackenzie, 1909

Ballads from Devil's Island
Helen Creighton

Helen Creighton began collecting folksongs in her native Nova Scotia in 1929 and in the succeeding years she garnered over four thousand songs, of which some seven hundred have been published in six major books. She has prepared two Folkways records, Folk Music from Nova Scotia *and* Maritime Folk Songs, *and her songs have provided the music for a folk opera,* The Broken Ring. *She has also collected folktales and superstitions, particularly those dealing with the supernatural, and has chronicled them in* Bluenose Ghosts *and* Bluenose Magic. *She gives a full account of her career in her autobiography,* A Life in Folklore.

Following in the footsteps of Roy Mackenzie, Dr. Creighton was overjoyed to find the wealth of songs still alive in the Maritimes, and she wrote colourfully of the many fascinating singers she recorded. As Professor John Robins of Victoria College noted in his preface to her first book, "There is an academic, clinical approach to folksongs, and there is a sentimental approach, maudlin or mocking as the case may be, but the ideal is a combination of the scientific and the sympathetic, and that is the one Miss Creighton has shown."

As an illustration of this approach, we have chosen an early article in which Dr. Creighton describes some of the fine singers she discovered on Devil's Island in Halifax Harbour and in Lunenburg County on the mainland. She emphasizes the excellent versions of Child ballads preserved by her singers and enlivens her account by mentioning local tales and superstitions. The songs she discusses all appear in her first book, Songs and Ballads from Nova Scotia, *originally published in 1932 and reprinted in 1966.*

At the mouth of Halifax Harbour there lies, all unknown to many people, a little piece of land called "Devil's Island." Where it got its name is a matter of doubt, but there is an interesting tale which relates that one of the earliest inhabitants once saw the Devil on the "banking"[1] of a house, accosting him in the form of a halibut. The following day the unfortunate man was found in his boat returning from Halifax. For no accountable reason, he was lying with his head over the gunwale in the water, and in this position he had been drowned. It was believed, of course, that the Devil had come to warn him of approaching death, and from this unhappy incident the island took its name. Other more plausible stories are told, but this is the most picturesque.

Devil's Island might go down through history unheralded except in times of danger, when storms lash it as they did two years ago when Mr. Ben Henneberry was nearly washed away in an attempt to rescue his own fishing boat. Such storms do not come very often; but the inhabitants know that no help can reach them from an earthly source while the elements beat about their little stronghold. For Devil's

---

1 On the island, seaweed is banked against the foundations of the houses to keep them warm in winter.

Island is only one mile in circumference and its highest elevation is eleven feet above sea level. It has hills and valleys in miniature, and reputed treasure sunk in a bottomless hole. There is a vale where a lake has been drained in the hope of finding treasure, but gold has not yet been discovered. It has a rock-bound coast, and a dangerous approach when seas run high. Yet unless treasure were actually found there, Devil's Island would still remain indefinitely an unknown spot where people actually live: although why they do so, those who have never visited the place cannot imagine. It happens, however, that it has a distinct and valid title to fame because of a treasure which is not to be computed by monetary values. For upon this little island and among its villages there are songs sung of such antiquity as can seldom be found today.

The reason for this lies pretty much in the manner of lives which these fifty people lead. Here the inhabitants fish for their daily living, taking their catch in to Halifax for sale. A few have gone away to distant seas, but for the most part their lives are spent, and very happily too, in their own little community. In summer there is a growing interchange of visitors to and from the mainland. In winter the fishing boats run back and forth, selling their produce in Halifax, but their owners do not linger long in town. Winter waters are treacherous, and fishermen's boats are small. Consequently, wise men plan to be home before darkness falls, and the result is that community life is all-important to the islanders. With such a paucity of outside communication, old customs have remained, and we today are to benefit through the survival of old songs.

The stock from which Devil's Island was populated is mostly Irish, and the predominant name is Henneberry. In the beginning of the nineteenth century some three hundred families immigrated from Ireland and settled on McNab's Island in Halifax Harbour. The Henneberrys moved from there to Jeddore, a few miles further down the eastern coast. Later they found their way to Devil's Island, and here they have remained. Faulkner, DeYoung, and Edwards are other island names, but they are in the great minority. Strangely enough, there has been little intermarriage among them, for wives and husbands have usually been taken from the mainland.

Of all the island inhabitants, there is none more interesting to the student of folksongs than Mr. Ben Henneberry, coxswain of the lifeboat, and independent fisherman. Mr. Ben (so called to distinguish him from the numerous others of the name) has a most retentive memory, recalling as many as ninety songs, many of which are of extraordinary value. To him they are just old songs which he loves to sing.

He unconsciously feels the beauty of their poetry, and is not altogether surprised to learn of their actual worth. In this article, I propose to say little of the folksongs which have come from him, from the lighthouse keeper Mr. Faulkner, and others, but to dwell principally upon the ballads which are still sung, beginning with that fine old piece, "The False Knight Upon the Road."

This is an excellent example of the riddle ballad. In remote days it sometimes happened that a clever lass won a crown by the solving of difficult riddles of State for her king. In this particular ballad, a child meets a knight upon the road who puts various questions to her which she must answer to escape his treachery. For instance:

"What is rounder than a ring? What is higher
    than a king?"
Cried the false knight to the child on the road.
"The sun is rounder than a ring. God is higher
    than a king,"
Cried the pretty little child only seven years old.

Many variants of this have been found, including several from this continent, but none is as fine nor so complete as this which comes from Devil's Island. Many of the questions asked are found in *Riddles Wisely Expounded*, revealing a close relationship with the oldest type of riddle ballad.

In this day and generation, with its countless diversions, the finding of a ballad is something of an event, particularly when the song is complete. Yet on Devil's Island we do not need to be content with one such song. All in all, according to the authority, Professor Child, there are only some three hundred [popular] ballads in existence.

There are many old songs, many genuine folksongs, ditties and many local songs which are spoken of as ballads, but the distinction is carefully defined. It is quite remarkable, then, that Devil's Island through its singer, Mr. Ben Henneberry, with the occasional assistance of Mr. William Faulkner and others, should contribute six, five of which are complete. These, of course, are variants of ballads found elsewhere; but where one is usually fortunate in picking up a stanza or two, the Devil's Islander recalls the full text.

Following close upon the heels of "The False Knight Upon the Road," the ballad of "The Cruel Mother" comes as second in importance. As we compare the wording of variants from different sources, many interesting features appear. Here the mother does away with her infant children, piercing their hearts with her penknife, and according to the Nova Scotia variant, the knife will not be washed clean since innocent blood has been shed upon it. This is an old superstition which Shakespeare uses in the sleep-walking scene in *Macbeth*. The magic stain caused by blood shed by a murderer's hand cannot be diminished by any amount of scouring. In Barry's variant from Maine this legend is given, and also in Sharp's from the Appalachians; but the

Nova Scotia text includes another superstition, the combination of which is unusual. In referring to the incriminating knife, the ballad says:

> Then she threw it far away,
> All alone and a-loney,
> The farther she threw it, the nearer it came,
> Down by the greenwood siding.

Another interesting phase of this ballad is found in the seven-year penances which the mother is to endure. These penances belong properly to the ballad of "The Maid and the Palmer," which is the story of Our Lord's meeting with the Woman of Samaria.

Then again, it is strange to find Robin Hood ballads sung on Devil's Island. Where did Mr. Ben get them in the first instance, and how does it come that he can sing them today as apparently nobody else on this continent can sing them? At least to the present time, no collection appears to have published it, yet "The Bold Pedlar and Robin Hood" is sung *in toto* by Mr. Ben, with an additional stanza at the end taken from another of the Robin Hood ballads, "Little John Goes A-Begging." His only ballad imperfectly remembered is "Robin Hood's Progress to Nottingham," of which only two stanzas and the chorus can be recalled.

Then comes "The Farmer's Curst Wife," probably the most widely current of all the old ballads, the legend of the old wife whom not even the Devil would take, being well known in the Orient and in Europe. Finally comes "Katherine Jaffray," which is the only doubtful piece in Mr. Ben's repertoire. It is evidently a much later variant of the old ballad which Scott used as the basis of his poem "Young Lochinvar." Whether it should actually be included among the genuine English and Scottish ballads is doubtful, but it is given the benefit of the doubt and added to the list. It bears a close resemblance to a variant in the Child collection.

Devil's Island is not the only source in Halifax County for ballad singing, but it seems to be the one most prolific. A few others have been found elsewhere, as well as many interesting folksongs. On the mainland at South-East Passage, close to the spot where a boat is taken for the island, there is a small community of people, Hartlan by name, whose progenitors were German. The present generation recalls little of the old German, but the deceased father and uncle seem to have retained much of the old country customs and speech, including an interesting superstition which dispensed with witches. When these unwelcome visitors came, the old uncle used to take nine letters from the German Bible and write on a board which he placed above the door. It was believed that the witch could pass over the door but not under, and as there was no access above the door, the family was left in peace.

It is rather difficult to discover just how it was that these German settlers, who came to Nova Scotia when Lunenburg was founded in 1750 and later moved up here, should be the singers of old songs of British origin. Yet many very good songs have been discovered here and two ballads, namely "Captain Wedderburn's Courtship" and "The Sweet Trinity." The former, like "The False Knight Upon the Road," is a riddle ballad. In this the hero wins his wife by answering difficult questions, a frequent custom in the old days. For instance:

> Oh it's for my breakfast you must get me chickens
>   without bones,
> And for my dinner you must get me cherries
>   without stones,

to which the man replies:

> Oh when a chicken is in the egg I'm sure it has
> no bones,
> And when a cherry's in blossom I'm sure it has
> no stones.

And so forth.

Other interesting ballads in the author's collection are "Lord Thomas and Fair Ellinor," "Little Musgrave and Lady Barnard," and "Sir Hugh; or The Jew's Daughter." The first is too well known to all students of the subject to be discussed in detail, except to say that Child considers Bishop Percy's variant the most beautiful of all ballads. The second is unfortunately remembered only in part. The third is extremely interesting not only for the text but for the story which lies behind it.

This ballad of "Sir Hugh; or The Jew's Daughter" was probably built upon some Italian legend, and bears a close resemblance to Chaucer's Prioress's Tale. For over a thousand years it had been believed that the Jews crucified children in contempt of Christ, enticing them into their homes for that purpose, although both Child and Percy absolutely discredit the legend. However, the story is a popular one, and the ballad is quite universal. It has even been heard sung by children on the streets of New York, and also by American Negroes. One stanza of the Nova Scotia variant describing the wiles of the Jewish girl runs:

> She gave him an apple green as the grass,
> She gave him a gay gold ring,
> She gave him a cherry as red as the blood
> Until she enticed him in.

The singer of these three ballads is Mrs. William MacNab, a Scottish lady whose family settled in Musquodoboit many years ago. She is living in Halifax now, and recalls still further a "Henery," one which is a variant of that charming ballad, "Lord Randal."

When the search for ballads and songs began, it was thought that a very wide field would have to be explored, many disappointments met, and countless discouragements faced. Such is usually the case, so it was really an excellent piece of good fortune that Devil's Island was so soon discovered with its adjoining district of German settlers. For in these remote districts where singing survives — and it is not every community that possesses its singers — the ballad singer is regarded still as a being apart from his fellows. He is looked up to as he was in the days of old when people gathered at one another's homes and through necessity provided their own entertainment, consisting very largely in the singing of old songs. Radio is coming even to the remoter districts now, and modern interests are creeping in; yet much remains still of old-time customs in Nova Scotia. When Mr. Ben Henneberry sings, his children, grandchildren and friends all gather about him with the same fascination their fathers felt towards the ballad singers of their day.

It is not the quality of Mr. Henneberry's voice that is so appealing, but his songs are all so interesting. Frequently he sings melodies which the listeners have heard before. This gives a pleasant sense of familiarity, since Mr. Ben never repeats himself to the extent of growing tiresome. On the other hand, he very often sings songs which they have never heard before. His companions who fish with him say that he is always singing in his boat, and even they who see him every day are constantly surprised when they hear him sing some new song. By "new" I mean new to them. Mr. Ben does not sing modern songs. Neither he nor other ballad singers can have any respect for them. His songs are all genuine old-timers.

It is sometimes curious, however, to find that something quite modern has crept in among the old stock. For example, Mr. Henneberry sings one song which is a highly technical piece of sea literature. Apparently somebody had read Walter F. Mitchell's poem, "The Tacking of a Full-Rigged Ship Off Shore," and had liked the sea phraseology it contained. At all events a tune was set to it and the dignified poem became a song. The first stanza, as it comes from Devil's Island, runs:

> The weather leach out topsails shiver,
> Bowline strain our lea shroud slack,
> Our braces taut and the least boom quivers,
> The waves was a-coming storm cloud black.

The same was done with a poem by Frederick William Wallace, the authorship of which has been credited locally to a mythical figure at Chezzetcook. Again the poem appealed to the reader, who adopted a tune and so set in motion a rollicking Nova Scotia sea song. It makes an excellent song, and the author has kindly given permission for its inclusion in the collection. The opening stanza runs:

> Come all you hearty haddockers
> Who winter fishing go,
> And brave the seas upon the Banks
> In stormy winds and snow,
> And ye who love hard driving
> Come listen to my lay
> Of the run we made from Portland
> In the *Mary L. Mackay*.

Melodies accompany all these songs, but of course cannot be given here. Suffice it to say that the tune to which the above is sung is one of the brightest and most singable in the collection.

These two songs are instances of adaptability, but there is no originality among folksingers. From the collector's point of view, this is a good thing because all wording remains as heard in the first instance. This is always a matter of wonder. Surely it would be much easier to substitute wording of one's own than to recall a forgotten phrase, but the ballad singer does not do this. He is extremely conscientious, and feels almost as if he were desecrating a sacred trust if he does not repeat a song exactly as his father or his grandfather sang it to him. He is very sensitive upon this subject. Occasionally other variants come to him, and he is quite disgusted when a line is sung differently from the way he has always heard it. A conventionalist is our ballad singer, and it is well that it is so.

Love songs, sea songs, nursery songs, indigenous songs, all are sung at Devil's Island and its environs, not only by Mr. Ben and the Hartlans but by others as well. Probably to Nova Scotians the local songs will be found to hold a particular interest for reasons both historical and romantic. Frequently sea tragedies and outstanding sea exploits have been perpetuated in song. A fisherman possibly has heard a thrilling tale. His imagination is fired, and he composes a ballad, so called, to describe the incident in such a way that it will not soon be forgotten. The melody is probably one he knows which fits nicely into his wording, or more probably he words his song with a particular melody in mind. It is a story which he sings and spreads widely. In the old days it was no idle boast that a song needed to be heard only once to be remembered.

From a literary standpoint, the song "Peter Rambelay" is probably the most interesting, one stanza being very reminiscent of the ballad of "Mary Hamilton." Others are valuable for local interest, and some for their historic value. For instance, there are three songs of the "Saladin" mutiny which give the last dying thoughts of three of the four men who were hanged for the horrible murders perpetrated on that ill-fated vessel, giving an account in detail of events which led to the tragedies. There is an interesting Newfoundland song of exposure to cold in a small dory from which two men were rescued. There is a delightfully frank song about a not-too-popular Halifax sea captain. There is a sad tale of two little girls lost in the woods near Preston, and another of the Tangier Gold Mines in the days of their prosperity. One might go on indefinitely.

One of the most interesting things about these local songs is that they are still being composed. Fortunately, there are not many hangings in Halifax today; but whenever one takes place, a "ballad" is sure to be written about it. Sea tragedies are still honoured by song, and it looks as if the art will be continued for some time. Eventually these will, no doubt, find their way to Devil's Island to be added to the repertoire of Mr. Henneberry. So this modest little island rises from its obscurity, and through its singers becomes a place of foremost interest in the Province of Nova Scotia.

Helen Creighton, 1933

Cruising for Ballads in Nova Scotia
W. M. Doerflinger

The third of our Maritime song collectors is an American, William Main Doerflinger. His contact with Nova Scotia songs came somewhat later than that of Roy Mackenzie or Helen Creighton and was less extensive. However, he did collect a sizable number of songs from Canadian sailors, fishermen, and lumbermen, which he later published in a fine volume titled Shantymen and Shantyboys (1951), later reprinted as Songs of the Sailor and Lumberman.

Mr. Doerflinger's article published in the Canadian Geographical Journal in 1938 is an account of a summer spent looking for ballads in Nova Scotia. His description of the old-time singers he met and the situations in which he heard the songs add much to our understanding of the way song traditions persisted in our eastern provinces, and his quotations suggest the richness and flavour of his collection. The full versions of the songs he mentions and the ones he quotes in part appear in the book mentioned above, along with similar songs from American singers.

Mr. Doerflinger is only one of a number of Americans who have been attracted to Canada's Maritime Provinces by reports of the rich store of folklore to be harvested there. R. W. Gordon, who edited a long-running column on *traditional songs in* Adventure Magazine, *called popular attention to this region, and Professor George Lyman Kittredge of Harvard had encouraged Roy Mackenzie's initial collecting in his home province. Elsie Clews Parsons, who had collected among the Micmacs, was responsible for sending Arthur Huff Fauset to collect among the blacks of Nova Scotia. More recently, MacEdward Leach of the University of Pennsylvania collected in Nova Scotia, Newfoundland, and Labrador, and Edward D. Ives of the University of Maine (Orono) has collected extensively in Prince Edward Island and New Brunswick. Many publications have resulted from this research (see Selected References), including Dr. Ives's paper in this volume (pp. 174-88).*

Nothing makes the trip more interesting than having some definite business in the country one is visiting. The random tourist sees the scenery, but he is apt to overlook less obvious things. Confined to hotels, golf links, towns, and highways, he lacks many opportunities to meet people unlike himself, while the traveller who must traffic with strangers on their own ground is more likely to come back knowing a country for what it is.

I have made tours by wagon along the dusty roads of Nova Scotia, for fun. I have gone cruising for the mere sake of being afloat and landing in new places. Those trips were well worth the making, but never, when afield in Nova Scotia, have I encountered as many interesting corners and people as when I went ballad recording.

Sea songs were the interest I had especially in mind when I decided to tour western Nova Scotia, combining vacation with a serious hunt for traditional balladry. What luck I should have it was hard to judge, but ballad recorders must choose their districts partly by instinct, as trawlers and whalers sometimes choose their fishing grounds. And thinking it over more carefully, I felt sure Nova Scotia would be a good place to hunt the ballad.

One's main clue, in such matters, lies in the history of a region, and thus considered, western Nova Scotia seemed almost perfect. Not only was it new territory but the entire coast, from Lunenburg to Shelburne and especially along the Bay of Fundy from Yarmouth to the head of the bay, was, during the last century, one of the world's important shipping and shipbuilding regions.

Let me roughly describe it. A broad belt of woodland and farming country, stretching inland from ten to twelve miles, extends about the western portion of this eastern-most province. Centrally, the country consists mainly of barren, rolling wilderness; but even on the bushy uplands, when the wind is right, one can hear, miles away, the Bay of Fundy foghorns blaring their warnings of a dangerous lee shore.

Forty years ago the seaports along this coast, tiny villages and larger towns, were places well known to most seafaring men. The names of such communities as Yarmouth, Digby, Shelburne, Annapolis Royal, Windsor, Maitland, and Kingsport, lettered boldly under the sterns of spruce full-rigged ships, trim barques, rugged brigs, brigantines, and schooners, were reflected in salt water all around the world.

Forty years have passed and the sailing trade is dying away. Only the cargo schooners are left, jogging along our coasts in thinning numbers. Judging from the signs, nonetheless, western Nova Scotia seemed a likely region, though the majority of the men who shipped under square-rigged sail can no longer gather on deck for the muster roll.

Digby, westernmost town on the Annapolis Basin, was

my headquarters, and from here I made various trips up and down the coast, later crossing over to Lunenburg County. Lunenburg is the home of one of the world's great deep-sea fishing fleets.

Such an expedition, easy enough to make, is an adventure for anyone interested in the sea and sea traditions. For the scholar it affords an opportunity to see how folk-songs are composed, how they are carried from section to section and are handed down through successive generations. More than literary curiosity is involved, however, for the recorder will find deeper interest in the sea songs themselves — records, expressed in common sailor's language, of seafaring life in the most eventful eras of our nautical history.

One of the most productive trips was that from Digby to Westport along the coast of the Bay of Fundy. Digby Neck, a rocky, wooded arm of the North Mountain, runs westward from Digby Gut for thirty miles along the receding shore of the mainland. This high geological formation continues in Long and Brier islands, ten and three miles long respectively, and the entire range, from Digby to Brier Island, is a region of thick woods, lonely farms, and small fishing villages.

One hazy summer morning, having made a quick trip from Digby, I stood with a group of men on the gravel road that runs beside the flats of Freeport Harbour at the western end of Long Island. There were Captain George Thurber, former deep-sea shipmaster, Leslie Nickerson, ex-mate, John Finnegan, Fred Thurber, Charlie Musgrave, and myself. Since my arrival in the village, sea songs and yarns had taken on new interest for the sailors of Freeport, and it was easy, that morning, to keep the talk in nautical channels.

"There was one old song, now," Charlie Musgrave said, "that was a wonder. Told about everything that happened on a voyage in a Nova Scotiaman — and I wish I could remember what it was she was called."

"Don't you mean Corbitt's barkentine?" Les Nickerson suggested eagerly. The little old man in faded dungarees, thin coat, and heavy shoes, with his spry and cheerful air and natural hospitality, was the best singer in the group. "The song about the barkentine *George E. Corbitt* of Annapolis Royal," he went on. "Never sailed in her myself, but I remember her mighty well."

"That's the same ship!" Charlie Musgrave exclaimed. "She's the vessel. Now I remember some of the song — it starts with Annapolis:

> "Come all you brave Annapolis boys, I'll tell you
> what I've seen
> On a voyage to Demerara in a fancy barkentine.
> The thirtieth day of August, boys, in eighteen
> eighty-three,
> The *Eva Johnson* took our line and towed us out
> to sea!"

"The old *Eva Johnson*!" Les Nickerson put in. "Towed out to sea by the *Eva Johnson*, the same's I've been many a time, Corbitt's barkentine — she was a hot packet, too, the song says — a regular old bloodboat."

By way of illustration, he went on with another stanza:

> "That night they picked the watches and unto us
> did say,
> 'If you can't do your duty, boys, she's the hottest
> out of the bay!'
> 'O Lord, O Lord, what have I done,' so bitter one
> did scream,
> 'That I should be shanghaied on board of Corbitt's
> barkentine?'"

The ballad turned out to be one of the best and most popular of Nova Scotian "come-all-ye's" dealing with local ships and sailors. The summer's haul included five such songs, which is especially interesting inasmuch as this type of sea ballad is seldom heard in other parts of the world. Corbitt's barkentine was an actual vessel, of course, and the song is a literal, though sometimes mildly humorous, account of her voyage, with its amusing and exciting events. It took some time, however, to secure a full version. My friends at Freeport, who remembered only scattered stanzas, eagerly suggested other men who might "know it all." Later other fragments were obtained by following such clues. Not until I went to Annapolis, however, did I meet by good luck the former owner of the ship and thus stumble upon the ballad in full.

Captain Frederick William Wallace, author of *In the Wake of the Windships* and other maritime histories of British North America, mentions in that book having heard the same old "come-all-ye" often sung in schooner forecastles. The reader will also find in Captain Wallace's book an account of the "fancy barkentine" *George E. Corbitt,* abandoned at sea in 1890 after a gallant career.

Leaving my Freeport boarding-house early one morning, I followed the harbour road, passing weatherbeaten frame houses, modest but substantial, which look across the water to the neighbouring town of Westport. For generations the men of the two communities have followed the sea, many as fishermen, hundreds more as officers and hands aboard windjammers and steamers sailing out of Yarmouth, Nova Scotia, Saint John, New Brunswick, and more distant places. Reaching Grand Passage, the channel between Long and Brier islands, I saw tangible evidence that this seafaring trade still goes on.

A tern schooner (or three-master) had arrived in the Passage the evening before and lay at the Westport wharf discharging her cargo of rock salt from Turks Island, British

West Indies. She turned out to be the *Leo le Blanc*, of Weymouth, Nova Scotia, commanded by Captain Henry Burke of Lunenburg. The ship has since been lost on Turks Island in a winter gale.

That evening, however, I sat with Captain Burke in her transom cabin and took down some half dozen rousing ballads full of the tang of sea wind and spray. There were "Roll, Julia, Roll" or "The Liverpool Girls," "The Schooner *Druid*," "The Soldier and the Sailor," "The *Ebenezer*," "The Schooner *Blizzard*," and a beautiful Lunenburg ballad, "The *Donzella* and the *Ceylon*." Captain Burke remembers only about fifteen stanzas of the last song, the rest having escaped his tenacious memory. The search for the closing stanzas, describing the *Donzella*'s homecoming and the wreck of the *Ceylon*, took longer. Burke was mate of the *Donzella* later in her career, which may explain his great liking for the old ballad, beginning:

> On the first of February from Lunenburg we set sail,
> Kind heaven did reward us with a fair and pleasant gale.
> We left the port of Lunenburg so early in the morn
> And side by side we sailed away, the *Donzella*
>   and *Ceylon*.

Wind-swept and rock-bound, the islands of Digby Neck are connected with the railroad only by motorboat and by bus transportation to nearby points where boats leave for the islands. Such outposts, many of whose citizens are apt to be older folk, make the best places for ballad hunting.

Even more surprising, therefore, was my meeting with the owner and driver of the Digby Neck bus. I could see that this obliging person had a remarkable memory merely by watching him deliver packages to his clients at crossroads, farms, and cottages all along the thirty-mile road. No errand or request seemed to stump Guy Morehouse.

I was hardly prepared, however, when I mentioned an interest in chanteys and forebitters, to hear him say: "Sailors' songs, eh? Well now, let's see. My dad was a deep-sea captain, and here's one he used to give us when he was home between voyages."

It makes a pleasant memory — Guy Morehouse bending over the wheel, the bus swaying and jolting along a wooded road, the driver's voice raised in a stirring old ballad of His Majesty's Navy more than one hundred and fifty years ago:

"It happened on a certain day
The ship *Ramilies* at her anchors lay.
That very night a storm came on
And the ship from her anchors cut and run—"

Then the chorus, symbolic of sailors' fortunes all the world over:

"So come all you girls, you girls that we adore,
Pray for the sailors that are on a lee shore."

Here, in the song's rough language, is the picture of the loss of H.M.S. *Ramilies* on the coast of Devonshire in 1760 — the month of February — with more than two hundred officers and men:

Then the boats we in so nimbly did toss,
Some jumped in, while others were lost.
Some in one boat and some in another.
While the watch down below, boys, they did smother.

"Talking about lee shores," as Nova Scotians would say, the rocks of this same coast along the Bay of Fundy have gnawed the timbers of many strong vessels carried to destruction by gales and tides.

It was August when I left the Bay of Fundy counties for Lunenburg County on the south shore. At Lunenburg, shipbuilders, fishermen, and veterans of the road around

Cape Horn and the West India trade all showed they could handle their grace notes and *basso profundos* as well as they could the marlinspike and heaver. All too soon, I "left the port of Lunenburg" to go inland to Lake William, where woodsmen from all parts of the province were gathering for the Guides' Sports.

Here at Lake William, log burling and canoe racing, wood chopping and buck-saw contests, were the order of the day. They attracted a set of men as much at home in the woods as Captain Henry Burke is at home on his quarter-deck. Many were former lumbermen. Lumberjack ballads — "The Jam on Gerry's Rocks," "Peter Ambelay," "Guy Reed," "The Death of Harry Dunne" are well known in wooded parts of Canada, although the heyday of the logging camp and river drive in springtime is over. At Lake William I heard some of these "shantyboys' songs" with their stories of heroism and tragic accidents among the big timber.

Woodsmen are apt to be great singers. One Indian guide at the sports, Peter Glode, formerly carried his song collection with him wherever he went. Joe Penault, the Micmac fiddler, can play "The Jam on Gerry's Rocks" with a lilt and swing fit to bring boisterous shouts of applause in any bunk house. Another Indian introduced me to Kenneth Zwicker, who was for many years a cook in the lumber camps.

"Got any of them old woods songs with you, Mr. Zwicker?" the Indian sang out as we approached.

"Why, sure I have," the little cook said, without showing the least surprise.

"Where are they?" the Indian inquired.

"Right in my head," Mr. Zwicker said with a wink. "Do you know 'The Shantyboys' Alphabet' now?

"So merry O, so merry are we,
There's no one on earth so merry as we,
I darey you up and I darey you down,
Give the shantyboys doughnuts and nothing
goes wrong!"

One evening when the cool mists were rising from the lake, John McEwan, chief of the Micmac Indians at Bear River, sang "Peter Ambelay," another favourite woods song, whose hero hails from the Maritimes.

"I was born in Prince Edward Island,
Down by the ocean strand,"
runs the traditional ballad, one of which Canadians can be proud. A stoic song, it tells how Peter Ambelay left home to join a logging crew, as many a young Prince Edward Islander has done before and since:

In eighteen hundred and eighty,
When the flowers were in brilliant hue,
I left my native country
My fortunes to pursue.

I landed in New Brunswick,
That lumbering countree,
I hired in the lumbering woods
To prove my destiny.

There's danger on the ocean
When the seas roll mountains high,
There's danger on the battle-field
Where the angry bullets fly,

There's danger in the lumbering woods
For death lurks on us there,
And I have fallen victim
Unto its murdering snare.

"No more I'll see those stately ships as they go sailing

by," Peter Ambelay laments as he lies wounded in some woodland camp, mortally hurt, dying far from the home farm and the salt tides of the Gulf of St. Lawrence. His thought, at that moment, of ships and the shore is very true to life in the Maritimes, where many men follow the sea one season and "hire in the woods" the next. Many of the older sea ballads, therefore, especially those which tell romantic stories of love, shipwreck, and adventure, are beloved ashore as well as afloat.

One afternoon, for instance, I met an old man up in the hills at Greenland, Annapolis County, Nova Scotia. He had never been to sea, never long away from his lonely farm, but he knew some of the finest sea songs it was my luck to hear in Nova Scotia.

We had come looking for his son, a former lumberman, but we found old Mr. John Apt alone, reading his newspaper on the front porch.

"My son's quite a singer," he admitted, "but he's away on a job. There's no one here could help you, I'm afraid." Presently, however, there was a pause in our conversation and Mr. Apt hummed a tune absently. Then, with a wink, he began that rare ballad of piracy:

"Bold Manning was to sea one day
    And a dreary day it was, too,
As dreary day as ever you see,
    All wet with fog and dew.
They spied a large and lofty ship
    About two miles ahead,
'Come, hoist up our main-topsail, boys,
    And after her we'll speed!'

He called unto his bo's'n,
    Whose name was William Craig,
'O Craig, O Craig, come up on deck

And hoist up our black flag.'
His bo's'n was a valiant man,
   His heart was stout and bold,
But when he saw his father's ship
   His very blood ran cold."

Stanza followed on stanza. Clearly, bold Manning's language was that of the true hellion, as having overhauled his prey and heard her name and port of hail, he proceeded with his bloody business:

" 'Oh no, oh no,' cried Manning,
'These things can never be true,
So heave your main yard to the mast
   And let your ship lay to,
And if you think my orders
   Are not fit to obey,
With grape shot and with canister
   I'll sink you where you lay!' "

"Yes," Mr. Apt said after his gory song, "I learned that years ago from a big coloured cook in one lumber camp. He'd been to all parts of the world, following the sea. We used to hear him sing 'Bold Manning' while he was scouring the big iron kettles, and he could roar a song out with a wonderful voice."

The ice broken, other nautical songs followed. Two of these ballads I had heard mentioned elsewhere, but never found in print. Nor had I met anyone who knew them. Until that chance meeting on the porch of the farmhouse, these fragments of our heritage were locked, as far as I was concerned, in the limbo of all-but-forgotten things. That, however, is a fair example of a ballad recorder's luck. Some twenty-five songs came to light which had never been printed, as far as I can discover — old British sea songs, ballads of the Western Ocean, the lumberwoods, and rural America, besides many other traditional songs known in other parts of the world but offering interesting variations.

Even in regions as promising as western Nova Scotia, ballad singers are few, and the track of a single elusive song often winds far and wide, through so many communities and personal contacts that the cost would seem high except for the incidental interests involved.

For pleasurable travelling, however, I can recommend the trail of the ballad to anyone with a month or two to spend, a liking for rhymes and history, and a willingness to meet all sorts of people. Since the eighteenth century, ballad recording has been largely a province of the scholar, yet it is also work well suited to the amateur.

Certainly more amateurs are needed. Technical knowledge, of course, is valuable in attempting to record folksong music, but if one has a fairly well-tuned ear or, better still, an electrical sound recorder, he can still do a good job. Most experts, indeed, prefer the latter method to any other. Sound-recording machines have recently been used with outstanding success, for instance, by John A. Lomax, curator of folksong archives in the United States Library of Congress, which is building up a permanent collection of phonographic recordings.

In Canada, collectors have discovered some of their most important and interesting material. Professors W. Roy Mackenzie and M. M. MacOdrum, to mention only a few contributors, have secured valuable collections in eastern and southern Nova Scotia, as has Miss Helen Creighton. The work of Marius Barbeau in this field is well known, especially his collecting of French-Canadian material.

Still much ground remains unturned. Many unspoiled regions in Canada and the United States have not been touched. There is a rich field for students to cover in the few years while the last deep-sea chanteymen remain on deck and old-time loggers, bards of the bunk-house, still recall the falling of the pine and the songs that rang so bravely through the clearing.

William Main Doerflinger, 1938

In Search of Inuit Music
Laura Boulton

Laura Boulton was an outstanding American ethnomusicologist who spent most of her life searching for and recording the music of people living in little-known parts of the world: the Arctic, Haiti, Nepal, Tibet, Thailand, Borneo, the Penguin Islands. She made twenty-eight extensive trips over thirty-five years, collecting some thirty thousand tapes and scores of musical instruments which became the heart of the Laura Boulton Collection of Traditional and Liturgical Music at Columbia University where she directed a research program in world music.

In 1941 and 1942 she made extended field trips across Canada, collecting among the Inuit, Northwest Coast Indians, and Iroquois, as well as Polish, Ukrainian, French, Acadian, English, Irish, and Scottish Canadians from the prairies, central Canada, and the Maritimes. These tapes are housed at the Centre for Studies in Ethnomusicology at Columbia University, with some found as well in the National Museum of Canada. She also produced seven short films for the National Film Board, and a Folkways record of Inuit music, "The Eskimos of Hudson Bay and Alaska." For a detailed list of her collection of tapes and films, see Jay Rahn's article, "Canadian Folk Music Holdings at

131

Columbia University," in the Canadian Folk Music Journal.

The following extract is from her autobiography, The Music Hunter, *which describes her search for music in all five continents. Between August 14 and September 4, 1942, she visited Inuit groups in Chesterfield Inlet, Southampton Island, and Baker Lake along the northwest of Hudson Bay. In an earlier passage, she described her reception as follows:*

> *Our ship hardly nosed her way to shore and anchored before groups of Eskimos scrambled on board for the mugs of sweetened tea and cookies sent up from the galley, a feast which had apparently become an annual ritual. They streamed about the decks, shaking hands with everyone over and over again, their impassive brown faces suddenly transformed by radiant smiles; all of them as simply, as openly delighted with the little ship's arrival as a child opening gifts on Christmas morning.*

When the time came for me to leave Southampton Island, I sailed down the western side of Hudson Bay in the Peterhead to Churchill. On arrival, I walked in on the American officer in charge of the U.S. Army camp there. He looked up from his desk and stared in amazement at me, in my Eskimo parka with white-fox ruff. Knowing full well that no ship or plane had arrived, he exclaimed: "How on earth did you get here?"

I pointed to the Peterhead bobbing in the harbour. "On that!" I said.

I explained to him that my project was jointly for the United States and the Canadian governments, the filming of various phases of the building of airstrips in the North as well as Eskimo life. In that difficult muskeg terrain near Churchill our officers were most co-operative in my enterprise; but afterward, back in New York when the war was well over, one of them I had met there invited me to dinner with his wife in their apartment. He laughingly told me that at Churchill he had been assigned not to assist me in my work, as I had thought, but to keep an eye on me (suspected as a spy, due to my unheralded arrival).

It was this same officer who had first asked me, "Do Eskimos have music?" — a question I have been asked many times since.

It is a joy to me to realize that there are no people without music; everywhere people sing when they are happy or sad; they praise or placate their gods; and they are born, marry, work, play, and are buried to some form of music.

The Eskimo is no exception. It is true he does not sing at his work like many primitives; his lungs would probably freeze if he did. In the winter, at fifty degrees below, the very breath he emits freezes instantly into a thick fog before his face. Most of his work involves the hunt for food, and in the Arctic, where a whisper can become a shout, silence is deeply ingrained in his nature.

However, the Eskimo welcomes any excuse for a celebration, and this always means music. After a summer feast, or during the long Arctic night, a dance song may continue for days. Nothing refreshes the spirits of the group more than dancing, drumming, and singing — or, as the traders put it, "whooping it up."

At the feast following the big walrus hunt which we filmed, it was old Eevaloo who began the dance, striking a few beats as if testing the drum. The *someak*, or drum, is the only musical instrument of the Hudson Bay Eskimos. In one of our films, *Eskimo Summer*, we showed Eevaloo in every step of making a drum while his wife, Tuktoo, sat beside him singing songs and telling folktales for me to record. While she sang and talked, she was scraping with her ulu the hair from a caribou skin that would soon form the drumhead, and carefully storing away the hair for use on some later day, perhaps for stuffing a pillow.

The frame of this *someak*, which I acquired for my collection, is a hoop about two inches wide and twenty inches in diameter. Once it was made only from whalebone or wood from the tiny willow that grows sparsely on Southampton Island; today it is more often made of some light, pliable timber bought from a trader. Over this the scraped wet skin is stretched tightly (a new membrane is fitted for every special occasion), and it takes several men to hold the skin taut enough over the frame while another draws a sinew cord around the rim, securing the membrane to it. The handle is a short, stout piece of wood notched at one end to fit the rim and lashed to it with strips of chewed-down sealskin.

The wooden drumstick is bound at the end with sealskin which has been softened to mellow the tone, and the drummer, holding the drum by its small wooden handle above his head, turns it from side to side and strikes, not the fragile drumhead but the wooden rim, first on one side of the handle, then on the other, producing a deep resonant tone as he beats a slow persistent rhythm.

As Eevaloo drummed the feast music, he danced around the ring of women singers, swaying with closed eyes as though entranced by their singing. He balanced first on one foot, then on the other, keeping time with the music. From time to time he lowered the drum, usually near the end of a refrain, and then raised it again as he began the next verse. When he was tired from dancing, or perhaps from holding the big *someak* against the wind, another drummer stepped in to take his place. One can imagine that in the long winter of darkness and blizzard there is plenty of time for such songfests and dancing.

One of the favourite songs recorded following the walrus hunt was sung by my Eskimo friends Polly, Mikusha, Atitah, and Billy Boy, all excellent singers. Each man has his own special songs, and most of them, with the exception of incantations and children's songs, can be used for dancing. Many of the dancing songs recount the experiences of the composer, usually the exciting events of a hunt during the brief summer.

One such, the "Johnnie Bull" song, is the sad song of a very old man who was once a successful and famous hunter; now his hunting days are over and he can no longer keep up with the hunters when they go out by dog sleds in the winter. Always he must remain behind, but he has his memories and proudly recalls the great hunts and the good days when he shot seal and caribou.

> I must think of what to put into the song
> That I should have out here in the wild.
> I have not much to tell.
> I gave a piece of lead [a bullet]
> To what will be a boot bottom
> [A bearded seal used for making boot soles].
> In the same summer I gave a piece of lead
> To a big horned animal [caribou buck].
> Though I go no more, I remember them, for
> Now I cannot leave the camp, even in the summer.

In Eskimo music there are found certain distinct influences of northeast Asiatic and American Indian music, and in later years increasing evidence of the whites' music as well. In Alaska and Greenland the music is more developed than in the Hudson Bay region, where there has been less contact with the outside world.

Among the Eskimos of the eastern Arctic, many songs — for example, play songs, lullabies, and story songs — have no accompaniment at all. The melodies are extremely primitive, the text meagre in the extreme, and nonsense syllables such as *aayaa, yaayaa,* and *yaiyaa* recur again and again, especially in the refrain.

Besides these, there are the conjurer's songs for healing or weather incantations, hunting songs by the score, songs of tender sentiment such as that I recorded from a sick old man who is begging his wife to find another husband quickly who will be her refuge, and animal songs in which all the creatures of the Arctic are imbued with human characteristics, suffer the same hardships, deride, torment, flatter and woo one another endlessly. Children as well as adults act out these folktales about animals; they are all born mimics.

The art of imitating sounds is no game for the hunter; it is a serious business. On Southampton Island I made some fine recordings of Harry, one of the crew on the Peterhead, imitating the calls of the Canada goose, the snow goose, and the swan, which brought the birds close to us. He could imitate with great accuracy the grunts of the seal and walrus, sometimes well enough to bring the curious animals within shooting range.

In a very unusual game song that I recorded, two girls about fifteen years old placed an open kettle on the ground and used it as a resonator; they bent down and breathed words or syllables into it. Their rhythmic, aspirated breathing cleverly imitated the sound of tools, among them the saw and the drill, which they had heard on a trip to the Hudson's Bay Company post.

The music of Eskimo women and girls is probably the most primitive type of music in existence. The songs I recorded were in a fast, even duple rhythm, so regular and driving that to my ears they resembled the chugging of a train. This panting music is also known in certain South Sea islands but it must be among the rarest musical effects in the world.

Storytelling, like singing and dancing, helps pass the time when the Eskimos are confined to their igloos. Sitting around on the skins spread over the *iglerk*, the sleeping bench of packed snow about one foot higher than the floor, the men smoke — one pipe sometimes passing clockwise from mouth to mouth. The women nurse their babies or chew skins, and the children sit on the blanket of skins listening intently. The elders are strict in insisting that the stories be told and learned correctly.

The storyteller, usually a respected older man, tells his tales with great deliberation and with many gestures and grimaces to suit the narrative: big eyes when the owl talks, peeping around among the rocks when the lemming is chatting to the weasel, showing wild excitement for the walrus hunt. All the birds and animals have their own story songs, so that it takes many days and nights to sing and talk through the whole cycle. From the men's hunting experiences and accurate observations, the habits and customs of the animals — the clever ones, the strong ones, the stupid ones — are explained and taught to the children by means of story and song.

Ashivoo, a great singer of hunting songs who belonged to the Caribou Eskimos, lived at Baker Lake in the Barren Grounds, west of Hudson Bay, where an old Eskimo culture was well preserved. It is believed locally that the hills west of Baker Lake were the favourite meeting place of the aboriginals. There were, until recently, four groups of Barren Grounds Eskimos and they literally live from one hunt to another, depending entirely upon caribou and fish for food, clothing, bedding, and tents; when the herds are frightened away from their ancient migration routes, the Caribou Eskimos face starvation. This barren country is wide open. The hunter has only scant cover behind which he can hide when pursuing his prey. Nowadays he uses a telescope, which has become almost as essential as a gun. When he sights a caribou, however, he resorts to primitive stalking methods despite his modern weapons. He will spend hours imitating the grazing motions of the caribou, crawling along on the tundra with arms and gun raised in imitation of the animal's horns until he is within shooting range.

Starvation conditions are so common in these regions of the Arctic that the people have developed a stoic calmness in the face of almost continual privation; it is small wonder that so many of their songs have to do with hunger, like this one:

> We were very hungry, our voices were weak,
> We were too weak to go out on the hunt
> But we went hunting.
> We shot two large caribou with much fat on them.

I found this song as well as the other music of the Caribou Eskimos to be even more primitive than that of the Hudson Bay people.

The religion of the inland Eskimos also differs from that of the sea people. Since the very precariousness of their living and the harshness of the continual struggle for survival allow them little time for anything else, there are fewer taboos to be observed here; even the customs regarding birth and death are much more simple.

The Barren Grounds Eskimos are far from the sea. However, when we were there, we found stories and songs of the sea that clearly indicated some contact with coast Eskimos. There was, for instance, the song about the polar bear that tried his strength against a bull caribou. . .and the girl who married a whale. . .and many others.

Although there are no tribes among Eskimos, there are distinct dialect or linguistic areas but no powerful chieftains as with most American Indians. The shamans or *angekok* (medicine men) appear to be the nearest thing to public officials in an Eskimo group. They are both priest and physician. Through the help of the spirits, shamans — usually male but sometimes female — are thought to bring aid to unsuccessful hunters. The shamans also diagnose the causes of misfortune and illness and intervene between the people and the spirits. They intercede directly with the spirits when bad weather prevents the hunters from getting seals and other game and when starvation threatens.

The usual procedure is for the shaman, in a trance, to utter phrases and produce songs that influence the gods in the desired way. Beside the much-feared sea goddess, who must be kept constantly appeased, the god of the winds and the god of storms are all-powerful. The gods of the sun, Venus, and the moon are also vitally important to these people — especially that of the moon, which is believed to bring luck to hunters and fertility to women.

Even on Southampton Island, where the outside world has brought changes to his pattern of living, the Eskimo still cherishes amulets. One boy we saw was wearing no less than eighty charms, including miniature whips to drive away evil spirits, the claws of the white owl, the front teeth of caribou to bring luck on the caribou hunt, and a musk-ox tooth for luck during salmon trout fishing.

The Eskimo also had charms for his songs. For example, the skin of the Lapland bunting, fastened in the neck of a coat, is thought to inspire good words for the composition of harpoon songs. One of these charm songs for hunters was translated for me as:

How shall I do it?
The animals were not influenced
By my song when I sang it.

On Southampton Island the shaman recorded for me a conjurer's song which dealt with the intrusion of outside religion into the Eskimo tradition. The shaman made this song just after he had emerged from a trance.

Before they came to this religion
They used to meet with strange things
Not seen by ordinary people.
The land moved. . .the rocks moved. . .
They used to meet with strange, strange things. . . .

Music and the primitive poetry expressed through it are an important form of Eskimo art. Because their song texts are so meagre, the audience is expected to be familiar with the subject and to fill in most of the meaning. Difficult though it was for me sometimes to grasp their meanings, the songs I recorded frequently contained profound and beautiful poetry, expressing the deepest thoughts and moods of these isolated people when travelling, while hunting in solitude in the icy waters, or when back once more in the warmth and safety of a tent or an igloo.

The dance songs were sung not only as a pleasant diversion, as an expression of joy, or as gratitude for a successful hunt, but in adversity were sung and danced as consolation for the sorrowing, to bring hope to the downcast, and as supplication to the gods. The longer one remains with the Eskimo, the more one realizes the power of his basic religion. Among some Eskimo groups there is always a moment of mute thanksgiving after the hunt. Ravenous though the hunters may be, the group will crouch about the body of the dead animal, and the one who killed it will make an incision in the body, draw out the liver, and offer a silent prayer of gratitude to whatever god blessed and rewarded the hunt. Only then is this delicacy, believed to house the soul of the animal, shared equally among them.

The Eskimo is not by nature voluble. Despite his ever-growing contact with the outside, his motorboats, his cigarettes, and his windbreakers, he is still a nomadic hunter and an unpredictable, charming creature.

Only when he sings do we learn something of what goes on in his mind; only through his rhythmic recounting of personal experiences can we gain an insight into his stoic life, into his inner feelings which he would be totally at a loss to express to us except in song.

Of all the music I recorded throughout the Arctic during the course of three journeys, none was more revealing to me than the Eskimo's songs of rivalry. These songs of derision are extremely important, acting as a form of contest between men who have become enemies. They perform a vital social function within the group by providing an outlet for pent-up anger. The men speak their minds in texts that are completely ruthless, abusive, and rude, but ridicule always predominates and the singer is required to be entertaining and amusing. As far as I could see, friendship was usually restored in the end. How enlightened it is to settle disputes by song!

It is not uncommon for a wrestling match to begin between rivals in the middle of a song dance, and this quickly becomes a formal contest — a primitive form of jujitsu brought with the Eskimos from Siberia. It lasts until one or the other of the combatants has fallen and been pinned to the ground, but more often until both are too exhausted to continue any longer.

The Eskimo has a wonderful word, a phrase really, which seems to embrace his attitude to the whole of existence in this vast white expanse which shuts him off from the rest of the world: *"Kooyannah ayornamut!"*

So complex, so tightly condensed is the language of these people that only a loose translation is ever possible. "Kooyannah ayornamut" was explained to me as: "It doesn't matter" or "It cannot be helped." This phrase seems to cover their inbred resignation to the overriding elements which always have the final word in anything they do.

"Kooyannah ayornamut!" covers a hunting accident, a drowning, the death of a child (buried in the snow under heavy stones to protect it from the ever-ravenous huskies), and even the rifling of some precious cache of food by an unknown traveller (a rare occurrence). If an Eskimo is the equivalent of our ne'er-do-well or sponger, he will rarely be criticized by his own kind; he merely "did not hunt or trap this year." When there is no food or clothing for his wife and children, some group member will sooner or later take them in.

Eskimos may be considered primitive by many, but I wonder. . . It seems to me that any people who have evolved a culture in which personal disputes, jealousies, and angers can be solved through song reveal a richly civilized attitude we might do well to study.

I remember one incident on a morning during the summer of 1942. Whenever we were at a post between stints of filming or collecting material, we would gather in an inner room for the eagerly awaited two hours each day when the post was in touch with the outside by radio. The war was then at a crucial stage, the battle of Stalingrad.

In the big community room beyond, Eskimos were coming and going, and one or two of the more curious stood in the doorway, fascinated, as always, by the white man's behaviour. At last one of them, unable to contain his curiosity, inquired what it was that held us all there listening so intently to a voice from the outside.

With infinite patience the post manager began to explain. There was a terrible war going on; many men were fighting each other with guns, many guns. Many people were being killed, and we listened because we wished to know how the fighting was going.

The Eskimo's impassive brown face was a picture of bewilderment. We looked at one another, vaguely self-conscious. How could anyone explain the malignancy of civilized warfare to one of these placid, naive people, whose only battle in life was against the elements? How could we explain this hideous, organized orgy of violence to men who for untold ages had settled their disputes in lusty song, more often than not re-establishing friendships in the last verse?

The post manager was doing his best, but when his voice ceased, the Eskimo still lingered outside the door, his face clouded with an effort to understand, his eyes studying each of us in turn, seeking a sign that might make some sense of the whole matter.

Suddenly, after he had exchanged a few quiet words with a friend, he turned to us and we knew that he was about to speak for the other.

It was a question at once so simple and so complex that everyone in the room knew there could be no really adequate answer. He said simply: "What do men fight about?"

Laura Boulton, 1969

D'Sonoqua
Emily Carr

*So many persons have written so many pages about the
Northwest Coast Indians that they are among the best
studied people in the world today. Study has not, in this
instance, produced widespread understanding, for few in
Canada or abroad know the intricacies and appreciate the
meanings of the elaborate and dramatic cultural traditions
of these native groups, popularly termed the "Totem Pole
Indians."*

*Much of the published material is anthropological or
sociological in nature, concerned with such distinctive
traditions as the potlatch or the renowned plastic arts, but
oral traditions — most particularly folktales — also figure
prominently in the studies. The following item relates to
one form of tale, the belief legend, though it does not give
an actual story.*

*In the course of her artistic development, Emily Carr
(1871-1945) made a number of trips among the Northwest
Coast Indians documenting their life and culture in sketches,
some of which she later used to produce paintings such as*
Big Raven *(1931) and* Potlatch Welcome *(1930-31) for
which she is famous. Years later, no longer able to paint,
she recounted her experiences with the Indians in writing.
Coloured by time and nostalgia, her recollections, published*

as Klee Wyck *(1943), stand as testament of the influence of foreign cultural traditions on this artist's sensibilities, orientation to life and artistic vision.*

Here Emily Carr captures in words the power and mystery of the supernatural bogey-man figure she had previously portrayed on canvas in Guyasdoms d'Sonoqua *(1929-30). This wild woman of the woods was traditionally used to frighten children into acceptable behaviour. The absence of a tale about D'Sonoqua in Carr's account reflects the decaying state of the culture she experienced, for a vestigial belief may remain, in memory at least, long after the story that supports it has vanished with the ancestors. For another discussion of the bogeyman tradition, see J. D. A. Widdowson's article, "The Function of Threats in Newfoundland Folklore" (pp. 277-88).*

I was sketching in a remote Indian village when I first saw her. The village was one of those that the Indians use only for a few months in each year; the rest of the time it stands empty and desolate. I went there in one of its empty times, in a drizzling dusk.

When the Indian agent dumped me on the beach in front of the village, he said, "There is not a soul here. I will come back for you in two days." Then he went away.

I had a small griffon dog with me, and also a little Indian girl, who, when she saw the boat go away, clung to my sleeve and wailed, "I'm 'fraid."

We went up to the old deserted Mission House. At the sound of the key in the rusty lock, rats scuttled away. The stove was broken, the wood wet. I had forgotten to bring candles. We spread our blankets on the floor, and spent a poor night. Perhaps my lack of sleep played its part in the shock that I got when I saw her for the first time.

Water was in the air, half mist, half rain. The stinging nettles, higher than my head, left their nervy smart on my ears and forehead, as I beat my way through them, trying all the while to keep my feet on the plank walk which they hid. Big yellow slugs crawled on the walk and slimed it. My feet slipped and I shot headlong to her very base, for she had no feet. The nettles that were above my head reached only to her knee.

It was not the fall alone that jerked the "Oh's" out of me, for the great wooden image towering above me was indeed terrifying.

The nettle bed ended a few yards beyond her, and then a rocky bluff jutted out, with waves battering it below. I scrambled up and went out on the bluff so that I could see the creature above the nettles. The forest was behind her, the sea in front.

Her head and trunk were carved out of, or rather into, the bole of a great red cedar. She seemed to be part of the tree itself, as if she had grown there at its heart, and the carver had only chipped away the outer wood so that you could see her. Her arms were spliced and socketed to the trunk, and were flung wide in a circling, compelling movement. Her breasts were two eagle-heads, fiercely carved. That much, and the column of her great neck, and her strong chin, I had seen when I slithered to the ground beneath her. Now I saw her face.

The eyes were two rounds of black, set in wider rounds of white, and placed in deep sockets under wide, black eyebrows. Their fixed stare bored into me as if the very life of the old cedar looked out, and it seemed that the voice of the tree itself might have burst from that great round cavity, with projecting lips, that was her mouth. Her

146

ears were round, and stuck out to catch all sounds. The salt air had not dimmed the heavy red of her trunk and arms and thighs. Her hands were black, with blunt finger-tips painted a dazzling white. I stood looking at her for a long time.

The rain stopped, and white mist came up from the sea, gradually paling her back into the forest. It was as if she belonged there, and the mist were carrying her home. Presently the mist took the forest too, and, wrapping them both together, hid them away.

"Who is that image?" I asked the little Indian girl when I got back to the house.

She knew which one I meant, but to gain time, she said, "What image?"

"The terrible one out there on the bluff."

"I dunno," she lied.

I never went to that village again, but the fierce wooden image often came to me, both in my waking and in my sleeping.

Several years passed and I was once more sketching in an Indian village. There were Indians in this village, and in a mild backward way it was "going modern." That is, the Indians had pushed the forest back a little to let the sun touch the new buildings that were replacing the old community houses. Small houses, primitive enough to a white man's thinking, pushed here and there between the old. Where some of the big community houses had been torn down, for the sake of the lumber, the great corner posts and massive roof-beams of the old structure were often left standing naked against the sky, and the new little house was built inside on the spot where the old one had been.

It was in one of these empty skeletons that I found her again. She had once been a supporting post for the great centre beam. Her pole-mate, representing the Raven, stood opposite her, but the beam that had rested on their heads was gone. The two poles faced in, and one judged the great size of the house by the distance between them. The corner posts were still in place, and the earth floor, once beaten to the hardness of rock by naked feet, was carpeted now with rich lush grass.

I knew her by the stuck-out ears, shouting mouth, and deep eye-sockets. These sockets had no eye-balls, but were empty holes, filled with stare. The stare, though not so fierce as that of the former image, was more intense. The whole figure expressed power, weight, domination, rather than ferocity. Her feet were planted heavily on the head of the squatting bear carved beneath them. A man could have sat on either huge shoulder. She was unpainted, weather-worn, sun-cracked, and the arms and hands seemed to hang loosely. The fingers were thrust into the carven mouths of two human heads, held crowns down. From behind, the sun made unfathomable shadows in eye, cheek, and mouth. Horror tumbled out of them.

I saw Indian Tom on the beach and went to him.

"Who is she?"

The Indian's eyes, coming slowly from across the sea, followed my pointing finger. Resentment showed in his face, greeny-brown and wrinkled like a baked apple — resentment that white folks should pry into matters wholly Indian.

"Who is that big carved woman?" I repeated.

"D'Sonoqua." No white tongue could have fondled the name as he did.

"Who is D'Sonoqua?"

"She is the wild woman of the woods."

"What does she do?"

"She steals children."

"To eat them?"

"No, she carries them to her caves; that," pointing to a purple scar on the mountain across the bay, "is one of her caves. When she cries 'OO-oo-oo-oeo,' Indian mothers are too frightened to move. They stand like trees, and the children go with D'Sonoqua."

"Then she is bad?"

"Sometimes bad. . .sometimes good," Tom replied, glancing furtively at those stuck-out ears. Then he got up and walked away.

I went back, and sitting in front of the image, gave stare for stare. But her stare so overpowered mine that I could scarcely wrench my eyes away from the clutch of those empty sockets. The power that I felt was not in the thing itself but in some tremendous force behind it that the carver had believed in.

A shadow passed across her hands and their gruesome holdings. A little bird, with its beak full of nesting material, flew into the cavity of her mouth, right in the pathway of that terrible OO-oo-oo-oeo. Then my eye caught something that I had missed — a tabby cat asleep between her feet.

This was D'Sonoqua, and she was a supernatural being who belonged to these Indians.

"Of course," I said to myself, "I do not believe in supernatural beings. Still — who understands the mysteries behind the forest? What would one do if one did meet a supernatural being?" Half of me wished that I could meet her, and half of me hoped I would not.

Chug-chug, the little boat had come into the bay to take me to another village, more lonely and deserted than this. Who knew what I should see there? But soon supernatural beings went clean out of my mind because I was wholly absorbed in being naturally seasick.

When you have been tossed and wracked and chilled,

any wharf looks good, even a rickety one, with its crooked legs stockinged in barnacles. Our boat nosed under its clammy darkness, and I crawled up the straight slimy ladder, wondering which was worse — natural seasickness or supernatural "creeps." The trees crowded to the very edge of the water, and the outer ones, hanging over it, shadowed the shoreline into a velvet smudge. D'Sonoqua might walk in places like this. I sat for a long time on the damp, dusky beach, waiting for the stage. One by one, dots of light popped from the scattered cabins and made the dark seem darker. Finally the stage came.

We drove through the forest over a long straight road, with black pine trees marching on both sides. When we came to the wharf, the little gas mail-boat was waiting for us. Smell and blurred light oozed thickly out of the engine room, and except for one lantern on the wharf, everything else was dark. Clutching my little dog, I sat on the mail sacks which had been tossed onto the deck.

The ropes were loosed and we slid out into the oily black water. The moon that had gone with us through the forest was away now. Black pine-covered mountains jagged up on both sides of the inlet like teeth. Every gasp of the engine shook us like a great sob. There was no rail round the deck, and the edge of the boat lay level with the black slithering horror below. It was like being swallowed again and again by some terrible monster but never going down. As we slid through the water hour after hour, I found myself listening for the OO-oo-oo-oeo.

Midnight brought us to a knob of land lapped by the water on three sides, with the forest threatening to gobble it up on the fourth. There was a rude landing, a rooming house, an eating place, and a store, all for the convenience of fishermen and loggers. I was given a room, but after I had blown out my candle, the stillness and the darkness would not let me sleep.

150

In the brilliant sparkle of the morning when everything that was not superlatively blue was superlatively green, I dickered with a man who was taking a party up the inlet that he should drop me off at the village I was headed for.

"But," he protested, "there is nobody there."

To myself I said, "There is D'Sonoqua."

From the shore, as we rowed to it, came a thin feminine cry — the mewing of a cat. The keel of the boat had barely grated in the pebbles when the cat sprang abroad, passed the man shipping his oars, and crouched for a spring into my lap. Leaning forward, the man seized the creature roughly, and with a cry of "Dirty Indian vermin!" flung her out into the sea.

I jumped ashore, refusing his help, and with a curt "Call for me at sundown," strode up the beach. The cat followed me.

When we had crossed the beach and come to a steep bank, the cat ran ahead. Then I saw that she was no lean, ill-favoured Indian cat but a sleek aristocratic Persian. My snobbish little griffon dog, who usually refused to let an Indian cat come near me, surprised me by trudging beside her in comradely fashion.

The village was typical of the villages of these Indians. It had only one street, and that had only one side, because all the houses faced the beach. The two community houses were very old, dilapidated and bleached, and the handful of other shanties seemed never to have been young; they had grown so old before they were finished that it was then not worthwhile finishing them.

Rusty padlocks carefully protected the gaping walls. There was the usual broad plank in front of the houses, the general sitting and sunning place for Indians. Little streams ran under it, and weeds poked up through every crack, half hiding the companies of tins, kettles, and rags, which patiently waited for the next gale and their next move.

In front of the chief's house was a high, carved totem pole, surmounted by a large wooden eagle. Storms had robbed him of both wings, and his head had a resentful twist, as if he blamed somebody. The heavy wooden heads of two squatting bears peered over the nettle-tops. The windows were too high for peeping in or out. "But, save D'Sonoqua, who is there to peep?" I said aloud just to break the silence. A fierce sun burned down as if it wanted to expose every ugliness and forlornness. It drew the noxious smell out of the skunk cabbages, growing in the rich black ooze of the stream, scummed the water barrels with green slime, and branded the desolation into my very soul.

The cat kept very close, rubbing and bumping itself and purring ecstatically; and although I had not seen them come, two more cats had joined us. When I sat down, they curled into my lap, and then the strangeness of the place did not bite into me so deeply. I got up, determined to look behind the houses.

Nettles grew in the narrow spaces between the houses. I beat them down and made my way over the bruised dark-smelling mass into a space of low jungle.

Long ago the trees had been felled and left lying. Young forest had burst through the slash, making an impregnable barrier and sealing up the secrets which lay behind it. An eagle flew out of the forest, circled the village, and flew back again.

Once again I broke silence, calling after him, "Tell D'Sonoqua—" and turning, saw her close, towering above me in the jungle.

Like the D'Sonoqua of the other villages, she was carved into the bole of a red cedar tree. Sun and storm bleached the wood; moss here and there softened the crudeness of the modelling; sincerity underlay every stroke.

She appeared to be neither wooden nor stationary, but a singing spirit, young and fresh, passing through the jungle. No violence coarsened her; no power domineered to wither her. She was graciously feminine. Across her forehead her creator had fashioned the Sistheutl, or mythical two-headed sea serpent. One of its heads fell to either shoulder, hiding the stuck-out ears and framing her face from a central parting on her forehead which seemed to increase its womanliness.

She caught your breath, this D'Sonoqua, alive in the dead bole of the cedar. She summed up the depth and charm of the whole forest, driving away its menace.

I sat down to sketch. What was the noise of purring and rubbing going on about my feet? Cats. I rubbed my eyes to make sure I was seeing right, and counted a dozen of them. They jumped into my lap and sprang to my shoulders. They were real — and very feminine.

There we were — D'Sonoqua, the cats and I — the woman who only a few moments ago had forced herself to come behind the houses in trembling fear of the "wild woman of the woods" — wild in the sense that forest creatures are wild — shy, untouchable.

Emily Carr, 1941

III. SURVEYS

"The Cut-Off Head Frozen On": Some International Versions of a Tall Tale
Herbert Halpert

Herbert Halpert was born in New York in 1911 of Hungarian parents. After graduating from New York University, he took his Masters at Columbia, studying with Ruth Benedict and George Herzog. His early collecting focussed on the Pines region of New Jersey, although he also collected widely in the Catskills, Pennsylvania, and various southern states.

He took his doctorate at Indiana University under Stith Thompson, where he initiated the Hoosier Folklore Bulletin. *Even when inducted into the United States Army, he continued his collecting wherever he happened to be stationed, gathering, among other things, an interesting assortment of tall tales from Calgary.*

After the war he taught at several American colleges until 1962 when he went to the Memorial University of Newfoundland. There his collecting and research led to the founding of the Department of Folklore in 1968. In 1979 he became Professor Emeritus, but has continued to work in Memorial's Folklore Department preparing his vast collections of songs and tales for publication.

Dr. Halpert was elected a Fellow of the American Folklore Society in 1954, served as its president in 1955, and was named an honorary president of the Folklore Studies Association of Canada in 1976.

An ardent bibliophile, Dr. Halpert has built up an extensive library of folklore materials, annotated many folktale collections, and published numerous articles that exhibit his bibliographic knowledge. In his introduction to Folklore Studies in Honour of Herbert Halpert, *Neil Rosenberg* noted:

> In 1956 he told the American Folklore Society, "It still amazes me that there was so little cross-fertilization between anthropology and literary scholarship in spite of the fact that Boas, as well as Child, was a founder of the American Folklore Society." He spoke as one of the first folklorists to embody these two traits. Equally as easy in the field and the library, he has stressed in his teaching and writing both the functional and comparative approaches.

The following article is a good example of his comparative approach. It illustrates the scope of his bibliographic expertise in tracing the history and variations of a popular folktale that has been told and retold in Newfoundland since 1795, if not before.

When the study of folktales became a scholarly practice in the nineteenth century, folklorists like Reinhold Kohler and Johannes Bolte of Germany and Julius and Kaarle Krohn of Finland developed the system of historical and comparative analysis of individual tales. They would seek out all the different versions of a particular tale wherever it had appeared, classify them chronologically and geographically, and compare them to see the kinds of variation that occurred. Here Dr. Halpert takes a popular Newfoundland tall tale and shows how it has travelled and changed since *its first appearance in a sixteenth-century German joke book, tracing it through France, England, America, Scotland, New Brunswick, and back to Newfoundland again.*

A tall tale, heard and recorded in Newfoundland in 1794 or 1795 by an English seaman, but not printed until 1968, reminded me when I read it several years ago of a similar tale, told in Indiana, which I had published in 1942. The striking resemblance between the tales, so separated in time and space, started me on the search for parallels which led to this compilation.[1]

The story, like most tall tales, is simple. A man has his head cut off, accidentally or deliberately; it is instantly frozen back in place by intensely cold weather and the man appears unhurt; and it falls or is thrown off when the man is exposed to heat and thaws.

Although I have found that the story has an international distribution, it does not appear in Stith Thompson's Type and Motif Indexes.[2] My Indiana version (1942) was abstracted and given motif number X1722*(b) by Ernest W. Baughman.[3] I have used "The Cut-Off Head Frozen On" as the working title for this tale.

In this article I shall reprint all the published texts I have located and several unpublished ones. All are told as true (actual experiences) and are usually well localized. Variations appear mainly in the manner of decapitation, and the way in which the frozen-on head is again separated from the body.

The tale recorded by Aaron Thomas in 1795 in Newfoundland is still told in this province, and I shall begin and end my presentation with the Newfoundland texts. Other versions, from Great Britain, western Europe, the United States, and the Maritimes will be cited more or less chronologically.

The first Newfoundland version is, so far as I can determine, also the earliest text found in North America. It was heard in St. John's in 1794 or 1795 by Aaron Thomas, an English able-bodied seaman, who wrote it in his journal, a fascinating record which was not published until 1968. His complete story is reprinted below, with the permission of the editor and the publisher.[4]

> I sat in company the other evening with a poor but merry Fellow who told me that a Brother of his had been killed in the Woods last Winter, and as it tends to show the extreme severity of the Climate here I shall introduce the anecdote.
>
> When the face of nature was cloathed with Snow in December last, two men of the names of Lacey and Connor went into the Woods to cut wood. It froze so strong that Icicles were form'd by the water that dropped from the Eyes and Nose. Lacey was bending his head down near to the Stick when Connor was cutting. Unhappyly the Ax missed the stick, struck the frozen Snow, rebounded and fatally hit the neck of Lacey. This sever'd his head from his body. But Connor immediately laid hold of the decapitated head, placed it on the body again, which *froze* and united the body and head, and for the present saved Lacey's life. After this Lacey and Connor carry'd their load of Wood to St. John's. Unfortunately Lacey went into a warm room where there was a good fire and, while he was relating the narrow escape he had had from death in the morning, he stooped

over the fire to take some Fish out of a Kettle which was boiling. In performing this office his head fell off (the warmth having thawed his neck), it fell into the Pott and his Trunk tumbled backward on the floor, and both perish'd at the same *moment.* . . . So much for Master Lacey!

This is a well-told yarn that retains some of the details and flavour of an oral delivery despite the introduction of a few literary phrases. It should be compared, however, with the transcript of a taped version from a twentieth-century Newfoundland storyteller at the close of this article.

Turning now to other examples, I shall begin with the variants in which the man is decapitated intentionally. I have three texts, from Germany, France, and England, which are the earliest versions of the motif that I have found to date.

Proceeding chronologically, the first story comes from sixteenth-century Germany. Since this is the period of the great German jestbook compilations, not surprisingly the tale comes from one of them: Hans Wilhelm Kirchhoff's *Wendenmuth*, Vol. 1 (1563).[5] I give it here in an English translation,[6] retaining the compiler's title.

Head Frozen Fast

I once knew a person who says in winter he once saw an executioner cut the head off a poor fellow who was standing up so quickly that it remained on the body and froze fast; afterwards he brought him home and sat him behind the table. Now when the poor man got warm and wanted to blow his nose, he flung his head behind the room door and only then died. Such people who can lie in this way must be of good complexion, since where they're selling such fantasies, the breath of life does not damage them.

This succinct yarn retains only the bare essentials of the plot, as one might expect from the fact of its inclusion in a large jestbook collection. Contrast it with the rich details given in the next version.

In this text the man's head is cut off by thieves rather than by an executioner. The original French version was published in one of the earliest European tall-tale collections: Philippe d'Alcripe's *La Nouvelle Fabrique des Excellents Traits de Vérité* (1579). Since Renaissance French is difficult to read, I present it here in Gerald Thomas' English translation with his express permission.[7]

About A Man Who Had His Head Cut Off

You will remember (I think) reading and seeing how a man from Tarmonstier in Christendom, while going through a wood one day, was met by some thieves who, to get his money, cut his head off, or at least almost off, so that it was only held by the skin on one side, and how he pinned it together for fear that it might fall to the ground. And because it was winter and it was freezing hard, it stuck and did not bleed.

After the thieves had ransacked him and stolen everything he had, they fled off fast and far. The poor devil came home and told his wife (crying the whole time) how he had been robbed and everything that had been done to him, and then he sat down on a stool by the fire to warm himself. But wishing to blow his nose and remove a snot hanging from the tip of it, he pulled off his head and the pin which held it and threw the lot into the fire. Thus did the poor devil die, without even being aware of it, leaving a wife and four little children. Oh! What a pity! To the Devil and Hell with thieves.

> While young and strong we think ourselves to be
> We often fall down dead, for all to see.

Despite the verse tag-ending, this text seems close to an oral performance. This style is one of the factors which led Thomas to suggest, in his excellent translation and study of d'Alcripe's book, that *La Nouvelle Fabrique* should probably be viewed as the record of the sessions of an early Liars' Club.[8]

The third version in which the victim is decapitated intentionally comes from England almost a century later than d'Alcripe's story. It is No. 384 in William Hicks, *Oxford Jests* (1671). I reprint it here from Zall's text.[9]

> Two men fighting together in a frosty morning, one struck the other's head off, but fearing the Law, took up the head again, being reeking hot, and clapped it on, which immediately was frozen on. Then they both went to an Alehouse to drink, and he whose head was fastened, his nose began to drop and he, going to blow his nose, his neck being thawed by the great fire, threw it quite into the fire, which saved the other's life. *Probatum est.*

Here again, as in Kirchhoff's version, the tale has been condensed. A jestbook compiler, with rare exceptions, prefers the "quickie" rather than a leisurely tale.

Zall makes some interesting observations both on the age of the jests in Hicks's collection and on the style.

> In effect this is a pool of the best English jests current since the fifteenth century. . . . Captain Hicks is not merely retelling old tales. He distills his 583 jests to minimum length. . .often neglecting form entirely to emphasize the point.[10]

For the variant in which the man is decapitated accidentally by ice, I have only two examples, both collected in

163

the twentieth century. The first, a brief version contributed to me by an Indiana University student, I published in the *Hoosier Folklore Bulletin* in 1942.[11]

A young man[12] went skating one day and was skimming over the ice with such speed that he failed to see an air hole in his path. He plunged through with so much force that his head was cut off by the sharp edge of the ice and kept going on. Not fully aware of his plight, the young man kept on skating under the ice, until, quite fortunately, he came up through another air hole just as his head came along. He went home and did not realize that his head had been cut off until that evening as he sat by the fireside. There he sneezed — and his head flew off behind the backlog.

The brevity of this Indiana version can best be observed by contrasting it with Alan Bruford's superb tape-recorded version from Orkney, published in *Tocher* in 1973.[13]

He was a graet lad for tellin stories, he had a graet lot o stories, and there was a New Year's Day, ice cam on the loch, you see, an aal the young fellows cam there skatin. They were aal oot there wan New Year's Day, ice on the loch, an they were skatin an there were wan of this body 'at geed a bit too far oot, and in the middle o the loch the ice was soft, you ken, an it broake wi him an he geed doon, doon in a hoale, and the other edge o the ice just catched him onder his chin. He slid away under the ice till he came to another hoale, and his heid did the same on top of the ice, and when they cam there his heid just stuck on again. . .the frost was that strong, you ken, till it just froze his heid on again!

In the evenin then they were sittin aroond the haerth tellin stories, and this boy was there too, and he was gotten some o the cowld wi his dip in the cowld watter, you know, and he start to sneeze. An he was gan to blow his nose — they just blow their nose wi their fingers then, you ken — an he was gan to blow his nose, an wi the haet, it was kind o thaaed the ice aboot his neck, you ken; he aimed his heid in the fire!

In a letter (November 21, 1978) granting me permission to reprint his story, Mr. David Work, Sr. (who is now in his eighties) added this delightful paragraph:

You will know as well as I do that it must be a lie, but it is as I got it from an old man from the Island of Sanday, and all I can say is just this. If it's lees, it was lee'd tae me.

The disclaimer in the last sentence is apparently a traditional one in Scotland. In a collection of tales set in the Scottish Highlands, the storyteller concludes with the remark: "And about the water horse, all I'm saying is that 'if it's a lie to you it was a lie to me.' "[14] Dr. Bruford, commenting on Mr. Work's saying, wrote (May 2, 1979):

. . .I heard a phrase much like "If it was a lee it was lee'd to me" used by a Scots lowland tinker a week or two ago. . . . The Gaelic equivalent is a commonplace in Ireland, and known I think in the Highlands: "If it is a lie from me it was a lie to me," literally.

The third variant of "The Cut-Off Head Frozen On" had the man accidentally decapitated by an axe or other sharp instrument. Aaron Thomas' story, quoted at the beginning of this paper, is the earliest example I have of this.

My second example of this category was published by "Elsie Crane Blossom" in Spring 1960 in *The Potash Kettle*, a small quarterly leaflet issued by the Green Mountain

(Vermont) Folklore Society.[15] In reprinting it, I have divided the original single paragraph into three for ease in reading.

Fifty Below Zero

"Yes, I guess you would call it cold with the temperature down to thirty-five below zero," Uncle Hiram Mills said, as he came in from the back porch. "But I've seen it lots worse. One winter the temperature went to fifty below right here on this farm. It stayed fifty below for three days. I was a young lad then, but I remember it because of an accident that happened during that cold spell.

"Pa had two men working for him chopping wood. They was two brothers by the name of Lafe and Hollis Hatfield. Powerful built men both of them. Well, on the morning of the first fifty-below-zero day, Lafe and Hollis, with their dinner pails and axes, set off for the wood lot two miles away. They had been chopping about two hours when Lafe leaned down to tighten a boot lace, and Hollis, not noticing, up with his axe and took Lafe's head off slick and clean. It scairt Hollis so bad he picked Lafe's head up and set it back on his shoulders, and the temperature was so low the head froze back on, in no time. 'You all right now, Lafe?' Hollis asked. Lafe, not knowing what had happened to him, said he was fine. So the two men went on chopping, stopping at noon to eat their lunch.

"They chopped until four o'clock, when dark started to settle down and they headed back home. Hollis kept looking at Lafe, but Lafe seemed as lively as usual. Well, when they came in, Ma had a good supper ready, so they sat down and ate with relish.

Then they went into the setting room and set down beside the hot stove and lit their pipes. Well, the heat from the stove thawed out Lafe's neck, and his head rolled right off onto Ma's braided rug. There was nothing we could do to save him."

According to her niece, Marjorie R. Russell, "Elsie Crane Blossom" was one of the pen names of Elsie C. Harrison (1885-1973), who was born in Pittsfield, Vermont, and died at the age of eighty-seven in Rutland, Vermont. Her writing over a period of fifty years included historical novels, short stories, children's stories, and a play.[16]

Aside from the fact that her story came from Vermont, there is no information on where or when the writer heard it. It is obvious, however, that she had a trained ear and memory, for the tale reads much like one told by an admirable yarn spinner.

In conversation with Sister Catherine Jolicoeur of New Brunswick at a meeting of the Folklore Studies Association of Canada, I inquired whether in her wide collecting she had ever heard the story of the cut-off head frozen on. She said that she had, but was unable to recall either who told it or under what circumstances. Although she was reluctant to give me a poorly documented text, she responded to my plea for at least one other Canadian report of the tale outside of Newfoundland. Here is the text as she sent it,[17] a third version of the head accidentally cut off by an axe.

The Lumberjack's Head

A young man, working in the woods, had an accident. The axe slipped from his hands and cut off his head. He picked it up and put it back in its place. It was such a cold day that the head froze and he was able to go on working.

When he came back to the camp at the end of the

day's work, he sat near the fire to warm himself up. His head started to melt. He then started to blow his nose with his fingers as was the custom then and there. He blew so hard that the head fell on the floor.

Sister Catherine added this note: "Heard somewhere in New Brunswick sometime between 1950 and 1970."

The text is unique in that it is the only one in which the man cuts off and replaces his own head.

A fourth version of this variant of the tale came from Shetland, as given in a letter of October 8, 1978, from Dr. Alan Bruford. After giving me permission to reprint David Work's Orkney text from *Tocher* (see above), he wrote:

Meanwhile I have heard (though not in circumstances suitable for recording) another version of the same tale, this time in Shetland a week ago from Charles Laurenson (some 30 years younger, also a stock-breeder but in this case of sheep, and a son of a well-known Shetland storyteller, Mrs. Kitty Laurenson, now deceased), Susetter, Voe. . .he heard it from the late Robert Robertson, Collafirth, Delting, who heard it told of himself by James Manson of Walls, who had been at the Greenland whaling.

He and a ship's cook had shot a seal and landed on the ice to cut it up and skin it with an axe when he saw a polar bear coming for them: his gun misfired, so he struck out at the bear with the axe and cut the cook's head off. Perhaps this frightened off the bear; anyway, he was able to stick the cook's head back on where it froze, and all would have been well if the cook had not blown his dripping nose as he sat by the galley stove and landed his head in the fire.

There are some nice local touches in this version not found in any of the other texts. Both the seal and the polar bear might well have appeared in a Newfoundland version of the tale — but we have no such example to date.

We turn again to Newfoundland for my last texts. The first was contributed in writing on March 4, 1974, by Mr. Howard Genge (then twenty-one years old) of Flowers Cove on the Northern Peninsula of Newfoundland. Mr. Genge was in my office at Memorial University on February 15, 1974, while I interviewed and recorded Dr. Harris, whose version of the story is the climax of this paper. After the recording session, Mr. Genge remarked that he had heard a similar story back home. He promised to write it down for me, giving as much context as possible.

Mr. Genge's folklore collection is now housed in the Memorial University of Newfoundland Folklore and Language Archive (MUNFLA) and the text is published with the permission of the Archive.[18]

> I heard this story one stormy day when a bunch of young men (eighteen or nineteen years old) gathered at the house for a game of cards and a good yarn. I was eight years old (about 1961). After the card game was finished, jokes were told for entertainment and I heard this.
>
> The characters in the story were given real names, but no names common to the people in the area. Since I don't remember the names, I will call them John and Bill. They worked in the woods, logging, for Bowaters Company at Camp Eighteen.
>
> It was a bitter cold day of about twenty below zero and the wind was from the north. John and Bill were cutting down a huge tree with a cross-cut saw. John cut Bill's head off and quickly put it back on. (The storyteller made a gesture of quickly putting his [the] head back on.) It froze immediately and Bill didn't even know his head had been cut off. That

evening after work they went back to the camp for the night. They were inside the camp about fifteen minutes when Bill decided to blow his nose (gesture of putting forefinger and thumb to nose). When he did — he t'rew his head into the wood box!

The man telling the story was my cousin. . . . He is considered a good storyteller. He made the gesture of blowing his nose. This made the story funnier and more effective because you could imagine Bill throwing his head into the wood box.

This story has been well-localized to the West Coast logging camp milieu, even to the use of a crosscut saw instead of axes for cutting down a large tree. It should be observed that this is the only text in this final group in which the saw has replaced the axe. Mr. Genge has also given us good contextual details, such as the storyteller's gestures. For this story in particular the gestures are obviously an important element of the storytelling situation.

The text I have reserved to conclude this paper is, like the one from Orkney given earlier, from a transcript of a tape recording.[19] It was told by Dr. Leslie Harris, Vice President (Academic) of Memorial University of Newfoundland, during a recording session on February 15, 1974, and the story is used here with his permission.

When I asked when and where he had learned this story, he said, "Well, I think I can remember the exact circumstances in which I heard that — on the first occasion. There was a small general store in Badger's Quay, Bonavista North, run by an elderly man, Skipper Nat Spurrell. . . . He had a dixie stove — a potbellied iron stove. And he sat by it, and there were always three or four chairs around it. . . there was always a group around it. . . . Now I was a teacher at the time, and I would come out of school in the evening and on the way home I would pass Skipper Nat's shop.

And I invariably dropped in and sat for awhile and yarned and listened to stories and so on. So that's where I heard that one."

In telling the story, Dr. Harris, as he explains, adopts the role of the storyteller from whom he heard it.

> This is Aaron Thomas' story in part. Although I heard it long before I read it in Aaron Thomas' diary. I'll have to tell the tale as I heard it told. So — this happened in Bonavista North, and say the man's name is Baxter (fictitious) and Baxter is telling the story and he begins:

> "Did I ever tell you 'bout the time I chopped off me father's head?" And of course his audience say — no!

> "Well, boy," he said, "'twas like this. We was in the woods now, we was up in the north-west arm, in by Ten Mile Pond. We in cuttin' spars for the schooner. . . . An' me an' me father was cuttin' down this bloody gert pine. An' we were choppin' away an' choppin' away, I was on one side of un an' father was on th' other.

> "And by an' by, I don't know what I was thinkin' about, I wasn't thinkin' at all I s'pose, but father was chopped deeper than I thought he was or I was chopped deeper than I thought I was, but in any case me axe goes right on straight through the tree, takes father in the neck an' off comes his head.

> "Now," he said, "'twas a bitter cold day. Wind was no'west, scatter snow squall. And the temperature — Oh Jesus, I don't know, perhaps 'twas forty or fifty below zero. I knows 'twas pretty cold. Anyway, I gets the fright but I jumps an' grabs father's head almost before he struck the ground, an' stuck un right straight back on his neck, an' Jesus!" he said, "he

stuck. An' father didn't even know he was off. Didn't know what happened.

"So I looked at un for awhile an' he seemed all right. So we went away, carried on. We limbed out our pine. An' we got un ready for haulin' out an' got the haulin' ropes on un. And [here a pause of about five seconds] be this time now it's gettin' late in th' evenin' an' we're on our way back to the camp.

"Now I was almost after forgettin' now," he said, "about father's head bein' chopped off. But suddenly it come in me mind: what's goin' to happen when father gets in the heat? This is goin' to thaw out. Now what I goin' to do?

"So," he said, "we goes back to the camp and soon as we gets back father said to me, 'Now, Baxter, you go down to the pond an' fill the kettle an' I'll light the fire.' An' I says, 'Father, no boy. No, you go down and fill the kettle an' I'll light the fire.' An' he said, 'Baxter boy, what's wrong with you? You knows I'm the hell of a lot older than you is.' And I said, 'Yes, father, I knows you are, but I'm tired this evenin'. You go down an' fill the kettle, and I'll light in the fire.'

"So," he says, "father goes off with the kettle, grumblin' away, an' he goes on down to the pond, an' I lights in the fire an' gets the fire started. An' bye an' bye sees father comin' back up the path. Comes up an' he lodges down the kettle an' he says, 'Baxter boy, this is goin' to be some good to get in 'longside o' that fire.' An' I says, 'Father, we haven't got enough wood for the night.' [The storyteller laughs] An' he said, 'Well, Baxter, what's wrong? We got thousands o' wood.'

" 'No, father,' he says, 'it's goin' to be a cold night. An' not only that, it looks like it might goin' be snow tomorra, we're not goin' to be able to get out. So we got to have a lot o' wood cut up. You go now,' he said, 'an' cut down a couple o' rampikes an' start gettin' some wood ready.' So," he says, "father grumbled, but he took the axe an' he goes off an' he cuts down a couple o' rampikes an' he comes back an' he starts in choppin' 'em up.

"An' bye an' bye he has a big pile o' wood cut up — enough for a week. An' he says, 'Father, are you sure we got enough wood?' [The storyteller laughs] An' father said, 'Yes, Baxter, we got enough wood for a week.'

"So," he said, "I didn't know what to do anyway so I had to let un come in. Couldn't keep un out any longer. An' bye an' bye he was goin' an' I'm watchin' un. An' he says, 'Baxter, that fire is some good!' An' I'm watchin' father all the time wonderin' what's goin' to happen.

"An' bye an' bye," he says, "there's a drop starts to gather on the top of father's nose. Like it would, you know, when you comes in out the cold. Anyway, I'm watchin' father an' I'm watchin' this drop on his nose. An' bye an' bye," he says, "up with his thumb an' finger to blow his nose, an' — away [very high pitch, strong stress, final syllable lengthened] goes his head over [in] the corner! [Storyteller laughs] That was the end o' father!"

With this text I conclude my presentation of all versions of "The Cut-Off Head Frozen On" known to me, having demonstrated that the story has been in circulation for several centuries and in several countries, and is still in active tradition. It will be interesting to observe how many other versions come to light in Canada and elsewhere and whether or not they introduce any new or different themes.[20]

Herbert Halpert, 1979

The Man Who Plucked the Gorbey
Edward D. Ives

Edward D. Ives, head of the Anthropology Department of the University of Maine, has collected extensively in the Canadian Maritimes. He is founder and editor of Northeast Folklore *and is noted particularly for his book-length studies of three Canadian songmakers: Larry Gorman, Lawrence Doyle and Joe Scott. Here he offers a fascinating compilation of material about the gorbey, more generally known on this side of the border as the Canada Jay or Whiskey Jack.*

The subheading of this article is somewhat misleading. "The Man Who Plucked the Gorbey" is not only a Maine legend: it is equally well known in New Brunswick, and, as Professor Ives suggests, it was probably carried to Maine by New Brunswick woodsmen.

After amassing over a hundred versions of this particular legend, Professor Ives classifies it according to region and significant details, cites literary versions and various parallels, and uses the distribution of this legend to substantiate his conclusion that "the folklore of Maine and the Maritimes is one folklore." He might have stressed also the effect of the northern lumberwoods on such folklore, a point Norman Cazden made in his article on "Regional and

174

Occupational Orientations to American Traditional Song"
in the Journal of American Folklore.

The Canada Jay labours under the official name of *perisoreus canadensis* but it is more commonly called gorbey, moose-bird, meat-bird, grease-bird, Whiskey Jack, Whiskey John, Hudson Bay bird, caribou bird, venison hawk, grey jay, woodsman's friend, or camp robber.[1] Maine woodsmen usually call it either gorbey or moose-bird. It is a native of the northern coniferous forests, which means that it is found all through Canada but only in the northernmost states of the Union. In the Northeast, it is found in northern Maine and over most of New Brunswick and Nova Scotia. Ernest Thompson Seton said it looked like "a magnified chickadee": it is a little larger than a robin and has thick, grey furry feathers over most of its body save for a white throat and forehead and a black cap. It will eat absolutely anything. It will peck at a deer carcass, steal bait out of traps, make off with soap and candles that have been left around a camp, and the Indians claim it will even eat moccasins and fur caps. It is a great hoarder and has a stomach that is bottomless. One story tells of a camp cook who threw out some stale doughnuts, only to see a gorbey fly down, put his left foot through one doughnut, his right foot through another, grab yet another with his beak, and thus make off to a nearby tree with three doughnuts. Over and over I have had woodsmen tell me how these birds would appear around a lunch-ground deep in the woods. There would only be a couple the first day, but more and more would gather as time went on, and they got so tame that they would sit on your knee or shoulder, eat out of your hand, or, if you were not careful, steal food right off your plate.

There are numerous stories about the gorbey. A ballad, "Tom Cray," local to northern Maine, celebrates the demise of a woodsman who worked on a log landing:

"He started for the landing, one morning quite late,/ But little did he think of his terrible fate,/ When down came two bluejays, a garbey and took/ The poor little landing-man on Beaver Brook." And it warns us all as follows: "Now it's young folks take a warning, of the fowls be aware,/ Of the young folks take a warning, of the fowls be aware,/ Of the bluejays and the garbies that fly in the air;/ When you go out-a-walking, be armed and keep look/ For the bluejays and the garbies upon Beaver Brook."[2]

Often in Maine I have heard the story that these little birds are the souls of dead woodsmen. While most informants have not wished to go this far, they have told me again and again that no woodsman will harm a gorbey in any way. Another belief is, as one informant told me, "Anything that you do to a garbie happens to you. . . . An exasperated woodsman kicked at one which was stealing his lunch and broke its leg; a day or so after that, the man got his foot caught in the trace-chain of a scoot and suffered a fractured leg." Another man threw a stick at one, broke its wing, and that afternoon he broke his arm. It is with a special version of this sympathetic reaction that I wish to deal here: the story of the man who stripped the bird of its feathers.

Charles Sibley of Argyle, Maine, now well over seventy, had worked for many years in the lumberwoods around Moosehead Lake. On 30 November 1958 he told me the story this way:

Ives: You were telling me the other day about Archie Stackhouse.

Sibley: Yeah.

Ives: Now where did you know him?

Sibley: Well, he used to be wangan man up in the woods there, and he'd watch camp and tote-teams; he used to stay up there the year round. Well, this is the story they told. Now I don't know whether it's true or not. The only thing I know about it — he didn't have a spear of hair on his head no more than you in the palm of your hand. Not a bit. And they said he took a — one of these gorbies, these meat-birds, you know what them are. Well, he took one of them and he picked him, all but his wings. In February. Picked him all off, feathers all off him, all but just his wings, and he said, "Go, you son of a bitch, and get you a new coat." And they said the next morning when he woke up, his hair laid right on the pillow, every Goddamned bit. Now, 'f they's any truth in that, I don't know, but I do know he didn't have any hair.

Angus Enman (*aet.* c. 75) now lives in Spring Hill, Prince Edward Island, but in his youth he worked in the woods of the Rangeley-Magalloway area of western Maine. On 18 August 1958 he told me the story as it had been told to him:

Ives: Did you ever hear the story about the fellow who pulled the feathers out of the bird?

Enman: Yeah, I heard the boys talking about that up in the woods. Oh, I never heard very much about it, you know. Up there, those moose-birds — you was lunchin' out, you know — they'd be thick, they'd be startin', they'd be right there, and they'd come right up on my feet. And, uh, there was an old fellow setting alongside of me one day, and I pretty near caught one. And he said, "Look," he said, "I could tell you a story about that." He said, "There was a bad fella, wicked sort of fella, and he caught one of the birds." And he said, "He picked the feathers off him and let him go in the cold of the winter. And he said, oh, he passed a remark — he was a wicked sort of a fella — he said, 'Let the old son of a bitch that put them on you grow them on again.'" He said, "He woke up in the morning bald-headed as could be." . . . That man told me that one day up there at the lunch-ground. . . . We was up in old Blue Mountain up back of Andover.

More often, though, the story is reduced to a single sentence, sometimes as simple a one as the following: "The story is that he had plucked a bird in the dead of winter and the next morning his hair was gone."

I had collected several versions of the story in my travels around Maine, New Brunswick and Prince Edward Island. Usually the man named was Archie Stackhouse and the locale was "across Moosehead Lake," until I was ready to title this paper, "The Legend of Archie Stackhouse." However, to check my findings, I wrote a letter asking for information on "the man who pulled the feathers off a bird and later lost all his hair," and I published it in every daily and weekly paper in Maine, New Brunswick, Prince Edward Island and northern New Hampshire and Vermont. As a further check, I published it in several of the larger papers in each of the Canadian provinces and upstate New

York. The result was a veritable avalanche of letters — over two hundred of them. Not all of them told me the story but almost every one had something helpful to say. I ought to add that I received only a couple of "wise-guy" letters (none of them very funny), three tracts, two offers to be penpals, but none of marriage. "Folklore by mail" has its drawbacks and limitations, but I think that in the present study it proved its usefulness.

I now have over one hundred versions of the story, varying in length from one sentence to several pages. Archie Stackhouse no longer occupies the centre of the stage alone; he shares that place with twenty-eight others. All but one of the versions have Maine or New Brunswick for their locale.[3] Within this area the story is widespread and homogenous, but it centres in six areas, each with its own local "heroes." Let us make a quick survey:

1. *The Upper Penobscot Basin.* Roughly, this area extends from Holeb through Moosehead Lake, Chesuncook Lake, Mount Katahdin to Millinocket. By far the largest number of stories, about a third of all I have collected, come from this area, and they almost invariably have Archie Stackhouse for the hero. One from Holeb mentions a Moses Comstock, while two more (located over near St. Zacharie on the Canadian border) name a Joseph Morin. Here also should be included the handful of versions that come from the Rangeley area.

2. *Eastern Maine between Lincoln and Danforth.* Roughly, this includes the Mattawamkeag-Baskahegan River basins. Here the hero, when he is named, is William Stinson.

3. *Northern Maine and Northwestern New Brunswick.* Perhaps this area should be divided into two, but the score of versions I have collected all come within an area of less than a hundred square miles. There are six different heroes here: Around Presque Isle, Maine, for example, he is always

Leonard Ireland (or a variation of that name: Linwood Allen, etc.); in Fort Fairfield, Benny Teague. Across the New Brunswick line on the Tobique River, he is usually Henry Boone, although one version named a man known only as Hickey and another said the man was Wilfred Gray.

4. *The Miramichi Valley in New Brunswick.* More often than not, the hero is nameless here, but when he is named, he is Alex Martin, Alex Grady or Joe Grady. A Richard Graves turns up in Newcastle Bridge, some twenty miles to the south, and since the headwaters of the southwest Miramichi lie close to the Tobique, perhaps Wilfred Gray from that area belongs in this group. All the names are close enough to make that idea attractive.

5. *Albert County, New Brunswick.* That is to say, the Moncton-Petitcodiac area. Out of the dozen versions I have from this area, Howard Beaman is almost always the man named. One version names a Millard Downing.

6. *York County, New Brunswick.* This area is a vague one, and the hero is generally nameless, except for one version from around Magaguadavic, where he is Bill Robson, and one from the Nashwaak Valley, where he is Judson Estabrook. One version comes from as far south as Bocabec on the Bay of Fundy.

This completes the survey of the areas where the story is known. Aside from this change in the name of the hero, there are practically no differences in the stories told in the different areas; a detail found north of Moosehead Lake is likely as not to turn up just as often on the Miramichi or elsewhere. The only other significant area difference is that in the southernmost versions (those from around Lincoln and Danforth in Maine and in Albert County in New Brunswick) birds like the bluejay, robin, chickadee and junco are often substituted for the gorbey, but here we are getting towards the southern edge of the gorbey's range.

However, even north of Moosehead Lake and in Aroostock County, we find the bluejay and even the robin occasionally.

The story has numerous slight variants, many of them only elaborations. In most of the versions the man pulls out all of the feathers, but in eight he leaves the wing and tail feathers. One version has him burn the feathers off, while another has him put the living bird in the fire (in this particular version, the man himself is burned to death a short while afterward). Most of the versions do not report his saying anything when he releases the bird, but about twenty percent have him say something like "Fly to Jesus," or "Go to Hell and get a new suit," while only two (one of them Enman's) actually show him as "wicked." "Calling on God," as a man from Cape Breton, Nova Scotia, reports it, "if he had the power he was credited with, to grow new feathers on the bird." Very few of the versions say anything about what the bird does, but eight have it fly straight up out of sight after being plucked. Seldom is the reaction of the rest of the crew mentioned, but when the storyteller does include it he always points out that they were horrified or, at least, uneasy.

The retribution almost always takes place "next morning," but some versions have it a few days, a week, or a month later, while one or two make it a point that the man received his punishment "before spring." Most of the versions just say that he lost all his hair, but some go into detail, adding "body hair," "eyebrows and eyelashes," "beard," and "even the hair from his nose and ears." An interesting detail that turns up in forty percent of the tales is the following: "And the next morning when he woke up all his hair was on his pillow." Many versions that tell the whole story in a sentence or two will still keep this one concrete detail. An interesting variant from the Nashwaak River says, "That man lost all of his hair within a year. If I remember right, on a hot day in summer he went to the spring for a drink of water and dipped his head in and all his hair came out." Two versions say nothing at all about the man losing all his hair, one simply stating "That night the man died," while the other says, "Hickey was drowned about a year after on the drive on Pokiok Stream. The story was that a squirrel was the cause of the drowning." About eighty percent of the stories stop here, but some follow through, adding that the man was forced to leave camp or that he always wore a hat, "even to meals."

A version from Monmouth, Maine, leads into the story in an interesting way:

> It happened on the Tobique River in Northern N.B. The bird was called a gorby. An old woodsman wouldn't hurt one. Sometimes play tricks on them by tossing out a piece of hot bun toasted over the fire and the first bird that got it got a hot beak and then would fly up in a tree and scold and it sounded as if they were saying "Jesus Jesus." . . . This man thinking he was doing something smart held one and picked all the feathers off but the wing feathers and tail feathers and tossed it into the air and said, "Now fly to your Jesus bare-assed." The others predicted something drastic would happen to him and the next morning when he lifted up his head all his hair was left on his heading which might have been his bag of clothes called a turkey, a folded jacket or a bunch of fir boughs. He left the crew soon after.

I might add that several people mentioned this matter of the bird's cries sounding like "Jesus." The late Herbert Rice, woodsman, of Bangor, claimed that when Archie Stackhouse held the bird in his hand it was saying, "Cold, oh Jesus, cold!" while another man remarks that after being plucked "the jack ran off hollering, 'Oh, it's chilly, bejesus!' "

I would like now to quote one version entire, both because it contains interesting details not found in other versions and because it is well told. It was sent me by Mr. A. Richard, fifty-eight, of Brunswick, Maine, "as it was told us when we were kids by my grandfather as a bedtime story."

In a large logging camp in the Maine woods, a crew of loggers were chopping for a logging company and under the leadership of a very cruel and brutal man named John? ? [sic] who was known to be able to beat up five to six men any time at the least provocating word or act. One night or early morning during a severe snow storm the men were in camp drinking or playing cards, not having been able to even step outside the doors for three days. These men used to very active work were all in a very bad temper, but none so bad as Big John, the camp boss; and Pierre LeBlanc, the camp cook, who was the smallest man in camp and who was always stating that some day he, Pierre, would beat the life out of Big John, to which all would joke about; on this particular stormy night Big John was sitting by a window when a little corberie came to peck on the window pane wanting to be let in out of the cold. Big John opened the window, and taking the corberie in, proceeded to clean off every last feather; then tossing the bird back in the cold night. The men stared in frightful awe at this cruel act, none daring to speak a word except little Pierre. Pierre, tiny alongside Big John, stepped in front of the cruel man and denounced him as only a Frenchman can do and then made his last threat to Big John. "John, you big brute, some day you will wake up and you will also be plucked clean of every last hair on your body."

In the early morning the men were awakened by an awful moan. Then tramping on the floor getting out of bed they saw an awful sight; Big John the cruel, and the brute of all the logging camps, was pacing the floor stark naked, and as hairless as the little bird had been featherless. At this time little Pierre came from his kitchen and taking one look at Big John said, "Now you big strong brutal animal, God has punished you, but not the way Pierre is going to do." And with that, he proceeded to give the big man the most unholy beating anyone had ever witnessed and every man stood rooted to the floor, unable to stop Pierre until Big John was whimpering and crying like a baby. When Big John was revived, Pierre fixed him a lunch and ordered him out of the camp with the warning never to return.

From that day on, no man in the Maine and New Brunswick camps would work for the once big woods boss, so the company passed a rule that Big John would have the rights to food and lodging for one night at any of their camps and Big John earned his keep going from camp to camp, not daring to stay more than one night, and making reports to the logging company on location of good wood lots that could be had for logging.

As might be expected, a good many of the narrators were skeptical, not wanting me to think that they believed the story. A great many more were simply doubtful. Both groups were apt to add something like, "At least that's the way it was told to me." On the other hand, I was not prepared for anything like the number of people who claimed to believe the story. Even if I discount as simple narrative devices a handsome percentage of such affidavits as, "That really happened, sir," or "That's not a story, that's a fact" (and a small percentage should probably be discounted as ploys in the great American game of "Let's-hoax-the-folklorist"), I am still left with enough evidence to show that the story is often believed to be true. I have only one letter from anyone who claims to have been an eye-witness, but many of the letters quote sources that are, or were certainly believed to be, unexceptionable: "My father was in the camp where it happened," "My grand-father knew the man," etc. One man said the story was told him by Archie Stackhouse himself. One woman gave me the following attest for her great-grandfather: "[Grand-mother] says she is quite sure this story is true as her father was a very truthful man and he told it to her. This happened in the same vicinity as the incident of 'Gerrie's Rock.' Her father was on that drive too." If anyone doubt that, let him be anathema.

There are several literary versions of the story, as might be expected. Stanley Foss Bartlett mentions it in *Beyond the Sowdyhunk,* a collection of stories about the Great Northern Paper Company lumber camps.[4] Sometime before that, he had published the same version in the Lewiston (Maine) *Journal* magazine section. Gerald Averill tells the story in Chapter Seven of his good book, *Ridge Runner.*[5] This chapter was published separately in *Field and Stream* under the title "Esau and the Gorbey," in the March 1948 issue. Both of these twice-published tales had wide circulation in Maine and probably have complicated the pattern of oral circulation somewhat. Generally, how-ever, it is easy enough to spot a version taken from one of these sources through certain persistent details. And while perhaps we cannot consider the following usage as literary in the strictest sense, the Reverend Alfred G. Hempstead has often used the story both as an anecdote in a talk on "Woods Superstitions" that he has given to service clubs throughout central Maine and as the theme for a sermon. Mr. Hempstead, by the way, brought a special authority to his telling, because during most of the twenties he had been in charge of the Social Services Division of the Great Northern Paper Company and knew the lumberwoods and the men who worked there well. More wonderful yet, on 6 November 1924, he officiated at the funeral of Archie Stackhouse himself up in Greenville.

The story of the man who plucked the gorbey has many parallels. There is a West Virginia version telling of a man who plucked a sparrow and was haunted by the sparrow's ghost until he went mad and died.[6] A Nova Scotia version tells of a fisherman who caught a gull, cut its feet off, and said, "Goddamn you, get out and get your living the same way I have to." When he died, his hands were shrivelled up to look like bird claws.[7] A man from Nelson, New Brunswick, tells our story, only the punishment is that his children are hairless. The same informant also tells of three boys who saw a bird's nest with three young in it. They cut out their tongues, and as a consequence their own off-spring were tongue-tied.

There are no exact parallels mentioned in the *Motif-Index,* and I have discovered only two Old World analogues, both of which were sent me in response to my letters to the papers. One man remembers his father in Canterbury, England, telling the story about a common sparrow, and another from British Columbia recalls the story as it was told in his native Ayrshire, Scotland, around 1918 or 1920, about a Quentin Young, who plucked a robin and woke next morning to find all his hair "lying on his pillow."

How far back does the story go? In 1902 the late Fannie Hardy Eckstorm published an article called "Concerning the Bad Repute of Whiskey John."[8] She makes no mention of the story at all, and I think we can be sure she would have, had she known it. Furthermore, she evidently knew nothing of the superstition that these birds were the souls of dead woodsmen, nor does she say anything about woodsmen never harming them. In fact, she curses Whiskey Jack roundly for being a thief and a pest. "How the native hunters always hated Whiskey Jack!" she says. "They never had a good word for him, and a bullet was their usual greeting."[9] The only indication that there might have been a superstition connected with the bird came when she offered two dollars apiece for the eggs but was never brought a single one. "On considering the evident reluctance of woodsmen to hunt up the nests of this bird," she says, "I have suspected that there may be some superstition connected with [it] . . . ." But she goes on to say that the superstition may be "similar to that which Mr. L. M. Turner records of the Labrador sub-species. The Indians there believe that if a person sees the eggs in the nest, and especially if he counts them, some great misfortune will befall him."[10] At any rate, there is nothing about our story, and it seems safe to say that it was not well known along the Penobscot at the turn of the century. Of course, it may go back further in other areas.

The answer to the question of the age, origin and distribution of the story may lie in a curious etymological puzzle: that of the name "gorbey." You will notice that Fannie Eckstorm did not use the term. Further, while most of the standard bird books list the other names I have given at the beginning of this paper, they all omit the name "gorbey."[11] But in 1949 Ralph S. Palmer spoke of it as "a New Brunswick name which is also used in a few Maine localities."[12] Yet it is the name I have found most frequently when collecting this story; in fact, I found it twice as often as all the others. Looking the term up in Joseph Wright's *English Dialect Dictionary,* we find the word "gorb" not only listed as Scots and Irish for "*glutton, a greedy person or animal*," but also as Scots and North-Country for "*an unfledged bird,*" and figuratively "*anything very young or bare.*" Both senses of the term certainly apply: the bird is greedy and he is unquestionably bare. Finally, when we know that the Scotch and North-Country English were very important in the settlement of New Brunswick (not to mention their settlements in the rest of the Maritimes and, to a lesser extent, Maine) and that thousands of New Brunswick woodsmen came to Maine in the late nineteenth and early twentieth centuries, our house of cards is complete and looks something like this: From Scotland or the North Country, the story came to New Brunswick, where it became associated with the Canada Jay (perhaps because this bird is easily caught). Through the story, the bird itself came to be called a "gorbey." New Brunswick woodsmen brought the term to Maine, where it flourished, partly because there was a well-known, utterly bald "character" named Archie Stackhouse in the heart of the busiest lumbering country in the Northeast. Admittedly, it is only a hypothesis, but it is just too attractive not to mention.[13]

Finally, the story can be used to point up something which is becoming more clear to me all the time: the folklore of Maine and the Maritimes is one fabric. I will not deny that there are differences, but they are slight in comparison to the similarities, and here in this one story we have an example of almost complete homogeneity in Maine and New Brunswick.[14]

Edward D. Ives, 1961

In Defence of Paul Bunyan [1]
Edith Fowke

Lumberwoods songs and tales form an important part of Canadian folklore and Paul Bunyan is inseparably linked with lumbermen. Unfortunately, Bunyan narratives fell into disrepute among folklorists when a number of popular authors seized upon the tales and published their own elaborated versions. In 1914 W. B. Laughead began publishing his series of pamphlets featuring the Paul Bunyan tales as a means of publicizing the Red River Lumber Company of Minneapolis. In 1924 Esther Shephard published one of the early full-length books of Bunyan tales, and the following year James Stevens published what was to become the best-known version of the tales. These literary treatments led Richard Dorson to condemn Paul Bunyan as a fakelore hero and to cite the stories about him as prime examples of fakelore — a term he created to describe author-composed material using folk themes.

Edith Fowke rebuts this position, noting that the Bunyan tales had long had an independent existence in oral circulation. She discusses their roots and persistence and cites examples from right across Canada, as well as numerous early American reports. She argues further that even the tales created by such authors as James Stevens and W. B. Laughead have also become part of authentic folklore because lumbermen have picked them up and retold them.

This piece was originally given as a paper at the American Folklore Society in Portland, Oregon, in 1974 and later printed in New York Folklore.

Because Richard Dorson chose the popular versions of Paul Bunyan stories as his prime example of fakelore, it has become customary to dismiss all Paul Bunyan lore as fakelore.[2] Dr. Dorson himself was careful to qualify, noting that there was "a slender vein of oral anecdote"[3] or "a slender trickle of oral tradition"[4] beneath the torrent of printed material. However, others who have followed him are more sweeping. In his widely used text, *The Study of American Folklore*, Jan Brunvand refuses to recognize any oral tradition, saying: "American folklorists sometimes use the term fakelore to disparage the professional writers' contrived inventions — like Paul Bunyan — which are foisted on the public as genuine examples of native folk traditions."[5] He refers without qualification to "the fakelore invention of Paul Bunyan,"[6] and again he says: "Without influencing public opinion in the least, folklorists have shown how the facts behind the giant logger identify him as a fake folk hero."[7] That, I maintain, is as much a distortion as to hold that the Paul Bunyan of James Stevens is folklore. Paul Bunyan was not a fakelore invention and he is not a fake folk hero, despite the misuse of his tradition by popularizers. There is good evidence that Paul Bunyan yarns circulated widely long before the first printed tales; some continued to be told long afterwards without reference to print; and some of the printed tales went back into oral tradition, thus qualifying in their turn as folklore.

Let's look first at the early oral tradition. Daniel Hoffman, whose *Paul Bunyan, Last of the Frontier Demigods* is the best survey of the subject, does not show that "the facts behind the giant logger identify him as a fake folk hero." In his introduction he notes:

> At first Paul Bunyan was but one of a large group of localized occupational heroes, most of whom were similar to him in size and prowess in their respective vocations. . . . In the years before 1910 when the exploits of few of these titans had broken into print and their fame was largely known by word of mouth, Paul Bunyan already had a great advantage over his fellow demigods. They were limited to one region: the sea, the Mississippi, or the south. But the logging industry spread clear across the continent from Maine to Oregon, and wherever the lumberjacks went they took with them their beloved jokes about Paul Bunyan.[8]

Does that sound like a "fake folk hero"? Later Hoffman specifically refutes the charge that Paul Bunyan did not exist in oral tradition before the tales were first circulated in print, citing the traditional nature of the stories which had been told independently of Bunyan for a century or more, and the testimony of six ex-lumberjacks from western Pennsylvania and New York State questioned by Dr. Halpert which demonstrate that Paul was known in that region between 1895 and 1907.[9]

In the first printed article, "The Round River Drive," of 1910, James MacGillivray merely strung together a number of tales he had heard when he worked in Michigan lumbercamps.[10] W. B. Laughead's original 1914 pamphlet, *Introducing Paul Bunyan*, is also based closely on the tales he heard when he worked in northern Minnesota lumbercamps from 1900 to 1908.[11] As Dr. Dorson admits, Edward O. Tabor's diary proves that he heard many of the common

Bunyan yarns in Palmer Junction, Oregon, in the summer of 1910.[12] In the 1916 *Transactions of the Wisconsin Academy of Sciences*, Bernice Stewart and Homer A. Watt presented tales taken down from the loggers of Michigan, Wisconsin, northern Minnesota, and from camps in Oregon, Washington, and British Columbia.[13]

In an article in the *New Republic* in 1920, Constance Rourke quotes Professor P. S. Lovejoy of the Department of Forestry, University of Michigan, who, she said, "has an inexhaustible fund of the Paul Bunyan stories, collected in a large experience with lumberjacks and in the lumber industry. . . . He has heard them at their best, which appears to have been in the last twenty years of the nineteenth century."[14] She quotes numerous examples of the yarns Professor Lovejoy heard and notes:

> It was in the bunkshanties at night that the stories got into full swing, with the lumberjacks sitting around the deacon seat, a cast-iron stove red hot in the centre, wet clothes drying overhead, the reek of Peerless in the air, and the bull-cook chopping wood for the morning's fire outside. The best audience included a few greenhorns, easy to string, who might be betrayed into asking guileless questions and who would be likely to accept or miss at least a few of the richer inventions.[15]

Thus we have pretty good evidence that Bunyan tales were told in Pennsylvania, New York State, Minnesota, Michigan, Wisconsin, Washington, Oregon, and British Columbia before they appeared in print.

In addition to these, which Hoffman lists among his primary sources, I would add some Canadian evidence. Mr. E. S. Russenholt, Secretary of the Canadian Cooperative Wheat Producers in Winnipeg, wrote me in 1956:

I first encountered the Paul Bunyan folklore in the summer of 1909 — that spring, with my father and brother I homesteaded in the Swan River valley eight miles east of the village of Bowsman. Late that summer big construction gangs began to dig drainage ditches throughout the area. On those gangs I drove teams of horses and then mules. We slept in tents — evenings and Sundays a good deal of spare time was spent in spinning yarns. In many of these Paul Bunyan was the central figure. That winter I went to a logging camp in the Steep Rock River in the Porcupine Mountains six miles northwest of Mafeking. For the next six succeeding winters I worked at logging camps and sawmills along that line of railways from Birch River north and west almost to Prince Albert. . . . Since those years I have heard Paul Bunyan yarns in construction and mining camps throughout the west from the Pas and Flin Flon to Fort Chipewyan on Lake Athabaska particularly.

Although the tales Mr. Russenholt remembered in 1956 were influenced by the printed versions, his clear identification of the summer of 1909 as the time he first encountered Paul Bunyan seems reliable. Similarly, Dr. E. A. Corbett, longtime head of the CAAE, told me that he had heard of Paul Bunyan between 1900 and 1903 when he was living in the Miramichi region of New Brunswick. He reported that Paul frequented a certain saloon in Newcastle and the proof is that he would jump up to the ceiling with his hobnailed boots and leave a print of a huge P. B. there — a tale common in the legends of other folk heroes. Again, as Dr. Corbett left New Brunswick in 1903, I think we can take it that Paul Bunyan was known there at that time.

Then there is John Robins, longtime head of the English Department at Victoria College, University of Toronto, who first heard Paul Bunyan stories between 1900 and 1907 when he lived at Goulais Bay near Sault Ste. Marie, in the Algoma district of northern Ontario. In 1926 he recalled those tales in an article in the *Canadian Forum* inspired by the spate of books and articles about Paul. He noted:

> When I first became acquainted with him some twenty-odd years ago and probably for forty years before that Paul Bunyan had become the conventional name attached to the central figure of a certain group of yarns and of a certain type of story, the story of enormous exaggeration then and possibly still popular in the lumber camps all across the continent.[16]

While describing the typical tales, he inserted various comments on them as he first knew them:

> Then there is the tall timekeeper whom Mrs. Shephard and Mr. Stevens call Johnny Inkslinger, but who was nameless in my time and locality. We knew some of his feats, however. He was so observant that on one occasion, finding a moose dead of old age, he was able in the course of one afternoon to track the animal back to its birthplace. He afterwards wrote a complete biography of this moose.[17]

And that's a story that Laughead first used in the 1944 edition of his pamphlet, attributing the feat to Paul. Again, Dr. Robins commented:

> Of course there are stories which account for the striking physical features of the continent as part of the terrific activity of the mythical Paul. These, however, were not told to any extent in any camp I ever knew, except one or two about the origin of Niagara and the Great Lakes.[18]

Dr. Robins also noted a possible link between Ti Jean and Paul, a theory that Gartenberg was to develop in the *Journal of American Folklore* some twenty-three years later.[19]

In 1958 A. D. Norton, a retired engineer from St. Lambert, Quebec, wrote me about the stories he'd heard when he worked on railway construction and in lumber camps "many years ago."

> In the main our tales were mostly about our work, similar to the stories about Paul Bunyan; most of the stories published in books are mere piffle for they are irrelevant to the bush; whereas the actual stories were exaggerated incidents in a lumberjack's life, though unfortunately because they were the relating of the technical details they are not understood by the outsider.

While none of those Canadians gave specific tales credited to definite informants, their evidence does indicate that the stories were told from New Brunswick on the east coast through Quebec, Ontario, Manitoba, and Saskatchewan, to British Columbia on the west coast.

Thanks to Kay Stone, I have one fresh story that predates Laughcad. When Kay asked her father to write about his childhood, he sent her this story that came from his father:

> My dad had worked in the lumbering forest of central Michigan so he told us stories of a giant who lived and worked there. He was so strong that he could chop down the largest tree with two strokes of his axe. He could eat two dozen eggs, ten pounds of bacon, and a bushel of potatoes for breakfast, besides a couple of gallons of coffee.

They had trouble with him for a while because he cut down more trees than they could haul away. Well, he got an ox as big as he was who could pull five big trees out at one time. The best a team of horses could do was one small tree. My father had us believing in this Paul Bunion, and that he was real true. He told us that Paul Bunion chased him out of the forest because Dad put a wildcat in his stocking and a skunk in his shoe! And he said he tied a bear to the tail of his (Paul's) big ox, and the ox ran through the camp and knocked all the buildings down.

Well, according to Dad (him being a little guy and Scotch at that), Paul couldn't catch him because he (my dad) could hide under the brush and couldn't be seen. That's supposed to be why my dad got religion and settled down in the English part of Detroit. Paul, being French, would not look for him there, so he started all over again and became a streetcar conductor.[20]

Kay noted that it would be 1900 at the latest when her grandfather heard the stories — and he told the story to her father in 1908. Confirming evidence that it is not contaminated by print is the fact that her father spelled Bunyan as Bunion.

In view of the scarcity of collected tales in North America before the 1920s, it is remarkable that we have any evidence at all of the pre-1914 Bunyan. That we have as much as we have proves, I maintain, that Paul Bunyan was a very vigorous and widespread part of our North American folk tradition long before Laughead, Shephard, or Stevens ever heard of him.

Furthermore, Paul continued in oral tradition without reference to print long after the fakelore tales appeared, as witness the tales in widespread oral collections. John Lee Brooks collected a number from oil men in the Panhandle oil fields during the 1920s;[21] E. C. Beck noted quite a few mostly from Michigan lumberjacks in the 1930s;[22] and Richard Dorson himself got several in Michigan which are obviously not from printed sources.[23] Herbert Halpert included a few in his "Tall Tales from Calgary, Alberta" in 1945,[24] and Helen Creighton gives a couple in her *Folklore from Lunenburg County* in 1950.[25] None of these shows any evidence of being contaminated by print, and more recently I got several in Ontario from Joe Thibadeau that are equally pure. Joe had served as a guide in northern Ontario for many years and used to entertain with stories like these:

> Well, he was quite a man, Paul Bunyan, and he had an ox he called the Blue Ox. So the river where he was and where I happened to be, this Blue Ox he had him tied up there to a tree. "Well," he says, "that river's pretty crooked, isn't it, Joe?" and I said, "O.K., you go ahead and straighten it out." So he gets a big loggin' chain and he hitches it around a tree on the bend of the river, and he says to the Blue Ox, he says, "Come on, Buck, get goin'!" And he drew out nine miles of bends with one pull. And that Blue Ox sunk to his knees right in solid rock!
>
> Paul says to me, one time, he says, "We can make a little bit of money now quite easy," and I says, "Yeah? How do we do it?" "Well," he says, "you know where Boyd's big island is on Pigeon Lake. Well," he says, "we'll move that big island 'way down into Gannon's Narrows, and we'll block the channel, and," he says, "then they'll have to pay us twice that much to get it back." I says, "All right," so he says, "What

you got to do, catch a lot of those mud turtles — those big snapping mud turtles." So I got about a thousand of them and took them up to old Paul, and he placed them in channels, you know, right all around the island. And they love bananas, mud turtles, so we got a long pole and we kind of hung some bananas on the end of this pole and held them out like that, and they come up and come up and come up to get the bananas, and we knew the way we wanted it to go, you know — south, and they just went right after those bananas, and accordance they did, they were hitched to the big island and they had to move it, and they walked right away to Gannon's Narrows with it. Well, we got five thousand dollars for that.[26]

When I met him in 1964, Joe was living in Bobcaygeon, a small town near Peterborough, and Pigeon Lake and Gannon's Narrows are local place names. Incidentally, Newbell Puckett, who used to spend his summer vacations at Bobcaygeon, also collected a number of Bunyan yarns from Joe which are now in the Folklore and Language Archive at Memorial University of Newfoundland. These are typical tall tales, using traditional motifs in original ways — the kind that have long been told about Paul without any influence of print.

Then there is the third group of tales which have been influenced by Laughead additions to the canon. Hoffman notes that Ida Virginia Turney's chapbook of 1916 has many parallels to Laughead's, but he credits this to the complex interrelation between printed and oral sources.[27] He also discusses the fine storytelling of Perry Allen, whose tales were recorded for the Library of Congress in 1938. Some of them incorporate Laughead motifs, but others have no printed sources. As Hoffman puts it, "At any rate, in Perry Allen's mouth they are transformed again into oral tales whose structure shows the dramatic accomplishments of a talented raconteur."[28]

The fact that a storyteller calls the Blue Ox Babe or refers to Johnny Inkslinger or Big Ole the Blacksmith doesn't mean that his story is fakelore: it has been influenced by print, but many of Laughead's additions have been picked up by the folk and have passed into oral tradition. In fact, his booklets served exactly the same purpose as the ballad broadsides — the ballads as printed were not folklore, but when the folk began to sing and to circulate them, they became folklore. I would have thought that the influence of print on oral tradition was too well known to need emphasizing, but there seems to be a tendency to ignore it when referring to Paul Bunyan.

So, to recapitulate: Paul was a folk hero long before the popularizers got hold of him, and he has continued to thrive in oral tradition right down to the present.

Edith Fowke, 1974

Dancing in Cape Breton Island
Frank Rhodes

Of all the genres of Canadian folklore, none has been so un-
justly ignored as folk dance. Religious beliefs restrained
dancing amongst some early Canadian settlers — Scots
fundamentalists in Nova Scotia and some Jansenist French
Canadians, for instance. But mostly Canadian pioneers
danced for casual entertainment, at community festivals,
singly, in couples, and in groups. Many of the dances
reflected the élite or court fashions of the home countries
or sometimes of the urban-dwelling upper classes in frontier
Canada. Others, though, originated among the common
folk, the genius of nimble-footed artists.

Some early documentors mentioned folk dance, while
others portrayed it in drawings and paintings. Yet true
study of dance was hindered by the absence of a means of
recording and explaining it concisely and precisely. Even
early collectors especially interested in dance, such as
Maud Karpeles in Newfoundland, shied away from it for,
as she said, "It was too difficult to write down." Today
folk-dance study remains an open field in this country,
scarcely touched anywhere but in French Canada. With the
aid of modern, international dance notation as well as
videotape machines, collecting should now proceed and
the scholarship develop.

Of the studies to date, Dr. Frank Rhodes' analysis of Cape Breton dance with reference to its Scottish precursors and parallels is particularly noteworthy. It is based on a 1957 collecting trip to Cape Breton during which Dr. Rhodes found, just as scholars of historic French have discovered in Quebec and Acadia, some antiquated material no longer used in the land of its origin. With deep emotional commitment, settlers preserve some of what they bring over from their homeland and almost religiously pass it on to their descendants. These cultural remnants, memories of the homeland of long ago, must (because of the bonds of identity they represent) stay alive even long after their demise in the ancestral land.

Dr. Rhodes's article, then, supports a central premise of cultural diffusion theory; namely, that the most archaic forms will be found alive in tradition furthest from the source or "home" of the material.

Cape Breton Island lies off the northeastern end of the Nova Scotian peninsula and extends about 85 miles from east to west and about 105 miles from north to south. Until the middle of the eighteenth century the settlers on the island were mainly French, the nearest British settlements being on the mainland of Nova Scotia and on Prince Edward Island. Then in 1758 British forces captured and destroyed the French fortress at Louisburg on the southeast of the island, and the ruined town became the centre of a small British community. The British settlements on the mainland of Nova Scotia increased steadily, and after 1769 so did those on Prince Edward Island. However, no corresponding development took place on Cape Breton

Island until after 1784, when the island was separated administratively from Nova Scotia and placed under its own Governor, who chose Sydney, in the east of the island, as his capital. Immigration now began in earnest, and between 1784 and about 1800 immigrants came from all over the British Isles to settle the eastern half of the island. In the next two decades large numbers of people sailed from the Scottish Highlands and the Western Isles to open up the west coast of the island and the country round Grand Narrows. Most of these early immigrants crossed the Atlantic during the summer months when sailing conditions were at their best, and thus arrived too late to start farming before the short Nova Scotian summer was over. Many of them therefore stayed with already established immigrants until the next spring, when they could begin the task of clearing the trees from new 200-acre lots to make their own farms. In the middle of the nineteenth century there was another burst of immigration when the mineral resources of the island began to be developed; this time, however, the immigrants were mainly Irish labourers and miners from England and Wales (19).[1]

The Highlanders who settled in Cape Breton Island at the beginning of the nineteenth century handed down to their children many memories of their life in Scotland and of their early days on the island, and many of these traditional memories were recorded in the 1920s. Such records show that even in the very beginning the settlers did not allow the hardness of their lives to prevent them from following the recreations of their forefathers, and dancing seems to have played just as big a part in their social life as it did in Scotland. *The History of Inverness County*, a book which records the details of those who settled the west coast of Cape Breton Island, contains, for example, the following account of one family (19).

MacMillans (The Dancers)

Allan MacMillan was born in Lochaber, Scotland. About the year 1817 he came to America, landing at Pictou and spending his first winter in the new world with relatives at the Gulf shore of Antigonish. In 1820 he came to Rear Little Judique in the county of Inverness where he took 200 acres of land.

On the eve of his departure he was married by Fr. William Fraser (afterwards Bishop of Arichat) to Catherine Rankin of Lochaber. She was a Catholic and he a Protestant. He remained in the Protestant faith until his last illness, when he became a Catholic, and received the last rites of the Church at the hands of Reverend Alexander MacDonell of Judique. He was a celebrated dancer, and after coming to this country, kept a dancing class in both the settlements of Judique and Creignish. He had four of a family, namely: John, Donald, Ann, Sarah.

From the same source we learn of Lauchlin MacDougall, who emigrated with his four grown-up sons from Moidart. Like the MacMillans, the MacDougall family spent the first winter in Antigonish; then in 1808 Lauchlin settled three of his sons, Alexander, Duncan, and Archibald, side by side on the last 600 acres at Broad Cove Banks, and his fourth son, Hugh, on another site at Dunvegan. It is recorded that Archibald had a son Lauchlin, "This Lauchlin was a particularly cheerful and pleasant man, with an immense fund of the old Scottish legends," while Duncan had a son John who was "a man of great industry and good judgement, a famous dancer, and withal a kind and genial host."

In Cape Breton Island, as in the Scottish Highlands and the Western Isles, a good deal of dancing took place in the people's houses. The early Scottish settlers built for themselves quite large frame houses with three or four good-sized rooms on the ground floor, and thus had much more space in their homes for dancing than in their old croft houses in Scotland. The only alternative places for indoor dancing in the early days were barns and schoolrooms, for public halls were not built until the early years of this century — the first in Inverness County was built about 1900. Among the younger people outdoor dancing was also common, the wooden bridges being particularly popular as dancing places; also, in the summer whole districts would organize "picnics," when large open-air dance floors would be built out in the forests for a day or two of merry-making.

The dances taken to Cape Breton Island by the Scottish settlers seem to have consisted only of "four-handed Reels," a group of solo dances, and a few of the old Gaelic dance-games.

Most of the various forms of four-handed Reel (described subsequently) danced in Cape Breton Island have close affinities with the old West Highland circular Reel — they consist of setting steps danced on the spot alternated with a simple circling figure, the setting steps being performed with the dancers either in a straight line or in a square formation. I also met one form of the four-handed Reel in which the dancers swung each other instead of setting and in which the travelling figure was performed by the diagonal pairs changing places. This last form, which is very similar to the South Uist version of *Ruidhleadh nan Coileach Dubha*, was described to me by the oldest of my informants, Mrs. Jack MacDonald of Scotch Lake (she was over a hundred at the time when I visited her, and she put aside the painting of her garden shed in order to dance for me). Another of my informants, Mrs. Archie Kennedy of Dunvegan, had actually performed a dance called *Ruidh-*

leadh nan Coileach Dubha to her mother's *canntaireachd* as a very young child, and although Mrs. Kennedy could not remember this dance in full detail, her memories of it fitted Mrs. MacDonald's form of the four-handed Reel. It seems very likely, therefore, that Mrs. MacDonald's four-handed Reel was in fact *Ruidhleadh nan Coileach Dubha*.

Up to about 1939 the Scottish Foursome Reel, with its "figure 8," was known only to those people on Cape Breton Island who had travelled outside the island, and I could find no evidence that it was ever danced at the ordinary dances among the descendants of the old Scottish settlers. The situation in Cape Breton Island thus provides strong evidence that about the period 1800-20 the Foursome Reel, with its 'figure 8,' was not used in the West Highlands and the Western Isles (and indeed in more central regions of the Highlands such as Lochaber), and that the common Reel for four in these districts at that time was circular in pattern. We thus have confirmation of the evidence in this direction gathered by Dr. and Mrs. Flett and myself from living memory in Scotland.

In addition to its "English" name, the Cape Breton Island four-handed Reel also had two Gaelic names, *Ruidhleadh Cheathrar* (Foursome Reel) and *Ruidhleadh Bheag* (small Reel).[2] The latter of these two names distinguished the four-handed Reel from the eight-handed "big" Reel, *Ruidhleadh Mòr*. The old *Ruidhleadh Mòr* was the dance which earned the title the "wild eight," and was a very boisterous form of the Reel of Tulloch in a circle. At some time in the middle of the nineteenth century the "wild eight" fell into disfavour with the priests, and this led, apparently on the instructions of the bishop of the time, to a temporary ban on all social dancing — in some parishes the priests even went so far as to collect and destroy all the fiddles. The "wild eight" in its original form does not seem to have survived the priests' ban, but the eight-handed Reels which were danced after the ban lapsed combined the alternate setting and swinging of the "wild eight" with quieter circle figures. These more recent eight-handed Reels were not fixed in form but varied from one district to another, and also varied according to the inclination of the dancers. Moreover, for as far back as living memory extends — from at least 1880 — it has been quite common for these eight-handed Reels to divide into two four-handed Reels near the end, just as in Scotland the modern Eightsome Reel has, since at least 1894, often divided into two Foursome Reels.[3]

The solo dances brought to Cape Breton Island from Scotland were taught by a number of men on the island. In Broad Cove, Ronald Kennedy told me of the dancing classes which his father had held in that district up to about 1900. Ronald was not himself taught by his father, but as a young boy watched him teaching others the Fling, the Swords, *Seann Triubhas*, Flowers of Edinburgh, Jacky Tar, Duke of Fife, and The Girl I Left Behind Me, each of these being a solo dance with twelve steps. Ronald Kennedy's father had been taught by his own father, John Kennedy, who emigrated from Canna in 1790, going first to Prince Edward Island, and then moving a few years later to Broad Cove, where he commenced the dancing classes which were continued by his son.

A little further north, in South West Margaree, one family has preserved some of the solo dances taught to an earlier generation by Donald Beaton, an itinerant tailor. The dances handed down from Donald Beaton were the seven noted above, and also Tullochgorm, Irish Washerwoman, and Princess Royal, all ten of these dances again having originally twelve steps (1). As with the Kennedys, dancing seems to have stayed in the Beaton family too, for sub-

206

sequent to Donald Beaton a schoolteacher Angus Beaton held dancing classes in the town of Inverness and on the bridge at South West Margaree (3). Again, in Creignish, where Allan MacMillan "the dancer" held one of his dancing classes in the early 1820s, dancing classes continued to be held up to about 1900, and there were also classes in solo dancing in Iona and Christmas Island (10, 14).

The majority of the steps used in the various solo dances which survived among the Scottish communities on Cape Breton Island are very uniform in style, and employ a form of stepping in which the dancer marks the rhythm of the music with toe and heel beats and brushing movements, the feet being kept close to the ground throughout.[4] Although this form of stepping is unlike that seen at modern Scottish Highland Games, there is no doubt that the Cape Breton Island solo dances originated in Scotland, and indeed some of these dances can be shown on internal evidence alone to be related to solo dances which can still be found in the Scottish Highlands and the Outer Isles. This same form of stepping was also very largely used in the setting periods of the Cape Breton Island four-handed and eight-handed Reels. In the Reels, however, the steps were much less regular in construction than in the solo dances, and each individual step consisted of a number of very short sequences of movements of a more or less standard nature, these sequences being joined together as the dancer pleased in order to match as far as possible the notes of the music. The style of stepping used in the Cape Breton Island Reels is thus in close accord with the style seen by Colonel Thornton in the Scottish Highlands in 1804, where the dancers "all shuffle in such a manner as to make the noise of their feet keep exact time."

When the solo dances taught by the dancing teachers began to be forgotten, extemporized stepping of a form similar to that used in the Cape Breton Island Reels came to be used in place of the solo dances in exhibitions and competitions, so that until very recent years the dancing on these occasions was quite dissimilar in style to that seen on similar occasions within living memory in Scotland. This discrepancy in style was not widely appreciated in Cape Breton Island until in 1939 the Gaelic College at St. Ann started teaching modern Highland Games dancing together with some of the Country Dances published by the Royal Scottish Country Dance Society and some of the dances collected by Mrs. Mary Isdale MacNab of Vancouver. Since then many people in Cape Breton Island have doubted the Scottish origin of the stepping, and either have considered it to be an importation from Virginia or have attributed it to the French settlers from Louisburg or later non-Scottish immigrants. While all these factors may have had some influence on the present-day style, it is certain that the roots of the step-dancing lie in the solo dances and Reel steps which were brought from Scotland early in the nineteenth century.

The step-dancing, whether of a formal nature as embodied in the solo dances, or of an extempore nature as used in the Reels, was always a source of competition between the men. One of the popular tests of skill was *Smàladh na Coinnle*, the "smooring of the candle," in which a lighted candle was placed on the floor and the dancer was required to flick off the top of the wick with his feet whilst dancing, without extinguishing the flame (16). In an alternative form of this test, the dancers were required to snuff the candle between their heels while dancing (6). Again, at the end of an evening's dancing the two best dancers were often made to "dance it out," taking it in turn to dance as many complete steps as possible on a block of wood 18 inches high and 12 inches in diameter (10).

Of the old Gaelic dance games which the immigrants brought with them from Scotland I could find only vague memories. The centenarian, Mrs. MacDonald of Scotch Lake, was the only person I met who had heard of *Marbadh na Béiste Duibhe* (The Killing of the Otter), *Tri Criodhan Caorach* (Three Sheep's Trotters), and *Cailleach an Dùdain* (The Old Woman of the Milldust), which last she thought to be just "a plain jiggling twasome." But several people knew of *Dannsa na Tunnag* (The Duck's Dance), both as a children's game and as a dance for adults, and one 93-year-old lady danced a bit of it for me (15). Another dance of which I found some memories was *Dannsaidh na Biodaig* (The Dirk Dance): one version of this was performed over a dirk stuck in the ground with the point upwards (5, 10), while in another version the dirk was sometimes flourished and sometimes danced over on the ground (2).

Between 1890 and 1900 a number of Square Dances — Quadrilles, Lancers, Saratoga Lancers, and the Caledonians — invaded the island. These new dances were danced with Waltz and Polka steps, and with a sedate walking step. Moreover, they had to be danced properly — when there was dancing in the houses the young people practised in a back room until they were proficient enough to join in the sets in the front room. At first the older people continued to dance the old Reels in their own homes, but when the first public halls were built in the different townships between 1900 and 1920 most social dancing was transferred to these, and thereafter the programs consisted mainly of square sets. For the dances in the public halls at this time the couples paid for their admission to the hall, and also paid an additional charge for each set in which they took part. Within more recent years the full repertoire of the square sets has gradually been lost until now each district has its own single-figure Quadrille which is danced with little regard for footwork or phrasing. In the village halls nowadays, this "square dancing" alternates with "round dancing," this latter term being used to describe a couple dance derived from the Waltz, the Polka, and the couple dances of the 1920s, danced to boisterous Canadian-Scottish tunes. Only in a few halls in the largest towns will returned wanderers dance Waltzes, Quicksteps, Slow Foxtrots, or jive.

It will be noticed that the step-dancing classes closed down soon after the square sets were introduced — the step-dancing was no longer required for use in the fashionable social dances. Now only a few people occasionally step-dance in the square dances, the stepping is passed on in very few families, and one of the best young dancers whom I saw had picked up his steps from the television.

In addition to the various square sets, there were also a number of two-couple dances used within comparatively recent years in Cape Breton Island which consisted of selections from the "head couple" figures of the Quadrilles. These dances, which were usually known by the generic title the "French Four," were derived either from the square sets or from the Parisian Quadrilles, a form of Quadrilles for two couples.[5] The various four-handed Reels are sometimes referred to as the "Scotch Four" to distinguish them from the French Fours, but both types of dance are referred to by different people as the "Single Eight." The situation is not made any clearer when one comes across versions of the French Four containing figures similar to the version of the four-handed Reel which involves swinging. However, there is no evidence to suggest any origin for the two-couple dances other than Scotland or the Quadrilles, and each collected two-couple dance fits naturally into one or other of these two categories.

It is significant that Country Dances were completely unknown among the Scottish communities in Cape Breton

Island until their introduction by the St. Ann College in 1939, for this indicates that such dances were not danced by the ordinary people in the Highlands and the Outer Isles about the period when the main Scottish immigration to Cape Breton Island took place. This is in agreement with the evidence gathered from living memory in Scotland that Country Dances were first introduced among the ordinary people of these regions about 1850.

In the old days in Cape Breton Island, the big occasions for dancing other than the summer picnics in the forest were the "milling frolics," when neighbours gathered together to "waulk" the new cloth, and the weddings. No one whom I met remembered the full set of dances of an old Highland wedding, but many remembered that the dancing began with *Ruidhleadh nan Caraid* (The married couple's Reel), a four-handed Reel danced by the bride and bridegroom with the bridesmaid and best man. This was followed by a second four-handed Reel danced by a set of relations of the bride and bridegroom, and after this everyone danced. Just one man (6) mentioned that later in the evening the bride and bridegroom danced another four-handed Reel, to the tune The Bedding of the Bride, and that from this Reel the bride was stolen away. As in Scotland, with the change in the fashion of dancing, the wedding Reel became in some places just a set of Quadrilles; but it is through the *Ruidhleadh nan Caraid* that the four-handed Reel is best remembered. The dancing at the wedding did not end with the end of the reception, for on their way home the guests "danced away each crossroads" before parting to go on their separate ways (10). A custom similar to this survived within living memory in South Uist, for there the bridal party, as they walked from the church to the reception, danced a Scotch Reel at each crossroads on their way, "to dance away the cross" (17).

I now give descriptions of the Cape Breton Island four-handed and eight-handed Reels, and I begin with the details of the figures, leaving until later the question of steps. I must add a warning here against too rigid an adherence to my descriptions, for within living memory the forms of the Cape Breton Island dances were much less clearly defined than was normal in Scotland, and the dancers varied the figures with much greater freedom.

THE FOUR-HANDED REEL

(1) *Circular forms.* The forms of the four-handed Reel which I consider under this heading are all true Reels, with alternating phrases of circling and setting; all display also the characteristic change of rhythm, for in each case they are begun to a strathspey and in the course of the dance the music changes to quick tempo. For the part in quick tempo the music usually consisted of one or more reel tunes, but Scotch measures and jigs were also played occasionally. The normal tempo for strathspeys was 44 to 48 bars per minute; for tunes in quick tempo the usual tempo at the beginning of the period covered by living memory was about 52 bars per minute, but in more recent years it has been 60 bars per minute.

In all the four-handed Reels the two couples begin in square formation. In the case of the circular forms of the dance, my informants were almost equally divided between those who described a dance which remained in square formation throughout, and those who described one in which the dancers moved into line. I describe the latter first (18).

In this form the two couples stand opposite each other, with the ladies on the right of their partners, as in Diagram 1 (a). Throughout this section I follow the usage suggested by this diagram and refer to 1st man and 2nd lady, and similarly 1st lady and 2nd man, as "opposites."

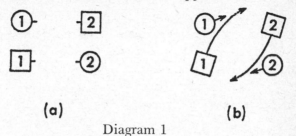

(a)   (b)

Diagram 1

Music Bars	*Description of the Figures*

1-8   All dance round clockwise in a circle, without giving hands; the ladies begin by passing to their left in front of their partner (Diagram 1 (b)). All end in a line, with the ladies in their original places and the men back to back in the middle facing their opposites. (This circle figure is the same as that in the old West Highland circular Reel except that there the men finish facing their own partners.)

9-16   All set to opposites.

17-24   All again dance round in a circle, the ladies moving off to their left and each man following his opposite. The ladies return to their own places, and the men finish facing their own partners. (The movement is again similar to that in the old West Highland circular Reel.)

25-32   All set to partners.

This 32-bar sequence is performed first in strathspey tempo and then in quick tempo; some of my informants said that it should be performed twice in strathspey tempo and then two or three times in quick tempo, while others told me that the number of repetitions varied from one occasion to another. The setting periods were also sometimes doubled in length, and this depended entirely on the fiddler; the circular figure was invariably performed to one part of the tune and the setting to another, and if the fiddler chose to repeat the setting part of the tune, then the dancers simply continued to set until the end of that part. In any case, whatever the phrasing, the ladies always return to their places at the end of each circle figure, while the men set alternately to their opposites and their partners.

The form of the four-handed Reel in which the square formation is preserved throughout has a number of variants. In the simplest of these the ladies stand on the left of their partners and the dancers alternately circle clockwise and set to their partners (2, 10). In another variant the setting alternates with a travelling figure consisting of a circle clockwise round to places followed by another circle round to places with right hands joined in the centre. The dancers move slowly round the circle taking eight bars for each complete circle, while the lengths of the setting periods depend as before on the fiddler. There were generally four lots of setting in strathspey tempo and four in quick tempo (8).

In a third variant the couples face each other as in Diagram 1 (a), and the ladies begin by moving across to their left in front of their partners, who follow the ladies round the circle, exactly as in Diagram 1 (b). So far the movement is that of the old West Highland circular Reel, but in this case the circle stops when the ladies reach their own places and each man is in the place diagonally opposite to his own. This circling figure, which occupies eight bars, is followed by eight bars of setting to opposites (i.e., 1st man to 2nd lady, 1st lady to 2nd man), and then the circling figure is repeated to bring the men back to their own places, where they set to their partners. This whole sequence occupies thirty-two bars and is performed twice in strathspey tempo and twice in quick tempo (3, 7).

I am inclined to believe that the square form of the four-handed Reel is older than the in-line form, and that the latter arose through two sets of the four-handed Reel being danced side by side in the eight-handed Reel, and there being flattened out to give the dancers more space.

(II) *"Crossing" forms.* In some forms of the four-handed Reel a "crossing" figure is substituted for the circle (5, 12, 13). Starting with the two couples facing each other as in Diagram 1 (a), the two ladies cross to each other's place, passing each other with right shoulders. The two men then cross to each other's place, passing with right shoulders, then the ladies cross back, then the men do likewise, each pair again passing with right shoulders. The movements are continuous, the tracks of the dancers being two crossing ovals.

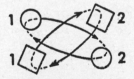

Diagram 2

It seems extremely probable that this "crossing" figure is a development from the circle; it will be noticed that in Diagram 1 (b) and 2 the initial tracks of the two ladies are roughly the same.

(III) *A form involving crossing and swinging.* This is the form given to me by the centenarian, Mrs. MacDonald of Scotch Lake (5), and is probably the same as the dance *Ruidhleadh nan Coileach Dubha* which another of my informants (2) had danced as a young child. It should be compared with the South Uist version of *Ruidhleadh nan Coileach Dubha*.

In this form of the four-handed Reel, the two couples face each other as in Diagram 1 (a), with the ladies on their partners' right. The dance is in quick tempo only, and is performed to any reel tune.

Music Bars	Description of Figures

1-8   The two couples dance the crossing figure as described under (II).

9-16   Partners swing each other, each having right hand on the other's waist and left hand on the other's right arm. The step here is either the pivot step or a walking step.

17-18   Set to partners while changing the hold to the opposite side (i.e., left hand on waist, right hand on arm).

19-24   Partners swing in opposite direction.

This sequence is repeated several times. The men might swing opposites alternately with partners or might swing partners each time.

I am not completely certain of the phrasing of the swinging. In the "square dancing" nowadays Cape Breton Islanders swing for as long as they feel inclined, and this seems to have been true in the latter days of this dance also.

THE EIGHT-HANDED REEL

The eight-handed Reel is in quick tempo and is performed to either reels or Scotch measures. The sequence and the phrasing of the dance are not fixed, and here I only give a typical sequence and indicate reasonable phrasing (13). The four couples start as in Diagram 3, with the ladies on their partners' right. As in the four-handed Reel, the dancers mark the rhythm of the music with their feet throughout the dance.

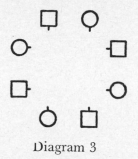

Diagram 3

Music Bars   *Description of Figures*

16   All join hands in a ring and circle to the left and back again.

8   All swing partners.

16   All dance a "grand chain" round to places, giving right hands to partners to begin (i.e., the ladies move round the set clockwise, the men counter-clockwise, passing each other with right and left shoulders alternately and giving right and left hands alternately on passing).

8   All swing partners.

8   Ladies stay in their places while the men set to and swing the next lady on their right.

16   The men set to and swing the next two ladies round the square.

8   The men return to their partners (who are still in their original places) and set to and swing them.

(In the preceding 32 bars the ladies also set to the men.)

16   All dance a "grand chain" as before.

8	The men join hands in a ring and circle to the left round to places, while the ladies step on the spot outside the men's ring.
8	The ladies join hands in a ring and circle to the left round to places, while the men step on the spot outside the ladies' ring.
8	The men dance right hands across, i.e., they join right hands in the centre and circle round to places, while the ladies step on the spot.
8	The ladies dance right hands across while the men step on the spot.
64	Two four-handed Reels dance side by side, adjacent couples dancing together. Any form of the four-handed Reel might be used.
64	Set and pass chain, i.e., all set to partners for eight bars, then pass each other and set to the next person, then pass again and set to the next person, and so on, taking eight bars for each pass and set. Continue in this way round the square, partners meeting again halfway round, and then back again in their places.

Setting steps for the four-handed and eight-handed Reels

The setting steps used in the four-handed and eight-handed Reels are mostly low on the ground and are built up from a number of basic movements which are adapted to any quick or slow Common time tune.[6] Ordinary hard-soled shoes are worn for dancing, and the feet are kept almost parallel throughout most of the steps; the body is held upright, the arms hang loosely by the sides, and there is almost no vertical movement of the body. The same steps are used by both men and ladies.

The reader who is accustomed to Scottish dancing will

need first to develop the art of beating out a rhythm with the toes and heels without ever having both feet off the ground. The four examples of one-bar phrases given below will help him to do so; they are used in various combinations to take up and maintain the rhythm of the dance when the dancer is not inclined to use more elaborate steps.[7] The counts are given for reels, and the movements are described for the right foot only.

Phrase A. Start with both feet on the ground.

Count 1 Rock forward to take the weight on the balls of both feet, then on the count beat the L heel on the ground, immediately lifting the ball of the LF just off the ground.

Count & Rock back on to R heel, immediately lifting the ball of the RF just off the ground.

Count 2 Rock forward on to the ball of the LF, lifting L heel.

Count & Rock forward on to the ball of the RF, lifting R heel.

Each count is marked with a distinct beat of the foot.

Phrase B. Start with the weight on the LF and with the RF just off the ground.

Count 1 Place the ball of the RF on the ground.

Count & Drop on to the flat of the RF, making a beat with the R heel, and at the same time lift the LF just off the ground.

Count 2 Place the ball of the LF on the ground.

Count & Drop on to the flat of the LF, making a beat with the L heel, and at the same time lift the RF just off the ground.

219

Again each count is marked with a beat. The feet are lifted only just enough for the dancer to be able to make a beat when they are put down again.

Phrase C. Start with the weight on the ball of the LF and keep it there throughout.

Count 1   Beat the L heel on the ground.

Count &   Beat the ball of the RF in 1st position.

Count 2   Beat the L heel on the ground.

Count &   Beat the R heel in 5th position.

The beats with the L heel are made by rocking the L foot, keeping the ball of the foot on the ground. The L knee is bent to lift the L heel — there is no vertical movement of the hip.

When the dancer needs to spring to change feet, or to hop as in the following phrase, the emphasis is placed on the beat on landing, and the vertical movement is kept to a minimum.

Phrase D.

Count 1   Hop on LF.

Count &   Brush RF forward, making a beat with the ball or heel of the RF as the foot moves forward.

Count 2   Hop on LF.

Count &   Brush RF backward, making a beat with the ball of the RF as the foot moves backward.

Here the hops can be replaced by rocking heel-beats as in Phrase C — the choice depends only on the lift of the music and the energy of the dancer. The brush forward may be in any direction, straight forward, diagonally outwards, or crossed in front of the hopping foot.

Phrase D can also be danced alternately on right and left feet, the first count then being a spring from one foot to the other. In this case the emphasis is placed on the first count in each bar, and the rhythm is similar to that of the *pas de Basque*.

More complicated steps are built upon the following movement. I here call it the "treble" because of its similarity to the treble found in Scotland — none of my informants had a special name for it. With the system of counting that follows, this treble movement occupies four successive counts, beginning on any one of the subsidiary counts "an." Using, for instance, the counts "an & a 2," we have:

    & a   1 an & a 2 an & a

Treble with RF. Start with the weight on the LF.

Count an Beat R heel in 3rd position.

Counts & a Beat twice with the ball of the RF in 3rd position, momentarily transferring the weight to the RF after the second beat.

Count 2 Beat with the ball of the LF in rear 3rd position, transferring the weight to it on the beat.

The two beats on the counts "& a" are made simply by tapping the ball of the foot on the floor; there is no forward and backward action as in the Scottish treble.

The treble is often preceded by a movement which in Scotland has the name "catch in"; again my informants in Cape Breton Island had no special name for it. The catch in is normally performed on the counts "& a 1," and is as follows:

Catch in with the LF

Count   Hop on RF and lift LF to semi 4th very low aerial position.

Count a   Brush the LF in towards 1st position, making a beat with the ball of the foot on the way in.

Count 1   Beat the LF in 1st position, transferring the weight to it on the beat.

Two common combinations of the catch in and treble are as follows:

Catch in with LF and treble with RF[8] (counts "& a 1.1 an & a 2"), then catch in with RF and treble with LF (counts "& a 2.1 an & a 2").

Catch in with LF and treble three times with RF[9] (counts "& a 1.1" for the catch in and counts "1. an & a 2"; "1. an & a 2.1"; and "2. an & a 2" for the three trebles).

The three successive beats on the one foot which occur in the treble are also used in the following movement (essentially successive trebles on alternate feet).

1. 1   Step on the LF in 1st position.

an   Beat with R heel in 3rd position.

& a   Beat twice with the ball of the RF in 3rd position.

2   Step on the RF in 1st position.

an   Beat with L heel in 3rd position.

& a   Beat twice with the ball of the LF in 3rd position.

The catch in is also combined with double beats as follows:

Count 1   an & Catch in with LF, as described above.

Count a   Beat R toe against L heel.

Count 2   Beat ball of RF on ground.

Alternatively, the two counts "a 2" may both be marked by beating the ball of the RF on the ground.

In all these combinations all the counts "1" and "2" should be emphasized.

It will be noticed that in Phrases A-D only the counts "1 & 2 &" are used, while in the steps constructed from the treble and catch in the full eight counts "1 an & a 2 an & a" are used. In general, the dancers endeavour to combine movements of the two types, i.e., those with counts "1 & 2 &" and those with counts "1 an & a 2 an & a," in order to follow the tune quite closely.

Such "beating" steps as these formed by far the greatest majority of the Reel steps used in Cape Breton Island within living memory. In particular, the treble and catch in were known to all my informants, and in the old days their use in the stepping seems to have been universal. In addition to such "beating" steps, there were also a few steps of the more conventional Scottish type; for example, the "backstep with a hop," and also steps similar to Strathspey step and Quick Reel step.

Travelling steps for the four-handed and eight-handed Reels

In travelling steps, as in the setting steps, the counts of the music are marked by beats. The walk, on counts "1" and "2" of a bar in reel time, becomes a "brush" walk:

Count 1   Step forward on RF.

Count &   Brush LF forward through 1st position.

Count 2   Step forward on LF.

Count &   Brush RF forward through 1st position.

This may be alternated with the *chassé*:

Count 1   Step forward on RF.

Count   &   Close LF to rear 3rd position (recall that the feet are almost parallel).

Count 2   Step forward on RF.

The *chassé* in turn has extra beats inserted either by brushing the LF forward on the last count "&" of the bar or by bringing the LF forward with the three "heel, toe, toe" beats of the treble on the last counts "an & a" of the bar. In the latter case all the eight counts of the bar may then be marked by doubling up the first beats of the *chassé*, giving altogether:

1. 1   Step forward on RF.

     an &   Close LF to rear 3rd position with two beats.

     a 2   Brush RF forward and step on it.

     an   Brush L heel forward through 1st position.

     & a   Brush LF forward, making two beats with the ball of the foot on the way forward, ready to step on the LF on the count "1" of the next bar.

Some dancers also used rather more springy steps, such as the travelling *pas de Basque*.

Frank Rhodes, 1964

Fiddle Music as a Manifestation of Canadian Regionalism
George A. Proctor

The fiddle is Canada's main folk instrument, particularly popular in pioneer times for accompanying square dancing. Most communities had a fiddle player or two, and many had their own fiddle-maker. Until recently folklorists paid little attention to fiddle music: the collecting emphasis was on songs which were normally sung unaccompanied. Today the fiddle is coming into its own: a number of performers have published collections of their favourite tunes, many articles have been written about Canada's most famous folk fiddler, Jean Carignan, and various scholars have begun to study regional fiddle styles and individual tunes.

George Proctor was one of the first to collect and write about Canadian fiddle tunes, and his pioneer article, "Old-Time Fiddling in Ontario," is still one of the few to deal with fiddling styles in depth. Back in 1960 the National Museum engaged him to spend a summer studying Ontario fiddling, and the resulting article described the practices he observed in the counties of Glengarry, Haliburton and Dufferin, and also provided a history of old-time fiddling with particular emphasis on the Scots style which has had the greatest influence on Canadian music. In the following article he goes on to discuss the differences that have developed in the various regions of Canada. This paper was originally presented at a conference on "Regionalism and National Identity" in New Zealand. When presenting the paper he played the examples on tape; here he cites the commercial records from which they came, with addresses where they may be ordered.

Those interested in the regional aspect of fiddle playing will find a list of records representing the various regions that Dorothy and Homer Hogan compiled for their article on "Canadian Fiddle Culture" in Communique: Canadian Studies.

Professor Proctor taught at the universities of British Columbia and Mount Allison before moving to Western University, London, Ontario, where he now teaches in the Department of Music History, Faculty of Music. He has recently published a book, Canadian Music of the Twentieth Century.

One of the most telling and most interesting barometers of Canadian regionalism is folk music — that is, the traditional music which the early settlers brought with them from their ancestral homes and modified or added to in the course of time. By folk music I refer to that which is created by a series of individuals over a long period, individuals who are largely unschooled in poetry and music, and which is passed on by oral rather than written means. Folk song is obviously one of the best manifestations of Canadian regionalism, some examples of which are the sea songs of Newfoundland and Nova Scotia, the milling songs of Cape Breton, the lumbering songs of New Brunswick and Ontario, the voyageur and children's songs of Quebec, the Ukrainian and Doukhobor songs of the West, and the indigenous songs of the native Indians and Inuit. A much smaller, less well-known, but equally interesting side of folk music is that performed by instruments. The music of the fiddle, the most important folk music instrument in North America, is the subject of this paper.

The term "fiddle" is one which often brings a smile of derision when mentioned in educated circles. Its association with unrefined music over the course of history has led to its less than respectable status. Most of this negative attitude dates from the seventeenth century and Puritan England, when the fiddle (or violin, which developed from the fiddle into its present-day form in the sixteenth century) was trying to make its way into sophisticated circles through the opera and court orchestras. In so doing, it displaced the more intellectual and aristocratic stringed instrument, the viola da gamba. The violin to the educated Englishman was considered only fit for use in the dance hall. This attitude changed gradually with the adoption of continental music after the death of Henry Purcell, but some of this prejudice has remained. In the past three hundred years the violin or fiddle has been required to serve two masters — namely, art music and traditional music.

Canada is a country rich in regional differences in fiddle music. Even though differences in folk song are more easily identified because of language, dialect and subject matter, it is possible to hear local or regional characteristics in fiddle music. A personal experience will illustrate this phenomenon. About twenty years ago I judged a fiddle contest in that part of Eastern Ontario (Glengarry County) which was settled originally by Scots following the American Revolution. This was announced simply as a fiddle contest but the organizers of the event knew or at least recognized only one style, and that was Scottish. As it turned out, the best fiddler in the contest was from neighbouring Quebec, and I and my co-judge awarded him the first prize. This was catastrophic to the organizers who had assumed all along that a fiddle contest was a contest in Scottish style. The fiddler whom we had chosen obviously did not know this style, even though, as I recall, he actually played a Scottish tune. Needless to say, I made a hasty retreat after the contest but not before the father of one of the Scottish contestants confronted me with the exclamation, "And to think I invited you into me hoose!"

In this paper I have chosen to discuss six of the fiddle regions of Canada: Cape Breton, Newfoundland, Maritime provinces, Ontario, the western provinces and Quebec.

1. Cape Breton

Cape Breton is an island off the northern tip of Nova Scotia which is joined to the mainland by the Canso causeway. Originally it was a separate colony, populated by Highland Scots and French Acadians. As an isolated and remote area, it served as a natural preserve for the folk culture of its inhabitants. The folk fiddling which is found here today is distinctive and closely tied to its roots in the highlands of Scotland. The period of original settlement in Cape Breton dates, by coincidence, from the period of "classic" fiddling in Scotland at the end of the eighteenth century, which is associated with such figures as Niel Gow, William Marshall and Simon Fraser. The fiddling tunes and performance style are closely linked to the social dances of the eighteenth century — namely, the strathspey and reel. Cape Breton style represents one of the most distinctive styles in all of Canada. This has been pointed up recently by the reprinting in 1982 of Simon Fraser's *The Airs and Melodies Peculiar to the Highlands of Scotland and the Isles* which was originally published in 1815 and revised by William Mackay, Jr. in 1874. This collection of some 230 tunes dates from the period 1714 to 1745 and is a nostalgic tribute to Scotland before the battle of Culloden. At the same time it has an interesting connection with Canada in that the editor was the son of one of Canada's pioneers, Simon Fraser, who fought on the Plains of Abraham and left his name on the mighty Fraser River in British Columbia. Thus the connection with Canada goes back almost to the origin of these tunes.

One of the fascinating aspects of the reprinting of the Fraser collection is that even though the tunes appeared in print in the early nineteenth century, they passed into the oral tradition and are remembered today by fiddlers who do not read music. Thus we are provided here with an opportunity to compare the written versions of over 150 years ago with oral versions of today. Listening to the examples as they were recorded in 1982 by Cape Breton folk fiddlers, one is astonished by the number and types of variations from the original printed version. While the broad outlines of each tune are unmistakable, the ornamentation of individual notes, filled-in passages or divisions, and rhythmical variations such as uneven playing of evenly-notated notes call to mind classical music practices of the eighteenth century. And precisely the same problems of interpretation are encountered in a modern rendition of this music as in baroque music, the only difference being that the fiddler has had an unbroken line of oral tradition on which to base his interpretation.

The tradition is to play these tunes in groups, the favourite medley being a slow strathspey, a regular strathspey and a reel. One medley performed in 1982 begins with a slow strathspey called "Dawted Mary." This tune has a modal flavour (Aeolian) and is also characterized by triadic outlines and scotch snap figures, as are many of the tunes. The uneven rendition of even notes in the score and the modal harmony, obviously derived from the bagpipe scale, are two of the most noteworthy features here.

Example I (a) — "Dawted Mary," from *Music from the Simon Fraser Collection*, Vol. I (Box 1654, Sydney, N.S., BIP 6T7). Reprint of Simon Fraser's *The Airs and Melodies Peculiar to the Highlands of Scotland* available from the same source.

The strathspey which follows, entitled "The Sportsman's Haunt," is in the same key as the slow strathspey and follows basically the same chordal progressions. As is the case with many examples in the collection, there is a close melodic similarity between the two strathspeys.

Example I (b) — "The Sportsman's Haunt," from *The Fraser Collection*.

The fast dance which follows is entitled "The High Road to Fort Augustus" and it too has the same harmonic pattern. Melodically this performance departs further from the written notation with uneven and repeated-note figures.

Example I (c) — "The High Road to Fort Augustus," from *The Fraser Collection*.

This process of comparing the nineteenth-century printed versions of these Scottish fiddle tunes with the oral versions of today in an isolated area of Canada is a fascinating one which bears further investigation. It also invites a comparison with field examples to be found in Scotland today, keeping in mind that another area of Canadian folklore, that of French folk song, apparently has survived more intact in Canada than in its place of origin.

2. Newfoundland

As Cape Breton has its Scottish ancestors, Newfoundland has its Irish, and the next example illustrates several aspects of that tradition. This piece, entitled "Le Sabot's Reel," is performed by a one-man three-piece band – fiddler, clogger and jigger. Clogging is produced by heel-toe tapping in rhythmic patterns by the fiddler himself and jigging by the singing or mouthing of the tune. The latter practice is often used in both Scottish and Irish-based traditions when a dance is called for but a fiddle or fiddler is not to be found. In keeping with the folk performer's lack of concern for the niceties of nomenclature, this piece is actually a jig, not a reel.

> Example II – "Le Sabot's Reel," from *Atlantic Fiddling*, CBC LM 470 (Box 500, Station A, Toronto M5W LE6).

3. Maritime

The three Maritime provinces of Nova Scotia, Prince Edward Island and New Brunswick, excluding the island of Cape Breton, retain a distinct "down east" style all of their own. This style, which was represented for approximately fifteen years on national radio and television by fiddler Don Messer (1901-1973), is characterized by neatness and smoothness as well as a certain degree of naiveté and simplicity. There is a decided lack of complex ornamentation, fancy bowing or double stopping in this style. It is clearly functional music in that it is very close to the square dances for which it is intended. (In Messer's case, he always featured a square-dance group which performed on his shows in a clean-cut style parallel to his music.) A feature of this style is the performance of newly created tunes which are often given names of local interest. Such would apply in this example, "Cape Blomidon," an original composition by a Maritimer, Ron Goodwin. Cape Blomidon juts out into the Minas Basin in Nova Scotia.

> Example III — "Cape Blomidon," from *Atlantic Fiddling*.

4. Ontario

As one moves farther west in Canada it becomes increasingly difficult to view distinctive folk elements, at least as far as the Anglo-Saxon communities are concerned. Several factors worked against the cultivation of a folk culture in Ontario, two of the most significant being the design of the farms in such a way as to inhibit social contact (the same applies in the West but to an even greater extent), and the attitude of the Protestant sects which discouraged folklore in the first instance. Most of the folk music in Ontario centred on the lumber camps, and when the forests became depleted in the early part of the century, the camps and folklore disappeared. The coming of the mass media in the twentieth century has tended to destroy the few isolated pockets which did survive.

The areas in Ontario which have tended to preserve both folk song and folk fiddling traditions are those with strong Irish and Scottish (Catholic) backgrounds. The early Protestant settlers who formed the majority of the population discouraged dancing and the associated activities of folk singing and fiddling, but not so the minority Catholic groups. In the early days many of these communities were ostracized by the Protestant majority; this, no doubt, encouraged them to practise and preserve their traditions even more. One such area is the Ottawa Valley, which not only preserved its folk traditions but also a distinct manner of speech. The following is an Irish tune, "Green Fields," played by a native of the Ottawa Valley, Graham Townsend, who, although he does not read music, is one of the few Canadian fiddlers who has made a career out of folk fiddling. This tune is characterized by modality and frequent ornamentation and double stops. The spirited bounce of an Irish dance is very much in evidence.

> Example IV — "Green Fields," from *The Great Canadian Fiddle*, Springwater Productions S6 (56 Clinton Street, Guelph, Ontario NIH 5G5).

Another tune from Ontario, "Boil Them Cabbage Down," shows much more the influence from Nashville, U.S.A., with its heavy guitar beat, repeated-note figures and back-bowing, the latter producing involved syncopated patterns much favoured by fiddlers in this style.

> Example V — "Boil Them Cabbage Down," from *Maple Sugar*, Springwater Productions S1/2.

5. The West

Most Canadian fiddlers pride themselves in being able to perform a wide variety of styles from their own country. This in itself is an interesting phenomenon. While they do in fact play the tunes, they usually put their own individual or regional stamp on whatever they do. For instance, one may find a French-Canadian fiddler playing an Irish tune which includes elements from American folk sounds. Such is the case with the "Winnipeg Reel" played by Jean Carignan, the most prominent Quebec fiddler of the past fifty years, who is accompanied on this recording by the banjo-playing of one of the most prominent American folk musicians, Pete Seeger. This example is typical of Carignan's style of playing, which is fast, aggressive and brilliant.

Example VI — "Winnipeg Reel," from *Old-Time Fiddle Tunes*, Folkways FG 3531 (632 Broadway, New York, NY 10012).

6. Quebec

This brings us to the last region for the present discussion, namely Quebec. Fiddling in the province of Quebec is interesting in that not only is it not related to language and thereby is readily accessible to all segments of the Canadian community, but it is the one area in Quebec folklore which has been influenced significantly by English-speaking Canada. Many of the tunes played by Quebec fiddlers can be traced to Irish and Scottish origins. The Quebec fiddler, as might be expected, has added his own touches for he generally plays the tunes at a faster tempo and in a more spirited manner. The ornamentation is also more involved and he makes greater use of scordatura or "mis-tuning" techniques. The Quebec fiddler frequently dazzles his audience with left-hand pizzicato and rapid string crossings as well as novelty acts.

An example of an Irish tune played by a Quebec fiddler is "Haste to the Wedding," a tune which is popular in English Canada as well. One feature of this example is that the variation of it comes before the tune itself. It also exhibits a common feature of American fiddle playing, which is to have a second fiddle accompany the main fiddle in a practice known as seconding. The joy of impromptu ensemble playing is one of the delights of fiddle playing, to which anyone who has witnessed one of these "jam" sessions can attest.

Example VII — "Haste to the Wedding," from *Old-Time Fiddle Tunes*.

In the "Reel du Pendu" (Hangman's Reel) Jean Carignan makes use of the scordatura technique for two reasons: to facilitate the playing of certain passages, but even more importantly, to create sympathetic vibrations. This technique dates back to the seventeenth century in classical music and one suspects that the same would be true for folk music as well. The altered tuning for the "Reel du Pendu" is to lower the top string of the violin down a major third to "C" and to raise the two bottom strings up a major second to "A" and "E." The open strings of the violin then sound an A-minor chord, which is, of course, the key of the piece. The resultant sound has an ominous tone, fitting for the subject of the reel, the hangman. The story behind this tune is that a young man was spared the hangman's noose by his playing of this tune on his fiddle. Bouncing bow and left-hand pizzicato are also techniques exploited in this piece, all for the purpose of enhancing the fiddler's supplication.

Example VIII — "Reel du Pendu" (Hangman's Reel), from *French-Canadian Fiddle Songs*, Legacy 120 (10920 Wilshire Blvd., Ste. 410, Los Angeles, CA 90024).

Where does this leave us, then, with respect to regionalism in Canada as seen in examples of fiddling? For one thing, it establishes that most of the ethnic groupings in the country have a unique type of instrumental folk music, fiddle music being the primary sub-category, and the transmission of tunes from one region to another is taking place all the time. The question as to whether the subtleties of style are successfully transplanted is more problematic. While the pervasive influence of radio, television and recordings works against the survival of regional differences in traditional music, the examples shown do indicate, in my opinion, that distinct regional differences continue to exist in Canada today.

George A. Proctor, 1984

A Survey of Folk Medicine
in French Canada
Luc Lacourcière

In recent years North Americans have experienced an
upsurge in the popularity of natural or traditional remedies
and at-home medicine. While the "health food"/ecology/
naturalist movement is partially responsible for this situation, the medical profession itself is, of late, displaying
increased interest in folk medical practices. Some medical
schools — especially those in areas with vital folk traditions
like Newfoundland and the Pennsylvania Dutch country —
even teach courses in folk medicine. As a result, folklorists
generally and other scholars as well have begun to show
more interest in this area of folklore.

In the past when doctors were not available to the
average person and since, whenever people have been
isolated from medical care, folk medicine and traditional
healers have come into their own. Like all areas of traditional belief, folk medicine incorporates two aspects: first,
those beliefs and allied practices that have been proven to
have some validity (like many Amerindian herbal remedies
and the ancient Greek practice of applying mouldy bread
to a festering wound); and second, those that are based
merely on faulty causal connections. The following article
documenting the history, extent and nature of folk medicine

in French Canada was prepared for a book surveying folk medicine in North America.

Luc Lacourcière is the senior Francophone folklorist in North America. In 1944 he was appointed to teach folklore at Laval University and went on to establish Les Archives de Folklore there; to bring out a series of monographs, Les Archives de Folklore; *to educate hundreds of dedicated scholars of North American Francophone popular traditions; to collect folklore throughout Quebec; and to present and publish many significant articles and books. He is a Fellow of the American Folklore Society, an Honorary President of the Folklore Studies Association of Canada, a Companion of the Order of Canada, and a Fellow of the Royal Society of Canada.*

To present even in its general outlines a panorama of folk medicine in French Canada seemed to me, after I had accepted the invitation to do so, a rash undertaking, as much from a historical as from an ethnomedical point of view.

Although the subject has always fascinated me, because of the family environment in which I grew up (as the son, brother, and brother-in-law of country doctors), as well as because of semi-professional circumstances, such as my participation as an ethnographer in the founding of the Canadian Society of the History of Medicine in 1950, I must humbly assert that my research on empirical or folk medicine and those who practice it has remained somewhat marginal to my major fields of study. My work on this subject has been confined to compiling bibliographical data and to collecting remedies and treatments, verbal devices, anecdotes, folk beliefs and traditions whenever the occasion has presented itself during field trips over the years.

I will not attempt to present here a complete picture of folk medicine from the early beginnings of New France in the sixteenth century to the present day, since such an undertaking also would entail, to some extent, the outlining of the main stages of the establishment of a formal system of medicine and its evolution into scientific medicine as we know it today. Consequently, I will limit my discussion of the early period to the mere mention of a few dates and references which will serve as historical background to certain observations and material based directly on field work.

The oldest folk remedy noted in the New World was given by the Indians to Jacques Cartier during his stay in Stadacona (now Quebec) during the winter of 1535-1536, when an epidemic of scurvy (*la grosse maladie*) decimated his crew. An infusion made from the bark of the *Annedda* tree proved to have "miraculous" healing powers:

> No sooner had they drunk than they improved in a manner truly and obviously miraculous. For, after drinking of it twice or thrice they recovered their health and were healed of all the disorders afflicting them. So much so that one of the men who had been suffering from the pox for five or six years was completely cured of it by the remedy. When this was seen and known, there was such a rush on the medicine that they almost murdered one another in their eagerness to be first served. So that in six days a whole tree as large and tall as any oak in France was used

up. And in those six days it worked more wonders than all the physicians of Louvain and Montpellier using all the drugs in Alexandria could have done in a year.[1]

This tree, identified as the white cedar (*Thuja occidentalis*), was called *l'arbre de vie*, or "the tree of life," by Cartier's contemporaries. However, the incident took place before the permanent settling of New France, and by the time Quebec was founded, the secret and the identity of this panacea were lost, a fact which Champlain was to deplore.

It was between the years 1608 and 1760 that French medical traditions, official or otherwise, were implanted in New France. The annals mention a good number of doctors, surgeons, barbers, and apothecaries established mainly in the cities and frequently in hospitals, notably the Hôtel-Dieu of Montreal, which have been in existence since 1639 and 1644, respectively. There numbered among these practitioners many worthy men, such as Michel Sarrasin (1659-1734) and Jean-François Gauthier (1708-1756), botanists and physicians of the king and both celebrated for having given their names to native plants, the pitcher plant (*Sarracenia purpurea*) and the wintergreen (*Gautheria procumbens*), which are currently used in folk medicine.

A medical historian of French Canada notes that besides these scholars, there appeared in rapidly increasing numbers healers and charlatans (*des guérisseurs, des charlatans, des "fratres"*), as they were called, who travelled about the countryside setting bones and selling herbs and panaceas.[2] Some of these folk practitioners have passed into history, but usually because of their unpleasant dealings with the authorities rather than their exceptional healing powers.

This is notably the case of the Breton Yves Phlem from la Pérade, a small village on the Saint Lawrence River. He signed a written agreement before witnesses and the parish priest to heal a certain Jean Bilodeau of a very advanced canker on his lower lip. However, Bilodeau died on May 10, 1736, in spite of eight months of treatment. His widow later refused to pay for her husband's treatments, hence the law proceedings in which she was sentenced to pay Phlem for the lodging and food given to her late husband but not for the treatment and care administered by the healer. The latter continued, nonetheless, to exercise his art among those people who still had faith in his healing powers.[3]

After 1763, under English rule, the position of official medicine gradually changed. It was not until 1788 that the law specified under the Medical Act that every candidate who wished to practise medicine, surgery, or obstetrics had to be examined by a board whose members were appointed by the governments of either Quebec or Montreal.

For those who were unable to go out of the country to study medicine, an apprenticeship took the place of academic studies. It was only in 1819 that medical instruction was officially offered by a group of doctors, and with the establishment at a later date of the universities, academic medicine continued to evolve. It is not necessary to follow its evolution here, but it should be noted that it would be erroneous to believe that scientific medicine completely supplanted empirical or folk medicine.

We will limit our remaining remarks to folk medicine and a consideration of the different types of healers and their arsenal of cures and treatments. First, what were and what are these healers to whom a clientele, much larger and more credulous than one would suppose, still turns?

There are healing saints who are solicited on certain

occasions or to heal specific diseases over which they have a sort of monopoly: Saint Blaise for a sore throat; Saint Apolline for a toothache; and Saint Geneviève, on whose feast day there is a distribution of miniature loaves of bread, to which the power of protecting pregnant women is ascribed. There are those of whom cures or even miracles are solicited in healing shrines: Saint Anne, Saint Joseph, and the Virgin Mary.

Mingled with an ardent faith, a kind of bargaining is done with Saint Expedit and Saint Jude, intercessors of urgent or desperate causes. Every day the local newspapers carry images of these saints or photographs of Pope John XXIII or less universally known benefactors as ex-votos for the fulfilment of promises made to them in return for the granting of favours, generally healing.

Next on our list of healers we would mention (in view of their religious nature) certain priests to whom extensive powers have been attributed. Placed at the head of parishes often lacking doctors, many priests gave medical advice which in the minds of their parishioners made them veritable healers. Their fame often extended far and wide, especially if they gave themselves up to the study of plants or herbs. The names of a few of these priests are found in history. For instance, Father Pierre-Joseph Compain (1740-1806) wrote down for the nuns of the Hôtel-Dieu of Quebec in 1799 his cure for cancer and a remedy for cankers in which spider webs played an important role.[4] People still cite as an effective cure "courvaline," a depurative decoction of different herbs attributed to Father Joseph-Claude Poulin de Courval, as well as the "holy water" of François-Xavier Côté, a preparation, primarily of colcothar, which is used in the treatment of wounds and inflammation of the eyes. Both of these remedies were considered so efficacious that they were included in a manual of therapeutics which was used at Victoria University in Montreal.[5] (It was at this university, no longer in existence, that my father studied medicine.)

As for the traditional healers whose gift is supposed to be hereditary — the seventh consecutive son having, like the kings of France, the mark of a fleur-de-lis under his tongue and *marcous* or posthumous children — they can be divided into two groups: bonesetters (or lay chiropractors) and faith healers.

Bonesetters generally limit themselves to setting fractures and dislocations. Many of them are well known, and people come from great distances to consult them, even from points outside of Canada, such as New England. They generally practise their art as a sideline to render service to the community. As a rule they do not accept money; that is, they do not set a fixed price, but they do not refuse gratuities.

Each region has its own bonesetter, and he is often a member of the third or fourth generation in his family to practise his occupation. This is the case for the Lessard family and the Lamberts of Beauce County, as well as the Boilys of the Saguenay region, whose reputations extend far beyond the area in which they live. For instance, a descendant of a certain Fabien Boily, who was a famous healer, has his picture published regularly in the Montreal newspapers with the brief notice "Still at the same address"; evidently this address is well known and has been for some time.

There is an anecdote frequently told in many areas to demonstrate the great skill of these bonesetters; Marius Barbeau has included it in his portrait of Fabien Boily:

> More than once Fabien Boily dared to measure his skill with that of a professional doctor. According to

Brigitte Desbiens, Boily had a bone to pick with the doctor of the Escoumains parish. The young practitioner had called him a charlatan.

Greatly provoked, the healer defiantly asked the young doctor, "Do you know cats?"

"Certainly I know them."

"If you do, then prove it."

Boily caught the black cat in the kitchen and dislocated its bones, except for those in the neck and spine, and placed the cat as an inert mass on the carpet in front of his adversary.

"You killed him, the poor beast!"

"Killed him? Go and look. If you know cats so well, revive him."

"But you're mad!" cried the bewildered doctor.

"Watch this," said the bonesetter.

He took the cat in his hands and while humming "Marie Calumet" [a folksong] he began to work his fingers. In a short time, as if by magic, the cat regained its form, shook itself on the carpet, meowed plaintively and got up and hid behind the stove, sending all healers, professional doctors as well as charlatans, to the devil.[6]

The same story is told of the bonesetter Noel Lessard of Beauce County, with the difference that the dislocation and setting of the cat's bones take place before a magistrate in a court of law. Lessard, who was without benefit of counsel, is reported to have said that the cat would be his lawyer; and it was in fact the cat that proved his case.

Faith healers who cure only by touching with the hands or include incantation or prayer in their treatment are more difficult to locate or interview since they dislike having field workers inquire into their affairs. They become known, however, through their numerous legal contentions with the College of Physicians. Since 1939, I have collected at random newspaper clippings of lawsuits which made the headlines of daily newspapers in Quebec and Montreal. The majority of these healers were fined for illegal practice or for extorting money from naive individuals. Those who have been duped have often revealed the unusual practices of the healer, such as those of a man (who shall remain nameless) whose healing power was to be found at the end of his penis and who sent the unsuspecting husband to collect herbs on a distant mountain while he administered his cure to the ailing wife.

However, many of these healers are too cunning to be caught. One such healer has practised for forty years and has had many lawsuits with the College of Physicians which have gone as far as the court of appeal, but he has always been acquitted. He has allowed himself the luxury of having a large volume of 427 pages edited with all of the testimony presented before the court, as well as a series of photographs and letters from individuals whom he has supposedly cured.[7]

Like other healers who exploit the public, he has a large personnel at his service, and he holds consultation in many cities, where his visits are announced months in advance. Apparently he merely tells his patients that he will think about them, and they have so much faith in him that they go away happy, although lightened of remunerations collected by his assistants. Since he is beginning to feel his age, this healer has recently announced in the newspapers his intention to retire, but he states that one of his nephews will succeed him, since he too has received at birth the gift of healing. This and similar cases leave one skeptical about the sincerity of such commercialism.

This type of faith healer contrasts with another category

of individuals who were forced by necessity, at least in the beginning, to intervene in the isolated surroundings in which they lived. These are *sages-femmes*, midwives or wisewomen of the rural milieus, many of whom have already confided their experiences to folklorists. They have existed since the beginning of New France, but they are beginning to disappear now that women generally have their children in hospitals.

Under the French regime, wisewomen were the object of rather strict regulations. We read in the ritual of the Quebec diocese published in 1704 that the priest must "make sure that no one undertakes this responsibility [that is, of being a wisewoman] within the entire parish without his having first examined her faith, good living and her ability to administer the sacrament of baptism in cases of necessity, and having then exacted from her an oath that she will duly carry out her duty." It is not known if these instructions were always carried out to the letter.[8]

From one of my notebooks used in field collecting, I excerpt a few of the reminiscences of an 88-year-old *sage-femme*, Mrs. Elzéar Gagnon, who lived in the mountain region of Charlevoix County.

> I began to attend patients in 1893 at the age of thirty-three. I went right up until last year [1945] when I delivered three sets of twins. I've never counted the number of children I've delivered. Over fifty-two years, that must make more than a thousand. I've never had any mishaps.
>
> When you go to a patient, you never know if it's going to be a boy or a girl. That's up to the good Lord.
>
> I never gave any remedies before labour. I prayed to the Holy Virgin. There were those who took

remedies, though; a growth which grows in the ears of rye is scalded and drunk as a tea. You take a soup-spoonful in a cup of hot water before giving birth. [Mrs. Gagnon uses the popular term *acheter*, or "buying," the child.] It prevents bleeding. When the woman lost a lot of blood, I taught quietness and prudence. Nothing unexpected. When there is something unexpected, children falling or a husband who talks too loud, well, the blood flows.

Mrs. Gagnon goes on to enumerate different remedies and foods which she recommends for the churching of the mother: "Teas which you make from seven types of herbs: juniper-berry, boxtree, white pine, white fir, red spruce. . . . You mix all that together. It's better when you add a little drop of liquor."[9]

I will not take the time to present interviews with other wisewomen or healers who have a special gift, such as blood-stoppers and those who "put out fire" (fever), cure toothaches, and remove warts. Nor will I discuss one of the most important folk practitioners, the blacksmith, since this topic would require a lengthy development. The black-smith played an important role in the community, where he was recognized as having great healing powers. The curative uses of the *eau ferrée*, or chalybeate water, of the blacksmith are well known.

I will close these few remarks on folk medicine with a brief consideration of the treatments and remedies most commonly practised.

First, it should be noted that the same remedies are often applied to both humans and animals, especially in the rural areas. This is documented in an old manuscript by a shoeing smith dated 1780 and entitled "Collection of remedies to safeguard horses from diseases and accidents which can befall them, enlarged by several remedies for the human body, prepared by me, Nicolas Joseph Neris, master farrier at Paris, residing. . ." (the bottom of the title page is torn, but the date 1780 is legible).[10] It is a manuscript of 295 pages; unfortunately, I have not had time to inventory it in its entirety. As a sample of its contents, the fourth section is presented as follows: "In which is contained various good ointments, poultices, plaster, essences, waters, powders, nostrums, as much for man as for horses; there is also contained herein remedies for different human diseases and mishaps."

This French manuscript, which contains many parallels with material found in French Canada, deserves special study and could easily be the object of an annotated edition. Similar works have been prepared in Canada. There is, for instance, a manuscript prepared in 1857 by Augustin Stanislas De Lisle, a notary and botanist of Montreal, entitled *Petite pharmacie végétale*. . . , which is a family guide to plants and their medicinal properties.

Our richest source of ethnomedical information is still, of course, oral tradition. An inventory of bibliographical sources for French Canada since 1900 reveals that folklorists and students of folklore have collected more than five thousand different folk remedies from Nova Scotia to northern Ontario. About two-fifths of these have been published; the rest are on file at Les Archives de Folklore. That means that a lot of work in the areas of both classification and collecting still remains to be done in folk medicine.

Those remedies which have been published to date have been presented simply as alphabetical lists under the name of the disease.[11] This is a cursory classification which is certainly not the most satisfactory. Other systems of classification now under consideration may give more information about the ingredients used, borrowings from the vegetable, mineral, or animal kingdoms, and so on. Even more satisfactory is the method which separates, wherever possible, remedies of a purely empirical nature from those based on magic and yet reserves an intermediate category dependent on both empiricism and magic.

I will not enumerate examples of medicines made of plants or certain animal or mineral substances. I would mention, however, that in the eighteenth century the correspondence of a nun of the Hôtel-Dieu of Quebec contains about ten remedies, autochthonous to Canada, which she sent to an apothecary in Dieppe, France; some of the ingredients used in their preparation were maiden-hair fern, maple syrup, ginseng, spruce gum, pine sap, the foot of a moose, and the musk glands of a beaver. All of these are still used today in folk medicine and even, at times, in official therapeutics.

The survival of remedies based on magic is still remarkably strong. It is only necessary to consider the frequency in remedies of odd numbers, especially three and seven; or the importance attached to colours — red flannel, white wool, and the dung of a black cow to prevent or cure sore throats, and so on; or the importance of gestures made with the left hand or foot; or movement in a certain direction, often in opposition to the orbit of the sun; or removing the bark from a tree in an upward or at times downward movement; or the days of the week and the months of the year which recall the fasts and the days of mourning of antiquity; or the many different kinds of amulets worn around the neck or carried in a pocket to ward off toothache or whooping cough.

Perhaps the most remarkable magic cures are those which propose the transference of disease to an animal, a tree, or another object. They are often accompanied by rituals or formulas owing as much to incantation as to prayer.

The belief in transference in folk cures is based on a simplistic conception of disease as a foreign element which has penetrated the body and can be extirpated by transmitting it to someone or something else. The removal of warts, for example, is accomplished by selling them for the low price of one cent; or if the sufferer encounters a funeral procession, they may be taken down under the ground by the dead person; or they may be thrown behind one's back along with peas or a piece of potato or pork with which the warts have been wiped.

The same thing applies to the removal of unwanted hairs. I quote a passage from a manuscript notebook written by a school teacher in 1939: "Have someone give you a piece of fresh pork and rub it on the part where the hairs are to be removed and bury it in the ground [where it is left to rot] and say, 'Cursed hair, remove yourself, just as the devil removes himself from the sight of God, and never come back again, never, never, never!' "

The transference of an internal disorder is somewhat more complicated. One can fasten a pain, such as a toothache, to the bark of a tree with the aid of pins, or get rid of a pain in the foot by stepping in peat moss and outlining the form of the foot with an object. But it is mainly in cures for rheumatism and similar disorders that this transference to a tree is most widespread.

To get rid of rheumatism, you must follow a path in the woods where no one is likely to pass; when you reach the foot of a tree, any tree at all, dig up the root with your left hand and, holding the tree root between your teeth, say, "Rheumatism, I leave you here and I will take you back when I pass this way again." Then bury the root with your left hand. If you take care to avoid this spot in the future, a complete cure is guaranteed.

Transference to trees has been recorded with fewer and greater numbers of variants by almost every folklorist who has studied folk medicine. However, transference to an animal seems to be less prevalent, at least in its sanguinary form, where the animal must be sacrificed. Two examples of this practice are the application to the body of a skinned cat to cure shingles (xona) or pulmonary disease, and the strangling of a mole or mouse to prevent certain disorders.

I have been mainly concerned in this paper with folk medicine in French Canada, but certainly many of the treatments and beliefs outlined here have parallels in other parts of the country, although not all of these folk practices are currently carried out in every area. For instance, Helen Creighton has found a considerable amount of folk medical material in English in the province of Nova Scotia;[12] and J. Frederick Doering has collected ethnomedical practices from the Pennsylvania German settlers of Ontario.[13] Parallels to the Canadian material and the principles on which it is based can be found, of course, throughout the world. But French Canada is rich in folk medical practices, and much important work remains to be done in this field.

To close, I will relate a short anecdote which illustrates, to my way of thinking, how people still respond to folk practices and are spontaneously filled with confidence.

One evening I was recording tales and folksongs in a family in a rural area of Bellechasse County. During a break, I noticed a delightful little girl, six or seven years of age, and wanted to ask her a few simple questions, but she clung to her mother and was visibly embarrassed by the presence of a stranger. Parents always respond when one takes an interest in their children. Noticing that the little girl had warts on her hands, I said, without thinking, "Come and see me. I can make your warts disappear." I had no sooner pronounced those words than the mother literally pushed the child into my arms, saying, "That man can get rid of warts. Go and see him." Not knowing just what to do, I blew on the little girl's fingers.

Well, the next time I went back to see those people, the little girl's warts were gone, and they brought me more children to have their warts removed! That happened twenty years ago, and whenever I go back to that area, people still mention that I have a gift for removing warts. That shows what great faith people have.

Luc Lacourcière, 1976

IV. ANALYSES

Buddhist Dirges on the
North Pacific Coast
Marius Barbeau

Charles Marius Barbeau (1883-1969) was the most import-
ant single figure in the history of Canadian folklore. In
1950 F. J. Alcock, curator of the National Museum, wrote:

> *Dr. Barbeau has been responsible for the develop-*
> *ment of folklore research in Canada, and the wealth*
> *of folklore material in the possession of the National*
> *Museum of Canada was largely collected by him and*
> *the numerous students to whom he transmitted his*
> *enthusiasm for this type of study.*

After studying at the universities of Laval, Oxford, and
the Sorbonne, Dr. Barbeau worked as an ethnologist with
the National Museum from 1911 until he retired in 1949,
and he continued as an active consultant for another
fifteen years. The list of honours he received would fill
a page: he was awarded the gold medal of the Royal
Society of Canada, received honorary degrees from the
universities of Montreal, Laval, and Oxford, and was one
of the first to be named a Companion of the Order of
Canada. After his death, the Canadian Press noted:

> *During fifty years of research, much of it on long and*

arduous field trips, he produced a wealth of knowledge concerning the Asiatic migrations to North America. He delved deeply into French-Canadian folklore and into the story of the Indian peoples, their legends and culture. He gave the National Museum a collection of 195 Eskimo songs, more than 300 Indian, close to 7,000 French-Canadian, and 1,500 old English songs. Many of them are still on the old tube-like records that came off his Edison recorder. . . "I would need two lives to process all my research," he once said.

The work he achieved in one lifetime is almost unbelievable. A prolific writer who was completely bilingual, he published some fifty major books, as many more pamphlets and monographs, and some seven hundred articles in over a hundred different periodicals ranging from scientific journals to popular magazines and daily papers.

One of his pet theories was that for centuries before the arrival of Europeans, nomads from Siberia were filtering across the Aleutian chain and down the coast of Alaska and British Columbia. He believed that these Asiatic migrants brought with them various cultural features including a clan structure and the totemic system. He also argued that Northwest Coast Indian songs and Asiatic songs are surprisingly similar, publishing various articles such as "Chanting Buddhist Dirges" (in Alaska Beckons), "Asiatic Survivals in Indian Songs" (in The Musical Quarterly), and the following piece from the Journal of the International Folk Music Council. In it he describes how he played Indian songs for Professor Kiang Kang-hu of McGill University and gives the professor's rather surprising reactions.

Later anthropologists have questioned some of Barbeau's theories about the Siberian-North American migrations, *but the relationship between Asiatic and West Coast Indian songs is striking and interesting, however it is to be explained.*

The idea of comparing Indian songs with those of Siberia and China as a means of discovering the origin of the former occurred to me only recently, that is since 1920, though abundance of materials has been at hand for years. Nearly 1,000 native songs of British Columbia and Alaska have been recorded for the National Museum of Canada since 1912, and many others are preserved in the collections of the United States and Germany. Many ancient Chinese and Japanese songs have been marketed by the phonograph companies. In addition, over 100 Siberian songs were collected by the Russian exile, Jochelson, for the Jesup Expedition more than sixty years ago, and the records were stored at the American Museum of Natural History in New York. I had duplicates made of these for our National Museum, and I understand that the original Edison phonograph records are now preserved at Indiana University.

When studying the Indian tribes of the Nass River on the Alaskan border some years ago, I heard on the phonograph a Japanese tune that arrested my attention. It closely resembled some of the songs of the Yukon and northern British Columbia, which I had been recording among the natives. At the beginning, the tune scaled a high curve, touched a top note, then dropped over wide intervals to the bottom, where it droned leisurely, just as do the tunes of a number of typical Indian songs. The melodic resemblance between the Japanese and Indian songs reminded me of other things: the nearness of Alaska to Japan; the Mongolian features of both natives and Japanese; the fan-like migrations of the Indians away from Bering, which I had been probing; and the cultural stamp of Asia noticeable on the whole northwest coast.

Incessant contacts tended to reunite the related peoples on both sides of Bering, long after they had parted, and those on our continent had strayed away to farther districts. Bering is only forty miles wide. It is dotted with islands, freezes over in winter, and can be crossed in a day or two. The American and Siberian natives kept in close touch with each other for barter. A trade route extended, since prehistoric times, from Siberia into Alaska, and almost as far as Hudson Bay. The strait was navigated in skin boats during summer, and it could be crossed, over the ice, in winter. No real barrier ever interfered with those widely scattered people, who sought each other seasonally for the exchange of commodities essential to life. Customs and culture passed back and forth also, slowly but surely. There was no complete break.

Recently, having transcribed nearly one hundred British Columbia and Yukon songs for publication, I showed about twenty of them to Professor Kiang Kang-hu, an eminent Chinese authority, now on the staff of McGill University at Montreal. The results of his inspection far exceeded my expectation, particularly when we came to dirge or funeral songs. I shall here recount several examples of these results.

The dirge of Raven drum: this funeral song is the exclusive family property of Kweenu, a Raven chief of the Kitwinlkul tribe, on the Grease-Trail between the Skeena and the Nass, in northern British Columbia. The ancestors of this family in the recent past migrated down from the north. Their traditional dirges were used only at the death of chiefs, and during the incineration of the body on a pyre.

"The Raven drum now has come back. We can hear nothing but its large voice. It is like a great brightness.

The great voice of the Raven, the cawing Raven all covered with pearls, is ahead of me. We can hear nothing but its large voice. . . ."

Professor Kiang said that this Indian song seemed to be similar to a Buddhist chant for funeral services, used among the nomads of Mongolia. I had not told him, up to this moment, that it was a funeral song of a family of American Indians whose home lies in the Canadian Rockies, on the Grease-Trail, running southwards.

The next dirge we examined was one that belongs exclusively to a branch of the Eagle clan of the Kitwanga tribe, in northern British Columbia. This clan participated in the most recent invasion from the north. It has belonged to this district for less than two hundred years.

The dirge of the Eagles (Geetanraet): "I looked up to the sky. Daylight came down early from the East."

This funeral chant reminded Professor Kiang "very much" of a Chinese ceremonial song he had heard coffin-bearers sing in the streets of Peking. So, from Mongolia we had proceeded a step farther into China to find further similarities with American Indian songs. But the next song brought us a real surprise. The very refrain was the same as that used in Chinese funeral songs.

Second dirge of the Eagles (Geetanraet): "Alas! alas! alas! alas! . . . (Hayu, hayu . . .). The chiefs mourn the last survivors of Geetanraet. Alas! alas! . . .

Now that the great chief has died, it is as if the sun were eclipsed. Alas! alas! . . .

My heart is full of grief, because the burial boxes of the other chiefs (unlike ours) are quite empty. Alas! alas! alas! . . ."

The words of the main section of this song were in a local dialect and referred to a fairly recent tribal event. But, to the singer, the refrain *hayu, hayu, hayu* was unintelligible, meaningless. Not so to Professor Kiang, who was amazed. *Hayu* means "Alas!" in Chinese and is exactly what dirge singers in China are accustomed to exclaim in frequent repetition. It forms an habitual part of familiar Buddhist rituals. The Indians of the northwest coast were singing unawares a Chinese religious refrain. This was, indeed, a significant and startling discovery.

Looking over a number of other songs, I find that the refrain *hayu* (alas!), wherever it appears, is used with the right context, that is, in songs of mourning for the death of a relative, and that, in every instance, it is employed by members of the Eagle and the Wolf clans, both of which were recent invaders from the far north.

The singsong-like way of moaning which I mentioned in *The Musical Quarterly* (January, 1933, p. 106) suggested other striking resemblances in mortuary customs. While I was at the Arrandale cannery, on the Nass River, close to the Alaskan border, during the fishing season of 1928, a tragedy brought grief to the natives stationed there. Several of them died of poisoning, after eating decayed salmon roe. Dirges broke out early one morning, and throughout the following days women could be heard moaning in the woods. As soon as the news of the misfortune broke out in the summer village, old women began to wail pitifully. Crouching on the ground in front of their houses, they tore their hair and beat the ground with their foreheads. For once in their lives, those Indians cast restraint to the winds and gave vent to grief. Professional mourners, like those of ancient Greece, rent the air with their lament and sprinkled ashes on their heads.

Weeping: Alas! alas!

ha - yu-gut-ku si - gu, ha - yu- gut-ku si-gwae, he he he he, ha - yu-gut-ku

"Just as it would happen in China," Professor Kiang added after I reported the occurrence to him. "There also mourners pound the ground with their foreheads, and they are paid for it. Quite typical!"

From the dirges, quoted above, Professor Kiang and I passed on to others. One of the most striking, because of its strange melody, was *Hano*! (*The Musical Quarterly*, 1933, p. 107). Somehow it seemed quite familiar to Professor Kiang. "It sounds very much like a Buddhist chant in a funeral service," he declared. "This chant comes from Hindu music." Another link in the long chain of origins: from Alaska, we pass on to Siberia, to China, to India.

Another Indian dirge of northern British Columbia, that of Small-Raven of Kitwanga, "sounds like a night watchman's song in Peking," said Professor Kiang. "The watchman goes out and shouts: 'Be careful of your fire and your doors! Beware of thieves!'" Drumbeats accompany the night calls. The rhythm of the American Indian dirge also is marked by drumbeats.

The dirge of Small-Raven (Hlkwaqaq):"Hohaleangwah, I bemoan the small human-like Raven of my sorrowful heart..."

The Raven here is the principal emblem of the singer's clan and is passed on to a new holder after the death of the head chief. The song includes the words: "I am left alone. Broken-hearted am I when I take his place, for I remember all my ancestors."

A lyric melody of the uplands, the "Fireweed" song of the Skeena headwaters, resembles a "Chinese street tune"; its first part certainly sounds exotic, almost European, if heard among other Indian songs.

"The Fireweed people will drink fermented juice with the Wolf and the Raven tribes. Why think you then that we know not how to brew it? We walk proudly, because we have made it for a long time."

The use of the drum in the Indian songs is an important element to consider in tracing their origin. The Indian drum of Alaska and the Canadian Rockies consists of a tanned skin dried and stretched over one side only of a closed circular band of wood. It is exactly similar to the instrument which the Koriak tribes of northeastern Siberia use in funeral rituals. Siberian drums, according to Jochelson (*The Jesup North Pacific Expedition,* IV), are "covered on both sides with hide, like those found among the American Indians. . . . Together with *drums covered on but one side*," they "are used in Siberia only by the Buddhists," in "their divine services." Even in size the Siberian and Alaskan skin drums are much alike. In northwestern America, the drums were used not only in "divine services" but in rituals on incineration. For dead bodies, as in Siberia, were burnt on a pyre surrounded by dirge singers and mourners.

In the light of these discoveries, a new field for fruitful investigation lies open before us. Theorists for many years have endeavoured to explain the independent origin in America of cultural features known elsewhere. Primitive men were supposed to find within themselves the faculty of recreating the same processes over and over again wherever they might chance to be. For lack of historical records it was impossible to check the application of the theory to features that refused to reveal their origins to investigators, and were accordingly swamped under a deluge of vague, if not sentimental, assumptions. But things may now take another turn, should the comparison of native songs on both sides of Bering prove that they go back to a common Asiatic source.

The new evidence under observation may turn out to be of an historical nature, should it be finally established that an early derivative form of Buddhism long prevailed, as now seems practically certain, in the mortuary rituals of the Northwest Coast Indians. Things like Buddhism and the Chinese mortuary rituals cannot be considered essential to human nature. They are a culture growth, largely accidental, like all other such growths. Besides, there is explicit evidence of the migrations from Asia of the people themselves.

Marius Barbeau, 1962

The Motif of the External Soul in French-Canadian Folktales
Margaret Low

While comparatively few European-derived folktales survive in English Canada as a whole, French Canada has an incredibly rich store of both these and indigenous tales. Les Archives de Folklore at Laval University contain more than five thousand versions of tales which Luc Lacourcière has described as "probably the most important collection of folktales in any language in North America." These tales are being classified and studied by various scholars, one of whom is Margaret Low, a researcher in Laval's CÉLAT. She has translated many French-Canadian tales into English, seven of which appear in Richard Dorson's Folktales Around the World, *and she is working with Luc Lacourcière in preparing an analytical, comparative and anthropological catalogue of French folktales in North America:* Le catalogue raisonné du conte populaire français en Amerique du Nord.

In the following article she studies French-Canadian tales that illustrate an ancient motif stemming from the belief of primitive peoples that the soul can be removed from the body to protect it. She outlines four different forms of this belief and shows how Canadian storytellers exploit this age-old motif for dramatic effect. This is a good example of the kind of analysis that proceeds past the classification by tale types to a study of cross-type motifs.

The idea that the soul, life, or heart of an individual may be placed in or bound up with an object or being other than his own apparently owes its origin in folktales to the belief of primitive peoples that the soul may leave the body without causing death. Consequently, as long as the soul remains safe, the individual is immortal; but as soon as his soul is touched, even at a distance, the individual suffers, and when his soul is destroyed, he dies.

The motif of the "external soul," to use the expression coined in 1922 by Sir James Frazer in *The Golden Bough*, is found in a whole series of folktales which are at once among the oldest and the most widely diffused tales in the world.

The external soul motif can be divided into four main types, all of which are found in the folktale tradition of French Canada. First, there is the repeated reincarnation or successive concealments of the soul; second, life bound up with a candle, light, or torch; third, life or soul in an egg which, in turn, is hidden in a series of envelopes or coverings; and fourth, life or soul in a bird.

We begin with the reincarnation of the soul since this form of the motif is found in the oldest known folktale dating from the thirteenth century B.C., the Egyptian tale of *The Two Brothers*, in which, as you recall, Batu, killed because of his treacherous wife, returns to her in the form of a bull. She has the bull killed but two drops of its blood fall to the earth and two trees grow from the spot. When one of the trees lets the wife know that it is her husband, she has them cut down. But a splinter flies into her mouth and she swallows it. Later she gives birth to a son who is no other than Batu himself.

The motif of the external soul which hides successively in the form of an animal, drops of blood, trees, splinters, and finally a duck rather than the rebirth of the hero, is found in the French-Canadian tale type 590A, *The Treacherous Wife.*[1] The characteristic form of the thirteen Canadian versions is as follows:

> At the instigation of an old man, the hero spends three nights in a haunted castle, thereby delivering an enchanted princess, as in types 400 and 401, and receives a cloak, which renders him invisible, and a magic sword.
>
> The hero conquers the King's enemies and wins the hand of the King's daughter. But his wife soon proves treacherous and reveals the secret of the magic objects to her paramour and has the hero killed.
>
> The hero's body is cut into pieces and tied to his horse. The animal returns to the enchanted castle and the hero is brought back to life by the old man or the disenchanted princess.
>
> Seeking revenge, he returns to his wife in the form of a horse but is recognized and killed.
>
> A servant, following an earlier request of the hero, buries three drops of the horse's blood from whence grow three trees. The treacherous wife has the trees cut down but the servant throws three splinters into a pond where they are transformed into three ducks. The wife's paramour tries to kill the ducks but one of them escapes and returns to shore. Regaining his

human form, the hero seizes his magic sword and slays his enemies.

The successive concealment of the soul is also found in Type 408, *The Three Oranges*, of which, however, only one version has been collected to date in French Canada. In this tale the heroine is transformed into a bird which is later killed. From the remains of the bird grows a tree which is cut down; but a splinter from the tree enables the heroine to regain her human form.

In the second form, the external soul is bound up with the life of a candle, torch, or light. In several versions of Type 708A*, *The Rose-Girl and the Queen*, a tale which will be discussed in some length later, the hero discovers in a secret room a table with three lighted candles and learns that the candles are the lives of three sisters who are fairies. He succeeds in blowing out the candles and the fairies die instantly. In a few versions the candles are also a life-index since the intensity of their light reveals the state of health of the three fairies, and the different lengths of the tapers indicate their relative life-span (as in Aarne-Thompson, Type 332, *Godfather Death*, although not in the Canadian versions).

In a tale recorded in 1914 by Marius Barbeau at Lorette, Quebec, from Mrs. Prudent Sioui, entitled: *Le diable et la bougie*,[2] a fisherman promises, in exchange for a boat-load of fish, to give to a stranger, who is of course none other than the devil, the first being who comes to meet him; and this is his son, rather than his dog as usual. However, his wife outwits the devil by making him promise to let her keep her child as long as a candle which she has just lit has not burned itself out. She quickly blows out the candle and the child is saved.

In another tale, *La femme plus rusée que le diable*,[3]

published by Charles-Edmond Rouleau, a man promises his soul to the devil in return for help in building a bridge. Once more it is the wife who outwits the devil. She asks him to wait and not take her husband until a lighted candle is consumed. She blows out the candle — and the devil is still waiting!

The same theme is found in a tale recorded by Luc Lacourcière in 1957 in Prince Edward Island, entitled: *L'homme qui voulait pas mourir*.[4] Here a rich but charitable man asks a monk to grant that he might live to be the last man on earth. The monk gives him a small piece of wood and says that he will live as long as the wood is not burned. The man hides the wood and lives for centuries and centuries. By that time, he resembles an old skeleton and his language is unintelligible. Finally, another monk who understands this ancient language comes to the man's castle. The latter entreats him to go and get the piece of wood where it is hidden. The old man throws the wood on the fire and is happy to die.

Another variant of the above tale was recorded by Jean-Claude Dupont in 1965 in Beauce County, Quebec.[5]

All of the tales in this section are to be compared, of course, to the Greek myth of Meleager (Type 1187). At his birth, the Fates declared that Meleager's life would last as long as a burning brand was unconsumed. His mother immediately extinguished the brand and hid it away in a chest. When, however, many years later, Meleager is responsible for the death of his uncles, his mother takes out the brand and, in her rage, throws it on the fire, causing Meleager to die a painful death.

The third form of the external soul is found in one of the most popular and widely known folktales in the world, Type 302: *The Ogre's (Devil's) Heart in the Egg*, in which, in the occidental form of the tale, the life of a giant or ogre is found in an egg which is in turn hidden in a series of coverings. In French Canada the egg is generally in a pigeon, which is in a serpent, which is in a lion or in a series of strongboxes, the whole being hidden far away in some inaccessible region.

With the help of grateful animals, the hero, who can transform himself to the animals' likenesses at will, succeeds in reaching the external soul. He kills the giant by breaking the egg, usually against the giant's forehead or some other spot of vulnerability.

Seventy-four versions of this tale have been recorded to date in French Canada, the majority of which are clearly derived from the French tradition, although a few versions have been influenced by the Irish tradition of Type 302.

The theme of the soul hidden in a series of coverings is found in a tale from the original collection of the *Arabian Nights* which is prior to the tenth century. This story, which was not included in Gallant's translation of the *Mille et une Nuits*, is found in Lane's translation (ed. 1883, III, p. 316ff.) and in the *Contes inédits des Mille et une Nuits* of Hammer and Trébutien (Extraits de l'original arabe par J. de Hammer et traduits en français par G. S. Trébutien, II, pp. 120-82). In this story of Seifol-Molouk and Bediol-Djimal, a genie sweeps down in the form of a cloud and carries a princess off to his palace.

The princess discovers the secret of the genie's external soul: warned by astrologers that he will be killed by a prince, the genie had his soul placed in a sparrow which is enclosed in a cage, the cage in a box, the box in a chest, the chest in seven other chests, the whole placed in a marble sarcophagus which is thrown into the sea.

The hero, Seifol, orders the external soul to appear by the power of Solomon's ring. When the sarcophagus is thrown up on the shore, he breaks it with his sword and takes out the sparrow which he cuts to pieces. The genie dies and is reduced to ashes.

This brings us to the fourth form of the external soul motif, which is usually thought of as the Asiatic form: the life of the antagonist residing in a bird (or insect).

This motif is an important part of almost all of the thirty-four French-Canadian versions of Type 708A*, *The Rose-Girl and the Queen*, by far one of the most interesting and best-told tales in French Canada.

I will outline this tale in its entirety since it is of such great interest.

A King who is on a hunt comes upon a cabin in a desolate part of the forest. The inhabitants are a very poor man, his wife, and their numerous children.

On seeing the eldest daughter who is, in spite of the rags she wears, a great beauty, he asks for her hand in marriage and returns with her to his castle.

One day, the King and his young bride set out in their carriage to visit the young woman's parents and discover on the side of the road a tablecloth or another object.

The King stops to pick up the tablecloth in spite of his wife's protests or because of her entreaties to do so. An ugly, old witch jumps out from under the cloth and says that he had no right to touch her property and must now, as his punishment, take her as his wife and abandon the young queen.

The witch takes out the young queen's eyes and abandons her in the forest. The witch then goes to live with the King in his castle.

Meanwhile, the young woman is found in the woods by a hunter or lumberman who takes her to his home where his wife will look after her. A few months later, the blind woman gives birth to a son.

The son reaches school age, is twitted with being a bastard by his schoolmates, and sets out to find his unknown father.

He reaches his father's castle, often with the help of a magic aid, an old man, old woman, or an animal, but does not reveal his identity. But the witch, of course, knows he is her husband's son and plots to get rid of him.

Feigning illness, she sends him on quests, often resembling those of Type 590, *The Prince and the Arm Bands:* to seek the milk of a unicorn or lion, the foam of seven wild horses, etc. The last task is to bring back to the witch her castle which is suspended by four golden chains over the Red Sea.

The hero receives from his magic aid a fiddle which compels those who hear it to dance, and a small boat, often of paper and small enough to carry in his pocket but which grows to normal size when placed on the water.

The hero reaches the castle where dwell the three daughters of the witch, and the latter are happy to see a handsome young man.

He convinces the sisters to show him the castle and finds there in a secret room:

the eyes of his mother, with an ointment to restore sight;

a lever to transport the castle at will;

a table with three lighted candles which contain the lives of the three daughters of the witch;

and a bird, usually an owl, which is the life of the old witch, and he learns that whatever is done to the bird happens also to the witch.

The hero plays his violin, compelling the three

sisters to dance until they fall to the ground exhausted. He then goes and blows their life-candles; the three fairies die instantly.

He then transports the suspended castle next to that of his father.

He seizes the bird and pulls off its wing. In the castle of the King, the witch's arm falls off, much to the astonishment of her husband and doctor. The hero then pulls off successively the bird's second wing and two legs, causing the same mutilations in the corresponding members of the witch.

When he enters the castle with the bird, the witch cries out: "Tit-Jean, come closer and kiss me"; but he wrings the bird's neck and the witch dies.

The hero returns to his mother, replaces her eyes and restores her sight, and she is happily reunited with her husband.

The hero, Tit-Jean, marries a princess, of course, and is happy; even the hero's wife lives happily ever after in spite of the fact that she is to have ninety-nine little princes and fourteen little princesses!

This tale has been recorded thirty-four times in French Canada to date but apparently has never been found in France or in Ireland. In fact, the other occidental versions, which are not numerous (three versions from Spain, two from Italy, and one from Chile), differ considerably from the Canadian. We classified the Canadian versions as Type 708A* (a type number added to the 1961 edition of the Aarne-Thompson because of the presence of the Spanish versions) to group the occidental versions of this tale together; but this was purely an arbitrary decision on our part since the Canadian versions belong equally to the Indic tale Type 462, *The Outcast Queens and the Ogress*

Queen, of which there are twenty-four Indic versions.

The comparison of the Canadian and Indic traditions of this tale is fascinating but we must get back to the matter at hand. The motif of the external soul is present in Type 708A* in two forms: life in the candles, as mentioned earlier (a form not found in the Indic variants of Types 462); and the life of the witch in a bird, as in the Asiatic tradition.

The hero makes his antagonist suffer as much as possible before destroying the external soul. This piecemeal destruction of the external soul is found in the Indic versions of Types 462 and 302, of which the best known is the story of the Indian magician Punchkin.

I will quote a brief passage to refresh your memory:

> "Give me my parrot!" cried Punchkin. Then the boy took hold of the parrot, and tore off one of his wings; and as he did so, the Magician's right arm fell off.
>
> Punchkin then stretched out his left arm, crying, "Give me my parrot!" The Prince pulled off the parrot's second wing, and the Magician's left arm tumbled off.
>
> "Give me my parrot!" cried he, and fell on his knees. The Prince pulled off the parrot's right leg, the Magician's right leg fell off; the Prince pulled off the parrot's left leg, down fell the Magician's left.
>
> Nothing remained of him save the limbless body and the head; but still he rolled his eyes and cried, "Give me my parrot!" "Take your parrot, then," cried the boy, and with that he wrung the bird's neck, and threw it at the Magician; and, as he did so, Punchkin's head twisted round, and, with a fearful groan, he died![6]

Here is a similar scene in a Canadian version of Type

708A* recorded in 1949 in Charlevoix County, Quebec, by Luc Lacourcière:

> "Le château s'en va au-dessus du château de son père . . . La bonne femme [la fée] sautait après le château pis a était toute prête. I' [le héros] prend la corneille qui avait les yeux en feu. I' lui casse une aile. La bonne femme a un bras de cassé en bas. I' casse l'autre aile. Elle sautait encore pareil. I' casse la patte. Elle sautait encore pareil. I' casse l'autre patte. Elle saute encore. I' la déchire en aiguillettes La fée s'écrase sur le bord du sable. Là, elle est morte."[7]

The successive concealments of the soul, life bound up with a candle, the soul in an egg in a series of coverings, and the soul in a bird and its piecemeal destruction, not to mention the related themes of unique vulnerability and the life-index, all of these motifs are found in the folktales of French Canada.[8]

The French-Canadian taletellers do not know that the term "external soul" was coined by J. C. Frazer, nor that the motif is probably derived from the belief of primitive peoples that the soul can be removed from the body for reasons of security; but the Canadian tellers do realize and exploit to the full the dramatic potential of this motif which still appeals to the popular imagination as it has for centuries and centuries.

Margaret Low, 1976

The Function of Threats
in Newfoundland Folklore
J. D. A. Widdowson

*Childhood lore in virtually every known society includes
frightening figures in one guise or another, used by adults
in dealing with children as well as by children themselves.
Decried by some yet, as is obvious from their persistence,
valued by others, the tradition of one sort or another bogeyman remains alive in Canada today. Widespread industrial-
ization and urbanization of the society as a whole and
heightened sophistication and worldliness among the youth
have not eliminated the need for and utility of traditional
verbal controls on behaviour.*

*As his doctoral dissertation, John D. A. Widdowson
undertook a thorough investigation of frightening figures
in Newfoundland folklore. Dr. Widdowson has long been
involved in research on Newfoundland traditions, particularly the dialect, because of his special interest and
training in the study of language. He has collected extensively across the island, served as Acting Chairman of the
Department of Folklore at Memorial University, and done
prodigious research for* The Dictionary of Newfoundland
English *among other books. He is Professor and Head of
the Centre for English Cultural Tradition and Language at
The University of Sheffield in Yorkshire.*

This study, a chapter from his dissertation, should be compared with Emily Carr's much more impressionistic description of a frightening figure among the native peoples in "D'Sonoqua" (see pp. 144-53).

Although the threatening figures used in Newfoundland have a wide variety of names, they have broadly similar functions. The choice of a given figure may depend on such factors as geographical location and social stratification. In Newfoundland the function of most of the figures is to encourage children to accept the authority of adults in matters of simple obedience and the like.

A group of generalized figures tends to be used in the threats directed against disobedience and misbehaviour. Some of these may also have a more specific function, such as deterring children from endangering themselves or from interfering with adult activities. Figures such as the boo-man and the bogeyman are normally used for general obedience but are also employed to deter children from going to dangerous places, to get them indoors before dark, to encourage them to go to bed or to sleep, and so on. In the same way the Devil or the Black Man may be used both generally and also against children who tell lies or act in an irreligious way.

Other figures tend to be limited to certain specific functions or are restricted to their roles in some other way. For example, fairies are used mainly to discourage children from wandering away on the barrens or in the woods, or from staying out after dark. Whether natural or supernatural, the Newfoundland figures have a special potency of action after dark. Their frequent association with dark or shadowy places reflects the widespread fear of darkness itself. The figures themselves are often described as being black or dark in colour and dress, which in western culture is ultimately suggestive of death and oblivion. Whereas the fairies, the bogeyman and other members of the boo/bogey group are primarily nocturnal in their application, the living authority figures, whose threatening function is closely connected with their occupations, tend to be used primarily in threats related to daytime activities. Ministers of religion are often used in threats against children who are behaving in some way which is thought to be immoral or contrary to the teachings of the Christian church, and teachers are the typical threatening figures for misbehaviour at school or refusal to do homework. The doctor, nurse and dentist are used mainly for reasons connected with children's health, such as refusal to take medicine, malingering, or refusal to eat. The policeman tends to be used when children are in danger of breaking the law, as well as for general misbehaviour. Some figures, such as Santa Claus, mummers and janneys, are restricted in tradition to a limited period in the winter months.

The figures used in Newfoundland for general disobedience, naughtiness and the like are characteristically conceived of as omnipresent, whereas those with more specific functions are often confined to particular locations or situations. The bear is associated with woods and lonely places; marine creatures such as the shark and the whale are naturally used in threats about the dangers of going near wharves, harbours and the like.

These two groups of figures have interesting parallels in Ranke's discussion of the German figures. He identifies as his first group those which lack a well-defined pedagogical task or mission (*Patronat*). Like the general figures in the Newfoundland material, these embody to some extent the moral principle in that they fetch and punish bad children.[1] The figures in Ranke's third group, however, have a more definite purpose, and their threatening role is exercised in certain places forbidden to children.[2] This group has obvious similarities with those Newfoundland figures which have specific threatening functions, although Newfoundland apparently lacks the corn-demons and other beings used to safeguard crops in the Germanic tradition and elsewhere.

It is interesting to note which areas of the young child's experience in Newfoundland seems to be subject to little or no control through threats. For example, there have been no reports of threats regarding care in handling potentially dangerous things such as fishhooks, splitting knives or boat-building tools and the like, with which children in many parts of the province came into contact quite frequently until very recent times. Further, although very small children may be threatened to keep them away from wharves and boats, etc., they learn to cope with these hazards at an early age. The tendency in Newfoundland is to warn very young children against venturing alone onto wharves or into boats, but when they are with adults they are expected to adjust to the new situation. Boys are thus initiated early into certain aspects of the adult world. In contrast, however, there are also occasions when children ought to be aware of danger and yet are not. Newfoundland children, for example, often seem oblivious of the perils of playing or walking carelessly on busy roads even though they are occasionally warned about such thoughtlessness. From this one might infer that certain acts or situations appear dangerous or frightening only when culturally controlled in some way — for example, by means of threats and other warnings which, through constant repetition, alert the child to the hazards concerned.

In Newfoundland, young children are protected from numerous dangers in the natural environment by means of threats which encourage them to believe that certain places are inhabited by some powerful and mysterious being. These locations are of four principal types:

1. Places of potential danger, e.g., harbours, rivers, ponds, brooks and wells; wharves and stages;[3] cliffs, rocks and caves; marshes, barrens and woods; old dilapidated buildings; root cellars.
2. Places where human beings often feel afraid or apprehensive, e.g., dark places, narrow lanes and paths, bridges, lonely places, graveyards, hollows, places shaded by trees.
3. Places from which children are forbidden, to prevent them from causing damage or otherwise interfering with adult activities,[4] e.g., vegetable gardens and fields of growing crops; barns and other buildings where animals are kept; workshops, storage sheds and various rooms, closets and cupboards inside the house itself.
4. Places associated with some unpleasant or frightening event, e.g., localities where a murder or suicide has been committed, where unexplained noises have been heard, or lights or other manifestations seen.

It is thought to be dangerous or inadvisable for children, and even sometimes adults, to visit some of these places, especially when alone. Danger might threaten there in many forms, whether from the natural hazards of the environment, or from robbery or the attack of some person or animal. In this sense, potential danger therefore links all four types of location where threatening figures are said to lurk.

Outdoor locations such as mountains, woods and water have their attendant spirits in the mythology of many cultures. A possible rationalization of this is that such lonely, frightening and dangerous places seem to be more out of man's control than those near at hand where he can prevent a child from being injured, or at least rescue him from danger. The threats used to effect such control imply that the further the child strays from the security of the home and the community, the more hazards he may encounter. An important function of such threats, therefore, is to prevent children from straying away from home and going to such places. The threats also serve to keep children within sight of the parents by warning them away from more distant places where, especially if unsupervised, they may make mischief or endanger themselves.

Nature figures, such as those which in Germanic tradition are said to inhabit mountains, woods and water, are rare in Newfoundland. Their place is often taken by the boo-man or some other figure which is also used in threats against many kinds of unacceptable behaviour. When invoked in threats concerning natural hazards, these figures apparently take on the characteristics as well as the function of nature spirits. In addition, some of the Newfoundland figures are associated with particular places in the natural environment. For example, mermaids are confined to the salt water, while fairies and the Jack o'Lantern are typically found near marshes, on the barrens or in the woods.

Whatever their location, many of the figures are represented as having the urge to take or chase children. They are often described as if they were expected to pounce on their victims unawares. This is especially true of the supernatural/invented figures. Sometimes they carry weapons to assist them in the chase, such as the "prong" carried by the Devil, the official "billyknocker" (i.e., truncheon) of the policeman, and the sticks, knives and similar implements carried by other human figures. They are presented as having the desire to injure children physically in some way, and especially to devour them. Perhaps even more terrifying for the child is the frequently expressed idea that he will be taken away from the environment which he knows, and in which he feels secure, to some unknown place where family and friends will be unable to find him. The figures are presented in the most frightening way possible so as to have the maximum effect in their threatening function.

Threatening figures in Newfoundland are sometimes presented in a hierarchy according to the age of the child. A very young child may be threatened with the boo-man or bogeyman; when he is older, the Black Man is used; later still, he may be threatened with the Devil. When the names of these figures, in ascending order of potency, cease to be effective, he may as a last resort be threatened with God. In order to fulfil their function, threats must evidently be expressed with increasing severity.

Newfoundland parents present children with various norms to encourage acceptable behaviour and to discourage what is culturally regarded as unacceptable. The child is encouraged to emulate the example of individuals or groups whose behaviour is praiseworthy or acceptable within certain social and individual behavioural codes. By contrast, various people who are not normal in some way are pointed out as examples of abnormalities which the child is actively encouraged to dislike and avoid and which he often comes to regard with apprehension. When the parent temporarily identifies himself as an authority figure in threatening his children with his own power or physical strength, he puts himself at a greater distance from the child. By employing the mechanisms of adult verbal control, he deliberately widens the gulf between the child's world and the adult world so that the child becomes at least temporarily less secure.

The power and authority of the adult world is also reflected in the fact that figures and motifs used in the threats are often said to be of large size. In the Newfoundland reports, the boo-man and the bogeyman, for example, are described as big and black, the Devil is said to have a big fire in which he will burn naughty children, and the policeman is said to be coming in his big car. When a living person such as a stranger is used as a threatening figure, his adult status is strongly emphasized and references are made to the "big man" who will take the child away. The adult's physical stature and proportions are commented on or exaggerated to serve the threatening function. The same is true of animals used in threats, and this is especially effective when a small creature such as a mouse or rat is presented as something of monstrous proportions which is more than capable of eating a child. The differences between the adult world and the childhood world are thus condensed into the idea of abnormally large size, and the bulky disguises which are often worn by the mummers, for example, may be frightening to a child simply because they distort the basic human form into something huge and grotesque.

Some Newfoundland informants reveal, however, that children are often not frightened when threatened. Even so, the threats may be efficacious. Threats can evidently be effective on several levels without necessarily being frightening. If one threatens a child who is already afraid, however, the threat is obviously more likely to fulfil its purpose. Direct physical action may also cause the child to obey; and although he may be resentful, upset or angry as a result, he may not necessarily be afraid.

The same child may himself already threaten other children, and later he will in his turn assume the full threatening authority of an adult. When Newfoundland children threaten each other, the threats are often playful. Sometimes, however, they are used in a deliberately bullying or spiteful way. Whereas an adult frequently withholds the full impact of a threat by modifying his tone of voice or giving some other indication that it may not be carried out, a child may threaten another in such a serious way that he is really frightened.

On the other hand, of course, children may make light of such threats. They often enjoy frightening each other and playing frightening games. In such games, the frightening is often simulated or vicarious. Children sometimes even appear to enjoy being shouted at or chased by people whom they tease, despite the fact that such people are often used as threatening figures and are made to appear particularly frightening.

Newfoundland adults themselves also use the verbal device of teasing in the social control of children. Whether teasing, threats, jokes or other linguistic means are used, however, their specific function is to effect control without breaking the bond between parent and child. The maintenance of these interpersonal relationships, despite the divisive potential of threats or physical punishment, is best summarized by Szwed in his study of Newfoundland's Codroy Valley.[5] In intrafamilial relationships such as those which Szwed describes, it is clear that threats and other verbal controls are constantly used by parents and other adults at all stages of a young child's development. The examples in the Newfoundland data, however, rarely identify precisely the age group to which individual threats apply.

***

Specific Functions of Verbal Social Controls

The specific functions of such controls as they operate at the family level have received surprisingly little attention. It is important to indicate the principal reasons for the use of threats in directing children's behaviour at the family level. The evidence at present available in MUNFLA[6] suggests that threats are used to control a considerable range of behaviour, from the general to the particular. In general terms, as one might expect, these functions reflect those which are given prominence in the various questionnaires. These are:

    a. Preventing or discouraging disobedience, general misbehaviour or "naughtiness."

    b. Keeping children away from dangerous or forbidden places.

    c. Preventing children from interfering with animals, crops and tools.

    d. Getting children indoors before dark and keeping them in during the hours of darkness.

    e. Getting children to bed and/or to sleep.

    f. Other miscellaneous or unspecified functions.

When a child disobeys or does something against his parents' wishes or without their approval, he is threatened that some unpleasant consequences may ensue. He is expected to "behave properly," especially when visitors are present in the home, and threats are directed explicitly against all forms of misbehaviour, naughtiness, contrariness, stubbornness, waywardness and mischievousness. A child who behaves in these ways is said to be "unruly" and is thought to be in need of disciplining. In these general threats, such figures as the boo-man, the boo-baggers, the boogeyman, the bully man and the policeman are typically used. The same figures are also used to keep children away from certain forbidden places. A wider variety of figures, including those typically associated with certain specific locations, is used to warn children away from dangerous places, and in addition to the general figures, such as the boo-man and bogeyman, figures such as the mermaid are typically used to keep children from beaches and harbours, the fairies and Jack o'Lantern keep them from getting lost in woods or marshes, witches and rats guard the wells, Mother Raw prevents them climbing a dangerous mountain, Henry Gouldwoody lurks on the barrens, and old buildings are haunted by ghosts.

The Newfoundland material includes comparatively few examples of threats used to prevent children from interfering with animals, crops, tools and the like. This may be partly due to the fact that few domestic animals are kept nowadays, and also because there is little farming in the province. The last thirty years have also seen a remarkable decline in the vegetable gardens which were once so important, especially in the outports. Children continue to be warned away from horses, sheep and other domestic animals, however, and are threatened if they torment cats or chase chickens. Sometimes the child is told that the animal itself will hurt him if he goes near it. Such figures as the bogeyman and the policeman are used to discourage children from damaging or stealing turnips, carrots, cabbages, potatoes and other vegetables, from raiding apple and plum trees, and also to prevent them from touching or playing with dangerous implements of various kinds.

One of the most common functions of threats in Newfoundland folklore is to get children indoors before dark and to prevent them from going out after dusk. Children are told to be in by a certain hour, or to be home before dark, and they are also told to come home early if it is foggy or stormy. Once indoors, they are warned not to go out into the darkness for fear of the various nocturnal figures which are said to be lurking outside. These same figures, especially those in the boo/bogey group, are also used to encourage children to go to bed and to sleep.

Threats are used to prevent or discourage numerous kinds of unacceptable or undesirable behaviour, many of which were not mentioned specifically in the questionnaire. In addition, threats are used to encourage children to co-operate by helping parents in the home and for numerous other functions. The examples quoted above are merely a representative selection of those in the Newfoundland Archive. They can do no more than hint at the wealth and variety of specific functions which a fuller and more intensive study would undoubtedly reveal. Some of the Archive reports comment on the fact that the threats are used mostly for the good of the child, although it is clear that adults also use them to encourage co-operation within the family group, and sometimes simply for their own peace of mind and as an outlet for their own hostility and aggression. Much depends on the mood of the adult, who may threaten the child either playfully or seriously, according to the situational context. Although the child eventually realizes that the verbal controls are merely a device to encourage acceptable behaviour, the more serious threats, especially in his early years, may induce him to believe in the existence of the threatening figures themselves. This belief, however uncertain and temporary it may be, plays an important part in ensuring that the threats fulfil their intended function.

John D. A. Widdowson, 1977

A Parable in Context:
A Social Interactional Analysis
of Storytelling Performance
Barbara Kirshenblatt-Gimblett

This discussion by Barbara Kirshenblatt-Gimblett is unusual amongst Canadian folklore studies in that it has had international significance to folklore theory. Most Canadian works are descriptive — collections and surveys of material — rather than analytical, and few indeed have contributed to the recent development of the discipline internationally.

This article concerns the role of one type of oral traditional material, namely the parable, in communication. It deals with such questions as why a person elects to use oral traditional materials in what situations to carry what messages. In all, it seeks to explain the function of this folklore in its performance context, using a specific group of people — members of the Toronto Jewish community.

Parables — didactic stories told to exemplify some moral — are a widespread folklore form. They are commonly associated with religious traditions and popular in Jewish folklore because of the rabbinical tradition.

Barbara Kirshenblatt-Gimblett was born and raised within the group she discusses, but has lived for many years in New York City where she now works at the Yeshiva Institute, directing its program in folklore study and propagation. She has a doctorate in folklore from Indiana

University and has taught the subject at several major American universities. She has numerous publications to her credit and is generally recognized as one of the major folklorists of the younger generation.

As early as 1925, Malinowski sounded a strikingly modern note in his classic essay, "Myth in Primitive Psychology," where he emphasized a performance orientation to the study of Trobriand folktales and stressed the importance of the social and cultural contexts of storytelling. Speaking of *kukwanebu* (fairy tales), Malinowski said:

> The text, of course, is extremely important, but without the context it remains lifeless. As we have seen, the interest of the story is vastly enhanced and it is given its proper character by the manner in which it is told. The whole nature of the performance, the voice and the mimicry, the stimulus and the response of the audience mean as much to the natives as the text; and the sociologist should take his cue from the natives. The performance, again, has to be placed in its proper time setting — the hour of the day, and the season, with the background of the sprouting gardens awaiting future work, and slightly influenced by the magic of the fairy tales. We must also bear in mind the sociological context of private ownership, the sociable function and the cultural role of amusing fiction. All these elements are equally relevant; all must be studied as well as the text. The stories live in native life and not on paper, and when a scholar jots them down without being able to evoke the atmosphere in which

they flourish, he has given us but a mutilated bit of reality.[1]

Ten years later, in 1935, Malinowski refined his notion of context when he discussed the contextual specification of meaning as part of his ethnographic theory of language and made a very important distinction between "the context of situation and the context of culture." He showed how the meaning of words, sentences, narratives and other genres of speaking was conditioned by "the situation in which the utterance is being made and the situation to which it refers."[2]

Folklorists and anthropologists since Malinowski have tended to study oral tradition in its ramified cultural context and general social setting while abstracting particular items of folklore from their immediate contexts of use.[3] At best, the investigator may specify the types of storytelling situations in general — legends were told "in homes, in stores and at ritual ceremonies"[4] and occasionally he may provide a brief description of what a typical tale occasion is usually like. This lack of interest in immediate contexts of use, in how one performer actually uses a particular tale on a specific occasion, reflects the preoccupation of folklorists with two important aspects of storytelling. First, in contrast with ordinary speech, folktales are preformulated. As a result, scholars have tended to view them as set pieces or autonomous entities and have recorded them most often in artificial interview contexts. Second, folklorists have concentrated on specialized storytelling events; that is, on speech events in which the focus is upon telling tales and narration is the dominant mode of discourse. Although in such narrative sessions, each of the preceding tales and non-narrative speech acts do create a frame of reference for the stories which follow, it is often the case that *there are several other narratives which could have served as functional equivalents for many of the tales actually told.*[5] This important feature of specialized story-telling events may explain in part why folklorists have treated narratives as set pieces and have stressed their invariant features rather than the performer's creativity in selecting the appropriate tale and in adjusting his rendition of it to each new situation. Thus, in accounts of storytelling, we generally find information about the broad cultural context of the tales and occasionally an indication or general description of the major types of storytelling occasions. Very rarely do we come across accounts of *actual* narrative events.

Furthermore, scholars have tended to neglect the type of narrative performance in which a narrator embeds a tale in a stretch of non-narrative discourse. In such cases, the raconteur will usually take considerable care to fit the particular tale to the immediate social context and because of this he may be hardpressed to find other tales which could serve as a functional equivalent. These are the story-telling performances which arise spontaneously and even unexpectedly in the course of conversation and which exhibit an especially close fit between text and context. Because of these characteristics, such performances lend themselves most dramatically to an analysis in terms of the structure of social interaction which is based upon a detailed description of the immediate context in which the story was actually told.

The present social interactional analysis of one perfor-mance in depth represents an attempt to examine folklore in its immediate context of use as a highly structured, integrated form of interpersonal behaviour. Rather than conceiving of context as a mass of detail which is relegated to a headnote or footnote as "background information" or "atmosphere," the "performance" will be my unit of analysis and I will try to show in detail precisely how a narrative event is structured and how a creative raconteur integrates a preformulated utterance such as a parable into a specific social interaction. I have chosen to analyze a parable because, being a didactic metaphor, it usually appears in the course of non-narrative discourse such as conversation rather than as a relatively self-contained unit in a specialized storytelling session. Like fables and proverbs, parables are a traditional technique for coping with problematic social situations. It is therefore especially appropriate to analyze the performance of a parable as an example of "interpersonal ritual behaviour" which attempts to restore harmony after someone has "made a scene."[6] This type of analysis with its emphasis upon the immediate context of use can also reveal how the social situation contextualizes the meaning of a tale and foregrounds the themes which are relevant to the narrator on a particular occasion. Thus, following Malinowski's later refinements on the concept of context, I will be analyzing one storytelling performance in terms of "the situation in which the utterance is being made and the situation to which it refers" in order to dramatize the structure of a storytelling performance, the integration of narrative and social setting and the contextual specification of meaning.

THE NARRATOR AND HER REPERTOIRE

Dvora Katz was born in 1915 in Brest-Litovsk, Poland, and came to Canada with her mother and siblings in 1929. Her mother, who died in 1949, is the chief source of the proverbs and parables in Dvora's repertoire. In the course of several conversations with me, Dvora revealed that she sees both herself and her mother as being especially skilled at getting along with other people, at resolving conflicts between others and "at putting things in such a way that no one is hurt." In her role as mediator, she frequently eases anxious social encounters by using about ten different parables and over one hundred proverbs which she remembers her mother applying to the foibles of human behaviour in the course of conversations which took place more than twenty-five years ago. Included in the parables which Dvora learned from her mother are:

Aa-Th 1682 *The Groom Teaches His Horse to Live without Food.* It dies.

In Dvora's version a stingy man is dismayed when, after weeks of reducing the horse's food, the animal is finally trained to eat nothing. "Just when I taught him to live without food, he goes ahead and dies." Dvora uses the parable to comment on the self-defeating nature of stinginess.

Aa-Th 163A* *The Bear Chases Away the Flies* that annoy his master. By chance he strikes his master dead.

Dvora uses this tale to make the point that a foolish friend can do more harm than a clever enemy.

Aa-Th 288B* *The Over-hasty Toad (Beetle)* is years ascending steps. On last step falls and curses haste.

Dvora's version is about a little girl who takes all day to buy a bottle of milk and drops the bottle just as she arrives home. She says to her mother, "Nothing good can come of rushing." Dvora's mother used to reprimand her with this parable when, as a child, she procrastinated about doing her chores.

***

TRANSCRIPTION OF NARRATOR'S REPORT OF HER PERFORMANCE OF ONE PARABLE

On March 24, 1968, I mailed a blank tape to the Katz family in Toronto, with instructions to record traditional narratives in the context of a festive social gathering of close friends and relatives. One of the texts recorded on this occasion was a report by Dvora Katz of how she used a parable on a particular occasion with reference to a specific social situation. The individuals referred to in the following text were present:

> Dvora: I have to tell you something and this was a true fact. Once I was at my brother's and the atmosphere was tense. My brother had promised the kids to take them to a show over and over again and he was busy in the office and he had no time. Are you listening?
> Al: Yea.
> Dvora: Next time. And he was busy and each time he made an appointment something else came up and the kids were disappointed. It was an afternoon show, a morning show. Nothing worked.
>
> I come in and my sister-in-law, Ruth, was upset and the kids were crying and my brother says, "O.K." This was nine o'clock. "We can go to a show now." Nine o'clock nobody wants to go to a show. It was late and there was just no point. So I saw there was going to be revolution because he couldn't understand why they can't go to a show. The kids realized that he should have gone when he made the promise to go so many times. Ruth felt that he was unfair and I thought at this point they need something to break the ice because the atmosphere was just too thick. So

I says, "You know, this reminds me of a story."

No. My brother comes up and he says, "Dvora, tell me. Tell me what is wrong with a father wanting to take his children to a show? What have I done? Have I committed a crime? I want my children to go with me to a show. They all say I'm doing something wrong. What's wrong?"

So I says, "I'll tell you. It reminds me of a story my mother used to tell me."

A man once came to a Rabbi to ask a *shayle* [question regarding ritual purity] forgiveness.

He says, "What is it? What did you do?"

He says, "I didn't wash. . . . I didn't say the prayer before the meal."

He says, "How come?"

He says, "Because I didn't wash my hands."

He says, "Well, why didn't you wash your hands?"

He says, "Because I wasn't eating Jewish food."

He says, "How come you weren't eating Jewish food?"

"Because I was eating in a Gentile restaurant."

He says, "How come?"

"Because it was *Yonkiper* [Yom Kippur, the day of Atonement, most solemn Jewish holiday and fast day, when every man's fate for the coming year is said to be decided] and the Jewish restaurants were closed."

So this, I said, reminds me of my brother, "Why can't I take them to the show?" Here he had made so many promises and so many disappointments. He couldn't understand how come the kids didn't want to go to the show.[7]

This parable is a formula tale employing a chain with interdependent members[8] and may be identified as the motif "Penitent in confession worries about little sins and belittles big ones" (Rotunda U 11.1.1.2.).[9] This tale has been recorded often from both Jewish and non-Jewish sources[10] and, in several collections, it appears as a framed narrative: the tale itself is embedded in a description of the social situation it reflects and in which it was reputedly told. Thus, Dvora is not exceptional in utilizing this particular tale as a parable, although the way she does so is unique. Furthermore, even *her report of her performance* is a traditional narrative since it constitutes a framed tale for which there are several analogues in printed collections.[11]

CASE HISTORY OF THE NARRATOR'S PERFORMANCE

As I was not present when the parable was originally told, what I am analyzing is *Dvora's report of her performance*. First, her account is a meaningful unit of analysis because it constitutes a culturally relevant case history in which she defines the natural boundaries — the beginning, focus and end — of a unit of spoken interaction: by unit, I mean "the total activity that occurs during the time that a given set of participants have accredited one another for talk and maintain a single moving focus of attention";[12] second, her report is valuable because of its subjective perspective revealing as it does how she sees her performance and what she considers important.

In order to construct a detailed case history of this particular event, I also elicited data in interviews which revealed points not explicit in Dvora's report of her performance; for example, her alternate courses of action and how she chose among them. Dvora's account of the social situation in which she used the parable and to which she applied it is an artistic narrative in its own right.[13] Without under-estimating the influence of the parable upon the narrator's original perception of the social situation, it is noteworthy that when later reporting on what happened, she tends to stylize her account of the social situation on the model of the parable in order to highlight the "appropriateness" and hence the effectiveness of her use of this story. Although her spontaneous report does reveal with particular clarity what she considers important about the social situation and what she thinks made the parable so appropriate to it, her account is a simplification. Therefore, I am supplement-ing her report with interviews in which I questioned her about the social context without reference to the parable in order to reduce somewhat the effect of stylization upon her description of the social setting. Throughout this analysis, then, I will distinguish between the informant's *performance*, and her *answers* in interviews to questions about her performance.

The following excerpts from the interviews (October 18, 1968; October 27, 1968, morning and evening; October 20, 1969) make explicit how Dvora sized up the situation; the focus of her performance; the alternate courses of action she might have followed; why she decided to tell a story; the appropriateness of the parable; and the effects of her performance. The emphasis in the transcription is my own.

Sizing up the Situation

Because of the layout of the kitchen, Ruth and Max, Dvora's sister-in-law and brother, were able to place them-selves in positions where they could not see each other; but Dvora, who stood in the doorway, could see them both. When asked, "Do you remember how people were standing or where they were positioned?" Dvora provided an emotionalized map in which positions were an expression of feeling:

Max was in his usual seat [at the head of the table] but he was standing because it was just too tense a situation to sit. . . He couldn't sit and argue. So he was standing up and arguing with Ruth, "Why doesn't she let the kids go?" . . . .

When I came in, she [Ruth] was near the sink clearing up and washing dishes and she was in no mood even to discuss anything. She was just too fed up. . . Ruth wasn't even talking. . . She had her back to him, but she, you couldn't help hearing her laugh [after the story was told] . . . .

I was facing the two of them. . . I stood like this [in the doorway] and I told the story so that each one could hear it. . . .

Interviewer: When you came in the door, who spoke to you first?

Dvora: Max. Ruth wasn't even talking. She was just too upset and too disgusted and she didn't have to tell me what preceded. She knows I know what the situation is at home all the time. When I came in, so he made the whole fuss. He wants to take them to the show. She won't let them [because of the late hour] and so on and so forth, and I listened and I knew exactly what had happened. I didn't need any explanations. *So after I saw what was going on and there was just no relief there because nobody's going to budge one inch. He wasn't going to say he was sorry* because he didn't intend to change his pattern. He was going to do the same thing next Saturday, so that I thought

that this was just the situation that needed this kind
of an example.

Focus

Interviewer: O.K. Now, when you told that story to
the Sokolovs and you were there, did you find yourself addressing the story to one person or another or
just to everybody?
Dvora: To Max, directly to Max. I addressed it directly
to Max but there was also the hope that the humorous
part of it would ease the situation, ease the tension
and it would make it light. . . I addressed actually the
story to Max because he tried too hard to convince
me that there is nothing wrong.

Alternate courses of action

A. *Take Max's side and convince the family to go to the
    movies*

Dvora: When I told the story I did not know how
Max would react. My first impulse and reason for it
[telling the story] was to reach Max. He has asked me
a question, "What is wrong?" and he didn't really
want me to answer because he knew what was wrong,
I am sure. He was in a dilemma. He wanted to appease
Ruth. His conscience would be eased. He would feel
much better if they would accept his last offer.
Interviewer: What did he think you would do?
Dvora: I don't know if he thought I would talk them
into it or whatever. Firstly, it was in desperation and
an opportune time — I had just walked in at that
particular moment — and he may have hoped I would
have some influence because on many occasions he

would turn to me and ask me to speak to Ruth. He may have thought I would take his side and perhaps talk to Ruth so that she would allow the kids to go out with him and I think that this was mainly in his mind. Everyone was against him and maybe he thought he could get me to agree with him because no one was on his side. I honestly think that this was a moment of desperation and he hoped for some approval on my part. . . .

Dvora: Now if I would have said to him, "It isn't such a drastic thing really. You should have taken them in the afternoon, but maybe something came up that you couldn't. So you could go now, but since they cannot, they're too tired or whatever it is, well, it's too bad but it isn't so terrible."

Interviewer: I see.

Dvora: That would have been the end of the whole thing and he would have been perfectly satisfied. . . If I would have done this, first of all it would be most hypocritical. It wouldn't be honest and it couldn't be sincere. So that would be for my part. There would be no satisfaction for me because I did not act sincerely. Three ways — there were three people involved: myself, Ruth and Max. So I would have done nothing for myself. Now I'll pass on to Max. You wanted me to appease Max, to tell him nothing was so terrible. I would have not fooled him in the least. He's smart and he would see right through this that I was just trying to humour him like a child, because firstly, he knows my feelings and it would be a farce. And he would realize that it would be a child's game to be hypocritical in a time like this. So that would serve no purpose whatsoever. Then comes in Ruth. She would have been most annoyed, justifiably so, because she would realize that this wasn't a sincere act on my part and who was I fooling. I would have achieved nothing except antagonize and act not sincere. Whereas what I did, I was able to bring some humour and laughter out of Ruth even for a moment. I was able to give an example to Max without directly hitting him — to let him reflect and left some food for thought. He would see it clearer, more objectively, without emotions, instead of directly hurting him.

B. *Tell Max bluntly he is in the wrong*

Dvora: Why did I show an example? Why couldn't I go right to the point and say, "You want to know, Max, what is wrong with a father not taking his children to the show and what is wrong with a father wanting to be together with his children, why you should be refused? I will tell you what is wrong. You are not a good father. You have promised your children many times. To you, your business is more important. You are greedy. You have a lot of money. You don't need all this. Your children don't want the *yerishe* [inheritance]. They want you now. They don't want the money when you are dead. They want to have your person." I would make him feel as cheap as a cent. I could do all these things. Now what would I accomplish? I would defeat the whole purpose.

C. *Tell Max a story instead of telling him straightforwardly he is in the wrong*

Interviewer: Why did you use a story instead of just telling him straightforwardly?
Dvora: I don't think he was receptive to a lecture and for me to tell him. He could give me all kinds of reasons

why he didn't keep his appointments last week and why he didn't start taking them to the galleries or wherever he promised for today. Why did he start now at eight o'clock to go to a show? *He could give me many many reasons and it would, I think it would just cause a lot of unpleasantness. . .* He had good reasons but they have reasons to feel the way they do. This would more or less illustrate it better than giving him a lecture. . . .

My, my main reason was that I wanted him to realize what he has done and I didn't want to come out and say to him, "You have done this and this and that." I didn't want to hurt him by emphasizing all these things. Neither would he be receptive, nor would he like it. It would only cause more guilt, as a result more anger and confused and emotional disturbance in him and then he wouldn't function at all. But by doing this [telling the parable], I thought it would ease that tension and I would be able to reach him to be able to see the situation and think about it and perhaps do something about it eventually and for the moment I wasn't even thinking about the future. I just thought for the moment this is the best way of answering his question and he directed it to me and asked me why. I thought if I'm going to tell him why, I'm not going to tell him what he did. I'm going to show him what somebody else did and maybe he can identify himself with that person and that way I'm not hurting him. I'm not saying to him, "You did this." I'm showing him "Someone else did it. Do you see any similarity?"

. . . I just thought that this was the best way I could handle this and I really felt sad for him. I felt really bad. As much as he was to blame, I felt bad that he was in this situation without being able to control it and being able to do something about it. . . . *If I gave him these arguments he would have to rationalize and come back with all kinds of excuses which were excuses. . . All I would do is strengthen Ruth's anger because I would put all the emphasis on the things she is already angry about* so I would only magnify them and agree with her that he has done so many things wrong which I don't have to. . . The questions he asked me — he knew the answers. *He just didn't want to face up to them. He knew all these answers.* Doesn't he know what he is doing to hurt his family? They've told him over and over again. But by doing what I did, I answered them without really hurting him. I spoke about a different, a third person and I illustrate a sample that he can mirror himself in it and see it and all the answers are there and it's done in such a subtle way as if I didn't touch him at all and I think that this had more effect on him and I didn't build up the case more for Ruth to make her flame more because she would have seen it even worse than what she sees it.

Appropriateness of the parable

Interviewer: Why does the man [in the parable] say that, of all the things he did wrong, why does the man pick the hands?

Dvora: He picks the least important.

Interviewer: Why?

Dvora: Because if you do something wrong, it is so much easier to approach it in this manner so that by the time. . .you slowly build it up to the important factor. He approaches him [the Rabbi] with a feeling of guilt and, uh, to come right to the point he feels that he's done a real bad thing, a real crime, but if he starts it with washing his hands, he also hoped that maybe it wouldn't, the Rabbi wouldn't go into all these details and he'd give him forgiveness for the smallest thing instead of for the biggest. But the Rabbi went from step by step to find out why, why, why, and he found out the original sin which was eating on *Yonkiper* which was a big one. . .

. . . I am sure he was fully aware of what he did. It was just a way of handling it to soften the blow or maybe it would never never reach to that stage.

. . . leading up slowly step by step and it eased it. Each time it became a little bit bigger, bigger, bigger and somehow it eased the way. It wasn't such a big blow right at the beginning. . . In relation to everyday life, in relation, it is a significant approach because we all seem to minimize the underlying causes. We sort of, you know, the last effect, the last thing that happened, this is what we. . . Somehow, it seems it's easier for us to do this than to analyze and to think what was preceded and treat the real root and the beginning of it all. So after a lot of things accumulate, we don't bother going to the beginning. We just say, *"Oh I can't understand why" for, for the last step, but, that is only an accumulated, piled-up situation.*

Effect of telling the parable

Interviewer: What effect did your story have on him?
Dvora: Being able to laugh made him able to see it [the situation] without being all wound up inside.

. . . And this was really my aim and it worked much, even more so than expected. Not only did, *did*

I answer him and *he laughed at it* and *accepted it without any kind of trying to rationalize* that *it also reached Ruth* and that the whole atmosphere was electrifying. It really was something that the response was beautiful.

. . . I can't tell you how receptive they received it. . . Max with his guilt feelings and angry feelings and what not just couldn't stop laughing. He thought it was really, uh, very funny. And Ruth, not even wanting to because being plenty angry, just had to laugh. She just couldn't help it.

. . . it was such a hilarious reaction. . .they understood it so well and even Max received it so that Ruth was pleased in a way. It was humorous and *she was also pleased in a way the situation was clear. . . With the explaining of the story she realized that we all knew what preceded* and she was in the clear so to speak. . . .

Interviewer: Do you think that Max and Ruth laughed at the story for the same reasons?

Dvora: I think basically so, basically so because firstly, the situation was so similar that you couldn't help even if you were angry, you still couldn't help to see the humour in it. . . It may have meant more to Max than it would to Ruth because to her you didn't have to explain. *The explanation had to be his. . .on his part because she knew what preceded, she knew why she was angry. He didn't understand why, so he had to be explained why. . . .*

Interviewer: What about this story? Could you have told this story instead of the one about the man not washing his hands?

A wealthy nobleman goes on vacation and while he is away he phones back to the mansion to ask the servant how everything is going.

The servant says, "Everything is great, only your favourite dog died."

The master said, "How did that happen?"

He said, "Well, he was trampled to death by the horses."

The master said, "How did that happen?"

The servant said, "Well, the horses stampeded when the barn caught fire."

He said, "How did the fire start?"

He said, "Well, they were burying your mother by candlelight when the barn caught fire."[14]

Dvora: No. It doesn't apply. . . .

Interviewer: . . . when you say Ruth responded to the humour of the story, now then if you had told any other funny joke, would she have responded as well?

Dvora: I don't think so because she was in no mood for jokes.

Interviewer: So then why did this joke. . .

Dvora: . . . it sort of hit home so directly. It was so typical of what is actually happening here and it clarified the situation. . . .

Interviewer: . . . Max after he finished laughing, what did he do?

Dvora: The whole, you know, the air was so clear. It seemed like everybody relaxed. He didn't take the children. They didn't go anywhere and we just sort of kibitzed.

Interviewer: Did he say anything?

Dvora: No. He laughed about it.

Interviewer: And did he. . .

Dvora: Made no comments.

Interviewer: Made no comments.

Dvora: Because I didn't want to dwell on it. . . .

Dvora: I think he really appreciated it. *We just didn't have to go into lectures and discussions and he didn't have to give all kinds of reasons for his behaviour.* It was a good thing.

ANALYSIS OF THE PERFORMANCE
AS A SOCIAL INTERACTION

This folklore event lends itself well to Goffman's analysis of inter-personal ritual behaviour.[15] Goffman's model is based upon the premise that the morality of an interaction inheres in the obligation to cope. When the orderly flow of a normal interaction is disrupted by an "incident," defined by Goffman as an event which increases the level of tension as a result of a breach of social norms, a corrective interchange is initiated which is supposed to terminate in the re-establishment of ritual equilibrium. The "interchange" consists of four moves, a "move" being everything conveyed by an actor during a turn at taking action:

I. *Orderly Flow of Normal Interaction*
    Children want to go to the movies.
    Max promises to take the children to the movies.
    The children wait for Max to take them to the movies.

II. *Incident* — breach of social norms which raises the level of tension.
    Max breaks his promise.

III. *Corrective Interchange*
    A. CHALLENGE — the participants take on the responsibility of calling attention to the misconduct.
        The children cry. They are disappointed. Ruth is

angry and argues with Max.

B. OFFERING — the participants, typically the offender, is given a chance to correct for the offence and reestablish the expressive order.
Max makes a new promise to take the children to the movies.

C. ACCEPTANCE — the persons to whom the offering is made can accept it as a satisfactory means of reestablishing the expressive order.
The family accepts Max's new promise to take them on an outing.

D. THANKS — the forgiven person conveys a sign of gratitude to those who have given him the indulgence of forgiveness.
Max is grateful.

IV. *Equilibrium Reestablished*
It is this pattern of challenge, offering, acceptance and thanks which re-occurred on many previous occasions when Dvora's younger brother Max broke his promise and thereby created an incident. The family presented their challenge to Max by expressing anger and disappointment, thus initiating the corrective interchange. Max then made an offering to them by giving his word that he would take the children on an outing some other time. In good faith, the family accepted his gesture. Harmony was thus restored until Max broke his new pledge and started the whole cycle over again. The night the parable was told, the family was fed up with Max's attempts to compensate for his broken promises. When he saw that Ruth would not accept a new offering, he tried to redefine the situation so as to plead innocent — "What have I done wrong?" — and thereby discredit the accusations

directed against him. Ruth refused to accept Max's redefinition of the situation and attacked him again. Again, Max redefined his position. This pattern of Ruth accusing and Max making excuses was repeated over and over again until Ruth, furious with Max's refusal to face his offences and unable to see any way out of the deadlocked routine of challenge and rationalization, ceased to cope any longer and withdrew from the interchange into silence. It is precisely at this point, where there appeared to be no way out of the disequilibrium — "because nobody's going to budge one inch" — that Dvora entered and told the parable.

Before Max could make an offering which Ruth would accept, he and Ruth had to reach a consensus regarding the definition of the situation. Perceiving this and wanting to be true to her own assessment of the matter, Dvora seized upon the parable as a "challenge" which would appeal to everyone. First, it would affirm Ruth's evaluation. Second, the story was sufficiently indirect, appropriate and humorous that Max, simply by laughing, could acknowledge that he understood the appropriateness of the analogy and accepted the definition of the situation it proposed. This was her way of making a "challenge" to Max which he could not rationalize. Thus, the telling of the parable was ingeniously integrated into the social interaction. It constituted a "challenge" which served to reinstitute the corrective ritual on a new footing and bring it to a harmonious resolution.

When asked what effect the story had, Dvora explained that everyone laughed uproariously, much more so than she anticipated. Laughter brought the discussion to an end and left Max with no comeback.

Further discussion would only have maintained the established frame and would have made it possible for the guilty one to respond with further rationalizations, thereby increasing the tension. The parable, however, introduced a new frame, in the form of a fictional story, momentarily distracted everyone's attention from the painful dominant encounter while this subordinate one was briefly allowed to hold sway, and by provoking laughter, neutralized the previously established frame of reference. While howling with laughter, Ruth could not remain annoyed and Max could not remain indignant. The parable constituted a displaced definition of the situation and, as Goffman points out, as it is safe to offend something no longer credited as reality, Ruth and Max were able to laugh at this depiction of the situation and Dvora achieved her aim. Max saw his behaviour clearly and unemotionally and Ruth was appeased.[16]

APPROPRIATENESS OF THE PARABLE I

Since the parable and social situation only hold certain features in common, the shared features are an index to what the narrator considers relevant and appropriate in this instance. The most important elements which the parable and the life situation share are first, the peculiar nature of the corrective ritual with its repetition of "challenge" and "offering"; and second, the manner in which the guilty person alludes to his offences, or, the nature of his "offering."

A. *The Corrective Ritual*

The parable provides both a microcosm of the life situation and a projected resolution. In both the social encounter

311

and the parable, the opening social frame consists of a guilty man recognizing but distorting the nature of his offences when he goes to a superior to restore the equilibrium. Like the real-life situation in which Max and Ruth were trapped, *the social interaction within the parable itself is a corrective ritual.* The fivefold incremental repetition of the "challenge" and "offering" moves of the corrective confessional ritual in the parable — the Rabbi asks, "How come?" and the parishioner answers, "Because. . ." — pinpoints the exact juncture in the real-life situation where the corrective ritual came to an impasse. The parable serves as a projected resolution by showing the guilty man confess his sins in full to the Rabbi, the institutionalized channel for restoring equilibrium.

B. *The Nature of the Offender's Offering*

Offerings may take various forms: one may try to re-define the situation so as to minimize one's offences; one may rationalize, place the blame on someone else or point out the extenuating circumstances. In the parable, the parishioner redefines his offences so as to minimize his guilt. First, narrating his series of sins in reverse order both of seriousness and chronology, he starts his confession with the last sin he committed which is also the most trivial. Second, each time he confesses to a transgression, the Rabbi questions him regarding the extenuating circum-stances. It emerges that what the parishioner offers as extenuating circumstances are really very serious trans-gressions themselves. Therefore, the definition of the transgression in each new offering is not only incompatible with the definition of the transgression in the preceding challenge but also progressively more serious. The fivefold incremental repetition of the "challenge" and "offering" moves in the interchange in the parable represent the attempt of the Rabbi and the parishioner to come to a consensus on the nature and seriousness of the man's transgression. It is only after the man has confessed to the entire chain of transgressions in all their enormity that the corrective ritual can come to a harmonious conclusion. Thus, in the parable the genre of speaking is the "confession" which is itself a special type of corrective ritual.

In both the parable and the real-life situation, the offenders make a similar mistake. They both distort the relationship between the final apparently trivial offences and the entire backlog of offences so as to make the final offence appear as a single instance, thereby making the trivial look significant and the significant look trivial. In the parable the backlog of offences is ordered in a hierarchical causal chain. The parishioner arranges his sins in reverse order of seriousness, in reverse chronological order, and in order of effect to cause. In the real-life situation, Max's offences occurred in a cumulative rather than hierarchical chain, since each of Max's offences is the same: he keeps breaking promises, whereas in the parable, one sin is intrinsically more serious than another. This difference between the parable and the life situation, however, is unimportant since Dvora emphasized that it is the generalized logical structure of the parable which is relevant; that is, the error of thinking that a person can evaluate the final offence in its own right without any reference to preceding offences, when in fact its significance rests upon its being the last of a series.

APPROPRIATENESS OF THE PARABLE II

To further clarify text-context fit, let us consider how the informant responds to an alternate story which is structurally similar to the parable in some respects only.

On the basis of the informant's response to the appropriateness of the alternate story, I will compare the parable, alternate story and social situation in order to reveal further features of relevance to the informant.

To determine how important the structure of the social interaction in the parable was to Dvora, I asked her if she could have substituted the tale about the wealthy nobleman whose servant tells him that his dog died when it was trampled by horses who stampeded when the barn caught fire during his mother's funeral. This tale employs a hierarchical chain identical in structure to the parable which Dvora used. Yet her response was "this story is not appropriate to Max's situation." When I analyzed and compared the parable and this tale, a striking dissimilarity appeared in the opening frame. In the Russian tale, a superior (nobleman) comes to an inferior (servant) and is mistaken in expecting equilibrium. The servant *then breaks the news of the calamities which have befallen the property and kin of the master.* In contrast, both Dvora's parable and Max's situation stress that an inferior (the younger brother or parishioner) comes to a superior (older sister or Rabbi), and *confesses his personal offences.* Thus, she considered the social situation in the opening frame and the structure of the social interaction conveyed in the parable essential features.

APPROPRIATENESS OF THE PARABLE III

The significance of a parable or proverb is not in the parable or proverb itself but in the meaning which particular participants give it in a specific context. Parables, like proverbs, are statements of group norms. And group norms may be defined as "ideas in the minds of members about what should and should not be done by a specific member under specific circumstances. ... Because norms are ideas and are therefore subject to elaborate qualifications, they can specify the many fine distinctions necessary to accommodate different persons, times, occasions and circumstances."[17] In order to appreciate the range of group norms which this parable can be made to express and the appropriateness with which this parable can be applied to quite different situations, let us examine the following report by Jack Starkman[18] of how Mr. Heller once used this parable:

> Interviewer: O.K. What about, like, Dvora has a lot of stories that she heard from her mother. Say, the one about the man who didn't wash his hands on *Yonkiper* and went to the Rabbi to ask forgiveness.
>
> Jack: Yea and this, this is, this is a classic, yea. It always applies because it was told to me here the same thing, so apparently it has accommodated many many generations, you see. I have heard it from a Mr. Heller who was a *mekhitn* [father of son-in-law or daughter-in-law] to my uncle, to my late uncle. You know, he was related by marriage. He was an extremely religious man. When I came home from work, we sat under the table and I was going to eat.
>
> So he says to me, this Mr. Heller, "My son, haven't you forgotten something?"
>
> And I looked at him and I says, "What?"
>
> He says, "You haven't washed your hands," for, for what you should do, wash, not like we usually wash our hands clean. I'd taken, I'd taken a shower previously. But he wanted me to wash my hands ritually, you know, just, a, this part of the fingers, the front part of the fingers. And uh, it is an *aveyre*

[transgression], you know, it is. . . .

So I says, "But this is such a small thing. It doesn't matter."

So he says, "Our Torah tells us that *aveyre goreret aveyre* [one transgression draws in its train another transgression].[19] That means, a small sin be. . .
Interviewer: Begets.
Jack: Begets another one, a bigger one. And I still expressed scepticism.

So he says, "I'll tell you something, my son." And then the story that you, that you heard. The way he told it, it had perhaps a little bit more *shmalts* [literally: fat, figuratively: elaboration] to it.

He says: This man came to the Rabbi *erev Yonkiper* [eve of the Day of Atonement] just like today, you know, a day before.

And he says, "Rabbi, I have sinned. Please, I would like to ask you for some kind of forgiveness, for penance, if you can." So he says, "My son. To forgive is God's, but let me hear what it is and perhaps I can help you."

So he says, "*Rebe* [Rabbi] I for. . . I finished a dinner and I'd forgot to say the closing prayer, at the dinner which is called *bentshn* [saying the benediction after the meal]."

So the Rabbi says, "Well, my son. It isn't a big *aveyre* [transgression]. I'll give you a penance for it. But before I do that, would you mind telling me why you didn't *bentsh*. Of course you could have said the *brokhe* [benediction]. It's a short time only."

So he says to the Rabbi, "I didn't *bentsh* because I didn't wash my hands prior and in the Torah, in the *peyrek* [chapter in the Mishna; the Mishna is the collection of post-biblical laws and rabbinical discussions of the second century B.C.], there is a saying, 'If you'd forgotten to wash your hands then you don't have to *bentsh*.'[20] One is tied in with the other."

So he says, "Well, this is also not a very big *aveyre*, but why have you forgotten to wash your hands? Were you perhaps in a hurry?"

So he says, "No, *Rebe*, it wasn't that I was in a hurry but I was in an environment where it wasn't nice for me to wash my hands."

He says, "Where was that environment?"

So he says, "It was in a Christian restaurant."

Then he says, "This already sounds bad. Why did you eat in a Christian restaurant?" He says, "You could have gone to a Jewish restaurant."

He says, "All the Jewish restaurants happened to be closed that day."

He says, "What was the day?"

He says, "It was *Yonkiper* and I had bacon and eggs in a *goyishe* [gentile] restaurant."

So this is what Heller meant to tell me. That if you skip the little *aveyre* you're gradually building up to one huge *aveyre*. Naturally the Rabbi couldn't give him a penance on that, I suppose. But yea, this must be a classic because it accompanied the generations and generations.

In the foregoing text, *the man to whom the parable was addressed reports upon the performance*. The parable was told to him as a warning in order to prevent him from committing greater transgressions in the future. In the parable the parishioner committed his greatest sin first. If he had not been eating on *Yonkiper*, he would not have had to go to a Christian restaurant where he had to eat non-kosher food and where because he could not observe the washing ritual he could not say the benediction. Nonetheless, Mr. Heller's point "that if you skip the little *aveyre* you're gradually building up to one huge *aveyre*," and the proverb, "One transgression draws in its train another transgression," indicate that Mr. Heller's focus is neither upon the particular chronological order of the sins committed in the parable, nor upon the nature of the parishioner's confession. Rather the general idea that one sin begets another (whether a large sin begets smaller sins or a small sin begets larger sins) is paramount especially because, in the parable, neglecting to wash one's hands ritually is the *last* and *least serious* sin in a series, whereas in the real-life situation not washing one's hands is the *first* and only sin to have been committed. Thus, the narrator is concerned with the notion that there are connections or links between one transgression and another, rather than with the order in which the sins occurred. In contrast, the essential points in Dvora's performance were first, the mistake of thinking that the final offence, which was also the least serious, could be evaluated in its own right without any reference to preceding offences; second, the opening social frame in which a guilty man confesses his sins in reverse order of their seriousness and occurrence; and third, the focus of the social interaction in the parable upon the repetition of "challenge" and "offering."

CONCLUSIONS

In this detailed study of how an individual actually used a parable on a particular occasion, I attempted to analyze folklore performance in its immediate context of use as a highly structured form of interpersonal behaviour. Dvora integrated her storytelling performance into the social interaction both by making her narration a move in the corrective ritual itself and by selecting a story which mirrored the precise point in the encounter where the corrective ritual had broken down. At the same time, her performance brought about the resolution which the parable itself had projected.

Consistent with the tenets of ethnoscience and the ethnography of communication,[21] I have given the cognitive processes of the narrator herself a central place in the analysis — what she considered relevant, what various courses of action were open to her and how she chose among them — in order to determine which of the alternate methods that I could formulate to account for this performance most closely approximates the model which she used. The series of comparisons represent attempts both to dramatize Dvora's perception of her performance and to show how Malinowski's notion of the contextual specification of meaning applies to folklore performance. The situational analysis and the comparisons reveal that the significance of a parable is not in the story itself — the narrative is not an autonomous entity which encapsulates one kernel of wisdom or a single "moral" — but in the particular and variable meaning which the participants give it in specific social contexts.

Barbara Kirshenblatt-Gimblett, 1975

The Ethnic Joke in Canada Today[1]
Robert B. Klymasz

Robert B. Klymasz is the leading authority on the folklore of Ukrainians in Canada. Until recently Canadians of Ukrainian descent formed our largest ethnic group, after the British, French and German. They have now been surpassed by the Italians, but their roots are deeper as most of them came to this country between 1890 and 1910.

Dr. Klymasz has collected widely in the three prairie provinces where most of the Ukrainians settled, and has published two books of their songs: The Ukrainian-Canadian Immigrant Folksong Cycle *and* The Ukrainian Winter Folksong Cycle in Canada, *and one on their folktales:* Folk Narrative Among Ukrainian-Canadians in Western Canada, *as well as other studies.*

In this article he describes and analyzes a type of folklore that is increasingly prevalent in contemporary society. In the United States ethnic jokes are usually known as Polack jokes but in Canada they are primarily Ukie, Newfie or, more recently, Paki jokes. Here Dr. Klymasz analyzes these Canadian cycles, noting not only how most of the jokes are easily transferred from one group to another, but also how certain jokes focus on supposed characteristics of

*the particular group being ridiculed. He goes on to discuss
how these cycles affect society as a whole and the groups
who are the butts of the jokes.*

Whether viewed in psychological terms as a veiled expression
of aggression, or in sociological terms as a convenient
mechanism for the sublimation of potential conflict and
hostility,[2] there is little doubt that the ethnic joke constitutes one of the most productive and prevalent forms of
verbal lore in the whole of North America today. Indeed,
the popularity,[3] potency and virility of this enormous
corpus of esoteric folklore have proved to be so disturbing
in some circles that, as witnessed earlier this year, efforts
have been made to enforce the Civil Rights Act in the
United States in cases where employers permit the telling
of Polish jokes around their shops when there are Polish
employees present.[4]

In Canada the ethnic joke — insofar as productive types
and formal features are concerned[5] — hardly differs from
its prototype, the so-called Polack joke cycles in the United
States, a phenomenon which only serves to give added
support to the contention that folklore tends to disregard
the artificialities of political and administrative boundaries
or demarcations.[6] Like the currently popular ethnic joke
cycles in the United States, the ethnic joke in Canada tends
to be terse, compact and epigrammatic in nature; and its
refined, direct, question-answer dialogue format[7] marks
the product of an urbanized society whose tight work
schedules allow little time for the flexible elaboration of
detail which characterizes a traditional storytelling session
in peasant or primitive cultures.[8] Perhaps the most import-

ant features to have paved the way for this affinity with ethnic jokes from the United States is provided by the convenient slot system which allows many of the jokes that are told about Poles in the United States to appear in Canada in the form of Newfie jokes, Ukrainian jokes and so forth.[9] For example, the image of two pallbearers carrying a garbage can at a Polish funeral in the United States[10] reappears time and time again in other ethnic cycles in Canada.

In contrast to the similarities in form and structure that promote this kind of mobile transferability, there are, of course, differences and distinguishing features. These are chiefly due to the specifics of the Canadian experience; and they emerge first and foremost on the level of content analysis where certain clusters of motifs reflecting established or, just as often, imagined folkways and traits tend to be held in reserve, as it were, for the portrayal and characterization of specific ethnic groups or communities and their milieu. The components of these individual clusters of motifs can vary from time to time and from place to place. Yet in terms of ethnic and/or regional distribution, the coexistence of various ethnic jokes at any one time initiates an attempt to turn each cycle into a kind of highly individualized screen which serves to project, support and, in turn, to help formulate and fixate certain popular notions about the given ethnic group and its behaviour. This process of attempted compartmentalization and categorization is illustrated by the following examples from seven different ethnic joke cycles in Canada:[11]

1. from the English joke cycle in French Canada:
   Q: What do you give an Englishman for a
        headache?
   A: Four aspirins: one for each corner of his
        square head.

2. from the French-Canadian joke cycle:
   Q: What is the dream of a pink flamingo?
   A: To have a little home with a French
        Canadian stuck into the ground on the
        front lawn.[12]
3. from the Ukrainian joke cycle in Western Canada:
   Q: How do you kill 5,000 Ukrainians at once?
   A: Plant mushrooms on the freeway.[13]
4. from the Jewish joke cycle:
   Q: How do you make twelve Jews get into a
        Volkswagen?
   A: Throw a penny into the back seat.
5. from the Newfie joke cycle:
   Q: Why did the Newfie want to move his
        house six inches off the foundation?
   A: To tighten up the clothesline.[14]
6. from the Italian joke cycle:
   Q: How do you break up an Italian wedding?
   A: Run in and say, "The cement's here!"[15]
7. from the Icelandic joke cycle in Manitoba:
   Q: What is the dirtiest fight ever fought?
   A: An Icelander and a sea gull fighting on the
        beach over a rotten fish.[16]

As a form of urban, mainstream lore, the immense popularity of the ethnic joke with its focus on ethnic differentiation appears at first glance to constitute a paradox: to clash, as it were, with the avowed pressures of homogeneity, standardization, conformity and uniformity in our civilization. Why is it, one may ask, that in our day and age it has suddenly become "fun to be a Polack,"[17] or that Poles have replaced elephants and morons as the leading butts of ridicule? Or is the ethnic joke simply a verbalized extension of the grand ol' American melting pot (*e pluribus unum*!)

reflecting a general intolerance for ethnic separatism?[18] Regardless of the interpretation one chooses, it can hardly be denied that the ethnic joke functions above all as an ever-ready vehicle for escape from the hum-drum monotony of daily urban life. The dean of "understanding media," Marshall McLuhan, has ascribed this kind of reaction against the strictures of a conformistic urban society to the influence of TV, which he finds "fosters many preferences that are quite at variance with literate uniformity and repeatability":

> It has sent Americans questing for every sort of oddment and quaintness in objects from out of their storied past. Many Americans will now spare no pains or expense to get to taste some new wine or food. The uniform and repeatable must now yield to the uniquely askew, a fact that is increasingly the despair and confusion of our entire standardized economy.[19]

With this new emphasis on novelty in our fast-moving Euro-American mainstream culture, the ethnic joke and its participants serve to transform the ethnically invisible workaday world into a kind of instant mini-dream world featuring a fantastic menagerie of somewhat amorphous, comical figures whose supposed idiosyncracies ostensibly surround us but which in actual fact are seldom, if ever, in sight. As such, the ethnic joke exploits the universal habit of wishful thinking by masking, repopulating, and re-organizing our social environment in such a way that, momentarily at least, the ethnically invisible is suddenly visualized and all attention is focussed on a new, multi-ethnic segmentation of the community — a process which transcends and replaces the easily recognized and usually acknowledged dichotomies reflected in our unicultural mainstream complex (e.g., economic and sexual differentiation). In the course of this sudden transformation, the banalities of mainstream conformity and homogeneity recede into the background and give way to a rich, albeit imagined, diversity in place of the real, dull conformity.

But besides all this, the ethnic joke plays still another role: for while it serves to provide a handy antidote to pressures of conformity, it simultaneously perpetuates the desire and the urge for identity, individuality, and separateness in terms of ethnicity. And even if we view the ethnic joke as a handy mechanism which operates for the harmless verbalization of inter-ethnic hostilities, it is important to note that the ethnic joke, although a mainstream form of folklore, is carried so that both sides of the fence tend to share alike in any particular given ethnic joke cycle or cycles, and to revel in them together. As a result, aside from its implications as a manifestation of contemporary mainstream folklore, the ethnic joke plays a special, crucial role within the minority ethnic group itself where its impact is largely but not solely degenerative in nature.

An important segment of most, if not all, ethnic joke cycles is the so-called "dialect"[20] or language joke corpus which always reflects some aspect of language breakdown. Collectively these amount to a vicious onslaught on the mother tongue of the ethnic group and point to its impotency in mainstream society. The entire ethnic heritage is further undermined by those ethnic jokes which deride various other aspects of the ethnic and his community. Corroded from the inside and ridiculed from the outside, the language and culture of the ethnic community is forced to retreat to a position of sterility with only negligible serviceability as an entrée into the attractive mainstream culture which surrounds it. At this point, the absence of a new and dynamic input jeopardizes the vitality of the entire ethnic cultural legacy which to a large extent remains grounded in a distant setting that with each successive generation becomes more and more alien, old-fashioned and irrelevant. It is hardly surprising, then, that the popularity of the ethnic joke within the ethnic community itself converts the joke into an agent which helps strip the old heritage of any aura of sanctity that at one time may have been attached to it. At the same time, however, it is just as important to note that the ethnic joke does not seek to destroy *in toto* the legacy of the ethnic community, but rather it reflects an attempt to purge the old folkways through a process of cathartic self-ridicule in the form of verbal lore.[21] For even as an expression of ethnic prejudice, aggression and ethnic self-ridicule, the ethnic joke gives tacit recognition to the problem of cultural continuity by heightening ethnic sensitivity. By so doing, the ethnic joke signals a transitional phase in the overall acculturative process and marks a kind of *rite de passage* in the in-group's reformulation of the ethnic cultural heritage and its transformation into a new complex that is geared to meet the challenge and pressure of the mainstream environment.

The manner in which the ethnic joke participates in the process of revitalization is suggested by its very designation: *ethnic* joke, *Polish* joke, and so on. That is, while it denigrates the ethnic community's folkways, the ethnic joke also brings to the fore the problem of ethnicity and ethnic distinctiveness which is usually couched in the form of an introductory, riddling question. The following are examples of such introductory questions taken from the Ukrainian joke cycle in Western Canada:

> How do you drive a Ukrainian crazy?
> How do you get a Ukrainian out of your backyard?
> How does a Ukrainian take a shower?

How do you keep the flies away from the bride at a
Ukrainian wedding?
How do you keep a Ukrainian busy?
Why does a Ukrainian have only two pallbearers?
How do you get a Ukrainian out of your swimming
pool?
What do Ukrainians use as bait to catch fish?
Did you hear about the Ukrainian who went ice-
fishing?
How do you get twenty-five Ukrainians into a
Volkswagen?
How can you tell which woman on the beach is a
Ukrainian?
Do you know why the Ukrainians are pock-marked?
Why do Ukies have round shoulders and flat heads?

As shown by the above examples, this particular ethnic
joke cycle can be seen to operate as a kind of concerted
attempt to present a comprehensive definition of "a
Ukrainian" in terms of specific, distinguishing ethnic
features and qualities. But in raising the question, the
ethnic joke side-steps the issue, fails to provide a satisfactory answer and only frustrates the attempt at definition
with its unexpected punch line; instead of a solution, the
ethnic joke offers a formulation that is distorting, absurd
and completely inapplicable.

In an effort to counter the negative image offered by its
own joke cycle, the ethnic community is pressured either
into succumbing to the threat of total assimilation or
meeting the challenge and creating a new, streamlined,
fully acceptable yet distinctively different cultural construct that is based on the ruins and fragments of its
shattered cultural complex. As such, the challenge of the
ethnic joke can mark a turning point in the life of the

ethnic community which must be prepared to turn itself inside out — to make overt that which had always been covert, to formalize the informal, to make exoteric that which would otherwise remain esoteric — in order to assert, expose, express and apply its own particular sense of ethnicity and pride.[22] This latter possibility, if pursued, entails a process of reformulation, reconstruction and rehabilitation which operates in a variety of ways and obtains on numerous levels of observation.[23]

The ethnic joke, then, plays a dual role: as an agent for breakdown and degeneration, on the one hand, and for breakthrough and regeneration, on the other. Ambivalence marked by antithesis and contrast — this is the crux of the ethnic joke as shown in its riddling format, its unexpectedly frustrating and hence humour-producing punch line, which functions to promote both dissolution and continuity. Against the backdrop of more traditional folkloric materials, the contemporary ethnic joke can hardly be viewed as merely a continuation of time-honoured efforts to seek amusement and satisfaction for various cravings in oral tradition and oral creativity. To be sure, if measured in terms of textual matter, the ethnic joke is but a minor genre and a modern version of *blaison populaire*. Its true dimensions, however, are almost monumental in scope, repercussion and impact.

Robert B. Klymasz, 1970

La Vie de l'Habitant:
Quebec's Folk Culture of Survival
Peter van Lent

The motto of Quebec is "Je me souviens" — I remember. One of the things Quebeckers obviously remember today is their folk heritage, for aspects of folk tradition pervade Québécois culture at all levels. One can still hear the habitant *songs sung in some homes, or see a troupe of professionals perform traditional dances at* Place des Arts; *one can hear* joual, *Quebec's folk speech, on the streets, or one can read it represented in internationally renowned works of authors like Roch Carrier. Folk traditions are clearly alive in modern Quebec, but in what fashion and to what purpose?*

In this article, Peter van Lent considers these questions, exploring in particular traditions of retention or survival as opposed to revival, and considering some of the economic, social, political, cultural and other factors involved in the relationship between Quebeckers and their folklore.

Northrop Frye in his book, *The Bush Garden*, one of the best-known studies of Canada and its arts, adopts a very critical attitude towards Quebec's folk culture. Damned by provinciality, Quebec has become, according to Frye,

> ... a cute tourist resort full of ye quainte junke made by real peasants, all of whom go to church and say their prayers like the children they are, and love their land and tell folktales and sing ballads, just as the fashionable novelists in the cities say they do.[1]

In recent years other voices have joined this criticism, accusing Quebec of everything from mass-marketing fake handicrafts to exporting would-be "folksingers" who are in reality chansonniers from Montreal's counterculture. There appear to be two general areas of criticism here. First, that Quebec has been culture-bound, unable and disinclined to transcend provincial themes to see beyond to the universal issues of great literature and the fine arts. Secondly, that Quebec has been only too willing to distort the representation of its folk culture whenever financial gain or political recognition was to be achieved by doing so. This article will attempt to put these criticisms in perspective: to justify the historical importance of folk art, crafts and the oral tradition in Quebec, to applaud sincere efforts to revive these elements of folk culture, and finally to deal with the problem of exploitation in recent years.

Perhaps the first thing one should posit when trying to understand why Quebec has always been identified with folk culture is that for over two hundred years that was the only culture Quebec had. While a few aristocratic administrators of the French monarchy and of the Catholic Church came to New France, as did a few noblemen to whom large holdings of land were granted, the vast majority of its settlers were members of the peasant class of Normandy, Brittany and other provinces of northwest France. These hardy, uneducated men and women of the land, who became known as "habitants," brought with them their folklore and their skills as artisans. Jean Talon, the King's Intendant in the 1660s and '70s, was quick to assess the value of these talents, and highest of Talon's priorities was the founding of a school where young habitants would learn traditional folk skills, especially wood carving. The year 1670 saw the realization of this goal when the St. Joachim's School of Art and Trades was founded at Cap Tourmente. In 1671 Jean Talon could brag to his king that

> I have the materials produced in Canada with wool from sheep with which to dress myself from head to toe.[2]
>
> If it is well administrated, I hope that this country will soon require nothing from Old France except a few necessary useful items.[3]

These statements are remarkable for two reasons. First, they show how early the art of weaving began in New France, a land where the traditional use of animal skins for clothing would have otherwise persisted for some time, as it did on the American frontier. Secondly, they show that self-sufficiency through home production of essential goods was an early goal for New France.

This self-sufficiency was to prove to be the most valuable legacy that France left to her habitant colonists, for after the defeat of Montcalm on the Plains of Abraham in 1759, France lost possession of Quebec to England. In the next few years many of the educated élite of Quebec's society decided to return to France. While some writers may have exaggerated the extent of this migration, it does seem safe to say that all of the government administrators, most of the highly placed clergy and many of the middle-class merchants chose to try their luck back in the mother country rather than to continue to live in a Quebec ruled by England. The consequences of this return on the history of French-Canadian folklore is obvious: a province already predominantly agricultural and traditional in its lifestyle became nearly exclusively so. After 1763 Quebec was populated essentially by scattered, uneducated farmers. Deprived of all cultural, artistic and commercial links with France, the habitants were now compelled to become totally self-sufficient with respect to their daily needs, their artistry and their oral traditions. Quebec became what George Woodcock calls "a closed little society"[4] separated by language and culture from its English captors and destined to evolve its own Gallic brand of the North American identity.

The years which followed 1763 were marked by a growing tension between the French Canadians and their English-speaking compatriots. When it became obvious that Quebeckers were determined to retain their own language and culture and not be assimilated into The British Way, the English began to condemn everything "different": that is, everything culturally identifiable as French. English noblemen visiting or appointed to authority in Canada deplored the folk level of the habitant's culture. Lord Durham, Governor in Chief of British North America, wrote in 1839:

> There can hardly be conceived a nationality more destitute of all that can invigorate and elevate a people than that which is exhibited by the descendants of the French in Lower Canada, owing to their retaining their particular language and manners. They are a people with no history and no literature.[3]

The Quebec reaction to this disdain was, of course, to increasingly value every aspect of their culture which was distinctive, and from this reaction there developed the *mentalité du terroir*, the homestead mentality. This ethic was to have a strong and durable influence on the habitants. It provided Quebec novelists with central themes for their works for nearly one hundred years, and its popularity as a dominant way of thought helped to solidify the Quebec identity. In simplest terms the homestead mentality advocates all things rural, traditional and integral to French Canada. Men and women should stay on the land and farm it, be as nearly self-sufficient as possible, raise large families, be good Catholics, and, above all, speak French. To properly discuss this homestead movement, so important to the evolution of Quebec's folk culture, is more than can be undertaken here. However, it must be noted that such a strong cultural movement does not come about without support from a broad base within a society. The Catholic Church in Quebec, strongly Jansenist in its doctrinal orientation, gave an early and vigorous blessing to the homestead ethic because its values were "simple" and close to nature and therefore to God. The Church held that when individuals in a society become urbanized, they slip more and more into a man-made world and lose sight of the divine plan. Quebec's peasant folk culture, impregnated with religion, was a far more nourishing food for habitant thought than the worldly, abstracted fine arts and urban pastimes already closely linked with commerce! A second force in Quebec society which strengthened the influence of the homestead mentality was the Nationalist political movement which obviously wanted to keep the habitants "down on the farm," for an isolated and self-sufficient Quebec population would remain French-speaking and culturally distinct from Anglophone culture which was making its self-proclaimed destiny so manifest throughout the continent in the early 1800s.

But man does not live by ethic alone. As the nineteenth

century progressed, a panic level of urgency arose among the homestead advocates, for the industrial revolution was well under way and young Quebeckers by the thousands were being lured away from the farms to urban areas where jobs in industry provided them with a seemingly glamorous life of bright city lights and wages per week which represented more cash than their fathers ever saw in a year. It was bad enough that so many young habitants were leaving the farms to work in Montreal, Quebec City and other towns in Quebec, but the worst blow for the Quebec Nationalist sentiment was that thousands of them were going beyond Quebec's borders, mostly to the mill towns of New England, where they were often learning English, living among Protestants and becoming United States citizens. The direct result of this industrial-urban population shift was the same in Quebec as it was everywhere: as society urbanizes, folk cultural experiences change. Manufactured goods replaced homemade items and the long snowy evenings were no longer devoted to *veillées* where folktales from all over France were blended with a touch of Amerindian lore to become perhaps the richest oral tradition in North America.[6]

With the advantage of hindsight, we know now how miserable life in urban areas usually was for these errant habitants. Packed into tiny rowhouses, exhausted by long hours of tedious work, branded and occasionally mistreated as "foreigners" in New England, many French Canadians found themselves caught in a socio-economic trap becoming, as one Quebec activist once called them, "The White Niggers of America."[7] Those habitants who came to New England may have eventually fared better than those who drifted to Montreal and Quebec City. By now many Franco-Americans are successful members of the United States' middle-class. Yet it took three or more generations for them to get there, and most of those who made it did so by abandoning many parts of their habitant heritage such as their language, their oral traditions and in some cases even their religion.

For those who remained in the cities of Quebec the cruelest moment of all occurred during the Depression in the 1930s. While their wages had seemed tremendous at first, the total dependency of their lifestyle left them very vulnerable in hard times. When many of them lost their jobs as one after another of the huge mills closed or cut back, these workers, landless and animalless, were left starving. And yet at this lowest moment of our story occurred one of the most fortunate events in Quebec's folk cultural history. Inevitably many jobless city workers returned to their ancestral farms in hopes of being taken back in by their families. Several enlightened craftsmen in the town of Saint-Jean-Port-Joli, seeing that many of these returnees lacked a definite livelihood, decided to revive the handicrafts which were traditional to this area of Quebec. Three pioneers of folk craft rebirth, Médard Bourgault, wood carver, Eugène Leclerc, miniature ship maker, and Madame Edmond Chamard, weaver, banded together to encourage, train and organize new artisans in their respective crafts.[8] At first the hard economic times meant few commissions, but after 1940 the reputation of these three craft masters and the acknowledgement of Saint-Jean-Port-Joli as the handicrafts capital of Quebec brought wide recognition. Support was given to the Saint-Jean-Port-Joli movement by the provincial government's Youth Assistance Bureau and the Quebec Department of Agriculture's Domestic Arts Section. But, lest their renewed interest in folk creation lead to an institutionalized phenomenon, it can be said to the credit of these artisans that they always insisted on individual creation, condemned the uninspired repetition of well-known patterns and urged their students to seek personal inspiration within the context of Quebec's true handicraft tradition.[9]

The rebirth of Quebec's handicrafts at Saint-Jean-Port-Joli was paralleled by, if not seminal to, a rebirth of interest in the province's oral folk tradition. Dr. Marius Barbeau had begun collecting folktales and songs since the first decade of this century, and as chief curator of Canada's National Museum, he gradually attracted scholars and collectors and formed a small but solid Folklore Division. The revived involvement in folk culture in the post-Depression years gave the work of these well-trained folklorists new impetus. Luc Lacourcière added courses in folklore to Laval University's curriculum in 1944 and shortly afterwards founded its Archives de Folklore. His colleagues have subsequently done an admirable job of collecting and classifying some 38,000 variants of songs, identifying more than 5,000 versions of tales in what Lacourcière calls "the most important collection of folktales in any language in North America."[10] The final evidence of the rebirth of folk culture in Quebec may be seen in the acknowledged influence of Quebec's oral folk tradition upon contemporary writers such as Roch Carrier. Mr. Carrier openly attributes the elements of fantasy, the role of supernatural forces and the passages of frenzied, violent action in his novels to the influence of the old habitant folktales which he heard as a child growing up in a rural Quebec village.[11]

The recent history of material folk art in Quebec has not been so positive. There do exist in Quebec many true folk craftsmen who are conservative in their creation, faithful to their folk aesthetic tradition with its characteristic concern for repetition and symmetry, and capable of achieving "complementary syntheses of the practical and aesthetic."[12] However, the exploitation of the folk culture

336

mentioned remains very problematic. When Montreal became the site of "Expo," the 1967 World's Fair, and again in 1976 when the summer Olympics were held in this city, hundreds of thousands of commercially produced items of supposed "folk artisans" flooded the retail market. Now surely the phenomenon of tourist or "airport"[13] arts is widespread and only to be expected at any event such as "Expo" or the Olympics which involves huge numbers of visitors. The problem of folklorists occurs when the integrity of the folk culture is compromised, when there is a breakdown in the distinction between these external or "tourist" arts and those items of material culture created both *by* and *for* the members of an ethnic group. Folklorists today try hard to avoid "value-laden" terminology and culturally tied aesthetic judgements when assessing commercial folk arts. Yet when the basic symbolic value of a folk craft item is completely lost due to adaptation to the expectations of an outside consumer, one cannot help but draw certain negative conclusions. The example of *catalogne* neckties is relevant. Originally *catalognes* were rag rugs woven by habitant housewives from scraps of worn-out clothing. Utilitarian in that, like any rug, they kept one's feet warm, these *catalognes* had a deeper symbolic content to the Quebecker who by creating them demonstrated resourcefulness, self-sufficiency and ingenuity — all traits highly prized in habitant culture, as we have already mentioned. A Quebec woman liked the idea that even when no longer wearable as clothing, fabric could still be made useful and even pleasing by its arrangement into attractive patterns and chromatic schemes. She confirmed a strong aspect of her identity from creating usefulness and beauty out of almost nothing. Today one finds offered for sale in the "old section" of Quebec cities men's neckties and place mats handwoven in a style made to imitate the traditional *catalognes*. The fabric used is not old, the utilitarian aspect nil, and finally, to the Quebec handweaver there can be little that expresses habitant culture in creating such an item which a visiting salesman can easily stuff into his suitcase. Beyond this souvenir level of exploitation there are many examples of outright folk fakery to be found in Quebec today. "Wood carvings" moulded out of plastic foam are sold as genuine folk creations in stores bearing names which use terms such as "cooperative" and "guild of wood carvers." Likewise, as mentioned, Quebec folksingers who normally wear the black turtleneck seen in the intellectual haunts near the University of Montreal suddenly don flannel shirts when performing in Europe and sing of the loneliness of vast frozen woods when in fact they may have only rarely been in a small Quebec village.

In conclusion, one must urge two words of restraint when condemning the exploitation of folk culture in Quebec. First, we cannot expect a folk culture to "stand still" technologically or aesthetically simply because it is reassuring for the cosmopolitan societies to have a base of simplicity and stability against which to measure our own progress or in which we can hide for a brief vacation.[14] If the use of Exacto blades and chemical dyes helps Saint-Jean-Port-Joli carvers and weavers to express the symbolic content of their culture in their creations, *tant mieux*! Even when the folk creator becomes aware of and accommodating to the reception of his creation on the commercial market, we must be careful before judging him to be sure that he is not merely expressing another traditional trait of his cultural heritage. This is, to a considerable extent, the case in Quebec, and this issue is closely related to the importance of projecting an ethnic image.[15] The whole issue of Quebec's political and cultural image is a complex and extremely vital one in Canada today. The greatest

Canadian national weakness may well be its lack of a distinctive identity, but in this respect Quebeckers are less weak than their Anglophone compatriots. Most Quebeckers know who and what they are. And, perhaps more important for the future, the rest of the world seems to have a sense of what Quebec is. Recently a rather asinine caricature of a "typical Quebecker" was portrayed on Canadian television. This character was a huge, bearded woodsman named Jos Ferrand who poured maple syrup on the pea soup that he guzzled by the gallon, blasphemed so energetically that it was difficult to tell his curses from his prayers, and spent his non-blaspheming hours singing "Alouette." And yet, as fatuous as this characterization may be, one must admit that at least there is enough that is distinctive in the Quebec identity that it can be caricaturized. What type of person would one use to parody an English Canadian? What typical name would he have? What typical food would he eat? What song would one have him sing – "God Save the Queen"?

Surely Quebec is guilty to some degree of exploiting its folk traditions, but we must be sensitive to the needs of this minority people who have emerged from years of repression with a firm sense of their own identity. For Quebeckers cultural survival has been a way of life for over two hundred years, and they are winning their struggle despite incredible odds. If we can approach the Quebec folk cultural problem from this perspective of survival, if for a minute we can appreciate that a popularization of the Quebec folk image does to some degree provide the province with an identity, the one thing that all Canadians seem to need most, then we can perhaps see even in this problem a certain historical continuity in the efforts of this resilient North American people.

Peter van Lent, 1981

The Ethnicity Factor in
Anglo-Canadian Folkloristics
Carole H. Carpenter

The folklore studies in a nation reflect, to some extent at least, the cultural concerns of that country. Folklorists have frequently been profoundly influenced by nationalist sentiments and other socio-political circumstances. Indeed, the scholarly development of folklore was intrinsically related to nineteenth-century nationalist movements in Europe, especially Finland and Germany. In such movements, folklore was used as a means to arouse popular nationalist sentiments, to uncover and express the true nature of the people — their folk soul.

Such use of folk traditions is one form of what today is termed applied folklore work. This approach to folklore has long been quite common in Canada; in fact, Canadians have tended to pay most attention to folklore when they have perceived a link between their concern and some social or political goal. The particular relationship between folklore and nationalism is not at all foreign to Canada: French-Canadian identity, for instance, is firmly rooted in widespread awareness, celebration and study of Canadien *folk traditions.*

The following article is an example — one of very few in the country — of applied folkloristics: that is, an inter-

340

pretation of aspects of the culture as a whole through the analysis of Canadian folklore work. Specifically, Carole Henderson Carpenter considers here the relationships between ethnicity — attitudes towards the identification with and expression of ethnic heritage — and Anglo-Canadian folklore-related activities, scholarly or otherwise. She develops the argument that association of folklore with ethnicity has been a key factor in preventing the majority group of Canadians from accepting folklore and its study as significant. Consequently, Anglo Canadians are less culturally aware than is desirable since they fail to recognize and celebrate their own folk heritage.

It has been said by a certain prominent Canadian that "... a democracy is judged by the way the majority treats the minority."[1] An understanding of Canada in many respects other than the merely political can be gained by investigating the majority's treatment of the various minority elements within the nation. Many of the central themes and concerns of Canadian culture are clearly reflected in Anglo-Canadian treatment of minority-group folklore. Indeed, Anglo-Canadian folkloristics — the collection and study of folklore[2] — has been profoundly influenced by the socio-cultural milieu.

This paper endeavours to identify the prevailing Anglo-Canadian attitudes which have prompted and directed studies of minority-group folklore, and to relate these attitudes to the socio-cultural milieu which shaped them. The most powerful influence on majority-group concerns with minority-group traditions has undoubtedly been associated with ethnicity. Meaning in common parlance

341

"apartness," ethnicity refers to that which delineates and characterizes separate ethnic groups both from within and without. Folklore has been a primary means for the majority group to distinguish different groups in Canada; in fact, the majority group has typically associated folklore with ethnic groups — first the Native Peoples and later the non-Anglo immigrant groups. Further, Anglo Canadians have focussed attention on these different groups in part because of and through oral traditions. In the following discussion, then, ethnicity will be shown to have been of particular importance in Anglo-Canadian folkloristics.

There has been a decided trend among Anglo Canadians interested in folk traditions to look beyond their own folk groups for material to study.[3] In fact, it is only since Memorial University of Newfoundland has been training Newfoundlanders and others in Folklore Studies (1962) that many academically-trained Anglo-Canadian folklorists have done research on their own traditions.

Anglo Canadians are by no means unique in this regard, for the same trend has existed until only very recently among most British folklore scholars. The various reasons for this common tendency among Anglo-Saxons to focus attention away from and, most often, to ignore the very existence of their own traditions are particularly illuminating in the context of this discussion.

Essentially, the reasons are derived from a perception common among Anglo-Saxons of themselves and their culture as the most highly advanced, the most developed of all creatures and cultures ever extant. In particular, nineteenth-century evolutionary thought, especially social Darwinism, combined with the rampant imperialism of the British Empire, gave rise to a persisting conception of British culture as superior to all others. Despite its strongly conservative orientation, British culture became, as a result of the Industrial Revolution, closely allied with progress and consequently with a liberal mentality.[4] The British consequently became increasingly alienated from their folk roots which were premised upon a conservative status quo-oriented mentality and which, therefore, came to be associated in the minds of the British middle and upper classes with the old-fashioned, the inferior and the obsolete.

Their transplantation to Canada did little to change the attitudes of most Britishers. Except for members of some delimited regional, and usually ethnic, sub-cultures such as Newfoundlanders or Nova Scotian Scots, most Anglo Canadians simply fail to identify folklore with themselves, and tend to consider folk materials to be the quaint, charming and decorative but ultimately unimportant possessions of the strange, foreign or "backward" people in their midst.

Anglo Canadians have been able to harbour such ideas because of their dominant majority-group position throughout most of the country. The majority of Anglo Canadians have not consciously felt culturally, economically, politically or socially oppressed or inferior. They have not, therefore, been motivated to seek means to express themselves in the nation through their unique traditions as have some peoples, both in Canada and abroad, as a result of positions of inferiority. Regional Anglo-Canadian sub-groups, ethnic minority groups (particularly the French and more recently others), and the Native Peoples have been prompted to attempt such cultural articulation through which they have achieved various degrees of general recognition in the larger society.

The basic British propensity to ignore their own folklore has been compounded in Canada by several important aspects of the Canadian socio-political and historical situation. Since this country was, for many years, a colony of Great Britain, and increasingly since the 1940s has been an economic colony of the United States, Canadians have commonly looked beyond their borders for their cultural identity. They have, therefore, neglected to a certain degree the minority cultural groups within their midst. Only recently with the upsurge of nationalist sentiment has the attention of Canadians been directed inward in a search for identity.

Even more influential than the colonial mentality in forming majority-group attitudes to minority groups has been the garrison mentality instilled by the pattern of settlement of the country and fostered by the subsequent socio-political circumstances in Canada.[5] As a result of their early settlement, primarily in isolated pockets surrounded by wilderness and/or aliens, Anglo Canadians developed a defensive stance towards the land and its other occupants. Therefore, small areas of civilization — "garrisons" — were in effect separated off and jealously guarded, primarily out of fear.[6]

Even today, Anglo Canadians retain such garrisons despite extensive settlement, cosmopolitan centres and the retreat of the true wilderness. The majority group remains challenged by the wilderness it has never fully conquered and, to some degree, feels threatened by it. Once actually the wilderness, this untamed entity has now become the society-at-large. In large part, this threat to the majority group — amounting to a sense of weakness, indeed almost inferiority in relation to the land — stems from the fact that the majority populace does not know either itself or the land it inhabits.[7] Those people who seem to know who they are, or at least who they once were, and who have distinct cultural traditions through which they can express their unique identities then also pose a threat to the majority group. The compensatory reaction to these feelings of inferiority amongst the majority are manifested in displays of paternalism — i.e., feelings of superiority — towards the threatening objects: the minority cultural groups and their traditions.

In essence, majority-group treatment of minority groups and their traditions has been characterized by three approaches: exploitation, sentimentalization and preservation. A brief general discussion of these approaches will be followed by a specific analysis of their effect on studies of Native Peoples' traditions, then a similar analysis concerning non-Native minority-group folklore studies.

The exploitative nature of Anglo-Canadian interest in minority-group folklore is evident from the fact that the majority group, major organizations and governments of Canada have only paid serious and concerted attention to these traditions when such interest has been either financially or politically expedient. Otherwise, throughout Canadian history, minority-group traditions have most commonly been treated as ephemera and exotica.

The sentimentalization of minority-group folklore has been a more complex process and one frequently related to the conception of Canadian culture as a mosaic. From the earliest years of this century, concern for and display of the traditions of minority cultural groups has taken many forms, but has consistently been a common occurrence in Canada. This visibility of minority-group folklore in the culture generally has promoted the mosaic concept.

It was an American tourist, Victoria Haywood, who first wrote about Canada as a mosaic culture.[8] She was fascinated by surviving traditions she encountered during her vacation forays into Eastern Canada. Sentimental romanticism pervades her writing and that of so many other people — her predecessors, contemporaries and even some successors

— who have been preoccupied with viewing alien customs, artifacts and other folk traditions as quaint.[9] The full influence of the mosaic concept on Anglo-Canadian folkloristics will be discussed subsequently.

Any number of people have been fascinated by the very "foreignness" of minority-group traditions and have been emotionally attracted to their study at least partially by this alien quality. This is true of Margaret MacLeod's interest in Métis songs, resulting in her book *Songs of Old Manitoba* (1959), and Helen Creighton's work with German Canadians in Nova Scotia, published as *Folklore of Lunenburg County, Nova Scotia* (1950). However, the considerable linguistic and cultural difficulties associated with concerted study of the traditions by most Anglo Canadians have led to the limitation of such interest to descriptive documentation, frequently inaccurate, editorialized, or at least incomplete.

Most commonly, Anglo Canadians have not considered linguistic and cultural communication to be quite the problem with the Native Peoples that it has been with non-Native minority cultural groups.[10] This fact has had interesting results. First, there are many more discussions of Native Peoples' traditions by Anglo Canadians than there are discussions of non-Native minority-group traditions. Second, despite or perhaps because of these numerous writings, there has been extensive and serious misunderstanding of many traditions, for example, the Indians' oratory rhetoric.[11] Third, the amount of Anglified materials concerning Native traditions available in the culture has encouraged many Anglo Canadians to adopt bastardized Native materials as their own, or as "Canadian" traditions. An excellent example of this tendency is the inclusion of Indian or pseudo-Indian legends, especially those referring to place names, within the traditions common to many western Anglo Canadians.

The Native Peoples and their cultural traditions have generally attracted a great deal of attention from many Anglo Canadians. The nature of, motivations for and impact of this attention reflect particularly clearly the attitudes of the majority towards minority groups and their unique cultural traditions.

From the early years of contact until well into the nineteenth century, the Anglo-Saxons freely exploited the Natives and their cultures while simultaneously romanticizing these indigenous people. The prevailing attitudes towards the Native Peoples tended to depend upon the proximity of the Anglo-Saxons harbouring the attitudes to the Natives; that is, Europeans abroad could speak and write of the "Noble Savage" while the British in North America had to deal regularly with the "Pesky Redskin."[12] The sentimentality inherent in the former attitude pervaded the works of many travellers, settlers and writers concerning the Native Peoples throughout the nineteenth century. This stance persisted in many of the numerous adaptations of Indian traditional narratives prepared mostly in this century and primarily for Anglo-Canadian consumption. Naturally, there are some non-sentimental and valuable nineteenth-century works dealing with Native traditions. Paul Kane's *Wanderings of an artist among the Indians of North America: from Canada to Vancouver's island and Oregon through the Hudson's Bay Company's territory and back again* (1859; new ed. 1925) is one of the most important of such works. Another is Sir John Franklin's *Narrative of a journey to the shores of the Polar Sea in the years 1819, 20, 21 and 22* (1823) concerning his expeditions in search of the Northwest Passage. It is particularly noteworthy that the authors of these, and most of the other nineteenth-century and earlier works of real interest to the serious scholar of Native culture, were trained observers rather than commentators. In their reports they — unlike most others — emphasized the nature, milieux and apparent uses and functions of what they encountered rather than their reactions to these traditions.

Virtually contemporaneous with their systematic and self-righteous eradication of Native ceremonial customs central to these indigenous cultures (e.g., the Potlatch and the Sun Dance were both made illegal), some Anglo Canadians began to appreciate the value, indeed the desirability, of preserving their cultures, or at least some of their artifacts. In the latter half of the nineteenth century, many personal and institutional collections of Native artistic treasures were amassed, particularly in the West and especially of the Pacific North Coast materials. While it can legitimately be argued that such acquisition of artifacts has ultimately been beneficial to the Native Peoples,[13] this cultural robbery undoubtedly weakened any residual tendencies towards cultural maintenance still surviving among the indigenous peoples, and speeded the demise of the traditional cultures. Among those who participated in these "get-it-before-it's-dead" preservation activities from mid-century onwards were the Canadian Geological Survey teams which provided later scholars with much information in their reports, and some extremely valuable photographs and artifacts.[14]

Beginning in the last third of the nineteenth century, some truly academic studies[15] of Native Peoples' traditions were undertaken, although frequently not by Anglo Canadians. Americans,[16] usually associated with the Bureau of American Ethnology, the Smithsonian Institute or other organizations, commonly directed these studies. Until the establishment of the National Museum in Ottawa, they were also most influential in urging Canadians to undertake them.

Canadians became very actively involved in studying Native Peoples' traditions when C. Marius Barbeau and Douglas Leechman joined the staff of the National Museum in 1911-12. Some dedicated non-professionals as well as scholars in Canada then made serious efforts to preserve remnants of the traditional indigenous cultures. At the same time, however, governments and the larger society urged Anglo conformity — essentially meaning the rejection of traditions — among the Native Peoples. Additionally, sentimentalization and exploitation of the Native folklore by the majority culture persisted despite all the scholarly efforts concerning this material.

Mounting guilt among the majority group when faced with the obviously negative effects of their treatment of the Native Peoples has resulted in a literature of guilt and a generally self-deprecatory view of Anglo-Canadian involvement with the Native Peoples' cultures. Approximately ten years ago this Anglo-Canadian guilt was reinforced, indeed exploited, by the Native Peoples themselves when they began to perceive the necessity for a cultural articulation generated, directed and controlled by themselves. This movement — a compensatory expression by suppressed, repressed and misunderstood peoples[17] — represents a certain cultural threat to the majority culture. Previously, the Native Peoples had played a minimal role themselves in the study of their traditions or in the determination of the nature and extent of the exposure of these traditions to the society-at-large. Now the Native Peoples are striving to establish cultural sovereignty. They have been somewhat successful since many Anglo Canadians have become hesitant to study or to publish materials concerning Native folklore. As a result, many more of the recent publications on Native traditions are by Native People themselves.[18] Some of these works contain as many, if not more, distortions than the non-Native publications, and some are just as exploitative, because they capitalize upon the white man's guilt. Partly because of such failings in the Native-produced materials on their cultural heritage, but mainly because of prevailing attitudes among the majority group, Native cultural traditions continue to be misused and falsely represented in the larger society.

The majority group has felt quite free to adapt, adopt and otherwise use the Native Peoples' traditions without ever fully understanding them or granting their bearers truly equal status within the society. Generally speaking, Anglo Canadians have displayed greatest interest in Native Peoples' traditions for commercial or cultural purposes. For example, Anglo Canadians readily adopted Native transportation equipment and methods during the frontier times, and have just as readily in modern times adapted Native art, for instance, to their use for the tourist trade and for international display as Canadian art.

This essentially pragmatic approach is, and long has been, typical of the majority-group attitudes towards minority-group traditions and their bearers. Generally, applied folklore activities — interest in and socio-cultural use of folklore for practical, non-scholarly purposes — have been and continue to be a prominent feature of Canadian folkloristics.[19] Those majority-group activities concerning minority-group traditions particularly tend towards an applied approach. This tendency has become more apparent in recent years when the majority group has come to consider the traditions of non-Native minority groups as they have long seen the Native Peoples' traditions — useful to the majority, especially for the identification and display of Canadian culture.

Examples of this pragmatic majority-group attitude towards minority-group folk tradition can be found early in this century when there was considerable concern for the vast numbers[20] of non-Anglo, non-French immigrants who had entered Canada towards the end of the nineteenth century and in the years of this century preceding World War I. Socio-political events and related cultural beliefs and movements have promoted and validated this utilitarian approach. Illustrative of the concern demonstrated towards minority-group traditions are the activities of J. Murray Gibbon, for many years the publicity director of the Canadian Pacific Railway.

A close friend of Marius Barbeau, the Dean of Canadian folklore, Gibbon became interested in the so-called National School of music, popular in the late nineteenth and early twentieth centuries. This school of thought, supported by such notable musicians and musical scholars as Bartok, Dvořák, Smetana, Tchaikovsky and Verdi, argued that a nation's music should be rooted in the folk music of that nation's people, and that through mutual awareness and understanding of their distinct musical traditions, the folk of a nation might evolve a national music reflective of their true nature.[21]

In keeping with these ideas, then, Gibbon endeavoured to cultivate inter-group awareness and a mutual tradition through exposure to and exchange of folk music among the people of Canada. Consequently, he organized a number of ethnic folksong, handicraft and dance festivals and concerts in the late 1920s. These performances were sponsored by the Railway,[22] and held at the company's famous hotels in various cities, including Quebec, Toronto, Winnipeg, Regina, Calgary and Banff. The express purposes of such public performances were the celebration of the cultural diversity of Canadians and the promotion of union among them through the mutual appreciation of tradition.

Gibbon achieved some national recognition for his well-intentioned efforts and for the resultant ethnic festivals which obviously appealed to a cultural predilection of his time:

> ... he [Gibbon] is coming to be regarded more and more as a champion of foreign cultures in Canada; and in this connection would appear to be performing a unique patriotic service, not only in entertaining the "Old Canadians" with the glamour, pageantry and melody of our "New Canadians" (as in the recent Folklore and Handicrafts Festival in Winnipeg), but, by this very means, making the "Old Canadians" more cosmopolitan and more tolerant — one might even say "less boorish" — towards the newcomer from various centres of Europe.
>
> It is felt that anyone who can do this is deserving of a niche in the Canadian Hall of Fame. In other words, it is felt that anyone who can help to enrich our native culture by bringing in contact with it that of foreign lands, at the same time showing up the picturesque, colourful and intriguing side of the newcomer, is doing something for this country.[23]

The tendency has persisted to concentrate on the "picturesque, colourful and intriguing" side of minority cultures in Canada, to consider such interest "a patriotic service," and to display the interest through public performances, not uncommonly, though not exclusively, in a manner and by persons foreign to the traditions involved. Demonstrations of ethnicity are commonplace in Canada today, very often taking the form of festivals involving folk traditions, and usually being directly or indirectly government supported.[24] A distinction can be made between folk festivals sponsored by one group, for instance, the annual Icelandic festival in Gimli, Manitoba, and multi-ethnic events like Toronto's Caravan. The former are usually more oriented towards the maintenance and communal sharing of traditions than are the latter, and less oriented towards demonstrations of traditions for non-members. A strong publicist element is, however, incorporated in virtually all ethnic festivals.

Anglo-Canadian interest in minority-group folklore has obviously been encouraged by the belief that if people can mutually exchange and participate in each other's traditions they will understand one another better and will create a community amongst themselves. Such thinking lies behind many of the current activities of the Canadian Folk Music Society, one of the very few organizations in Canada concerned with folk traditions. The formation of the Canadian Folk Arts Council in the mid-sixties was prompted largely by these same ideas.

Perhaps more influential in directing majority-group attention to minority-group traditions has been the general acceptance of the mosaic description of Canadian culture. The governments and people of Canada have clearly shown a willingness — indeed a need — to believe in and to foster the mosaic concept. In the effort to demonstrate the existence of the mosaic, both governments and the general populace most commonly point to the persistence and visibility of minority-group folk traditions or to the presence of minority-group members in important positions in a society essentially determined and controlled by the Anglo-Canadian majority. Minority-group traditions are, then, of peculiar importance in modern Canada.

The motives for the popular acceptance of the mosaic

and for the apparent willingness of Canadians to recognize folklore as a significant contribution by the minority cultures to Canada must be questioned. Essentially, the motives are derived from the intense, but generally covert, pressures towards Anglo-conformity in the country and from other cultural defensive reactions, i.e., measures undertaken by a cultural group to maintain its existence in the face of some threat. In Canada such measures have frequently been associated with nationalism.

In order to avoid compromising the basic structure of the country or jeopardizing its own superior position, the majority culture is quite willing to make concessions to appease the minority groups. Such concessions include not only displays but also studies of minority-group traditions. Multiculturalism — at least as it exists and is celebrated in Canada — is far less threatening to the majority culture, and therefore is considered preferable by most Anglo Canadians to nationally operative bilingualism and bi-culturalism. Hence, the mosaic is supported, as is scholarly activity that reinforces the concept.

In its search for a national identity, Canada has recognized the need to have native and/or national traditions. Since the mosaic demands that Canada's unity is in its multiplicity, minority-group traditions — or some selection of them that is acceptable in the society-at-large — thereby become Canadian traditions which can be utilized in the articulation of a distinct Canadian culture. Such articulation is demanded by one of the deepest needs of the Canadian psyche, namely to be different from Americans. The celebration of the mosaic is a compensatory expression of the Canadian culture believed by many Canadians to be distinct from and somewhat superior to the threatening American counterpart. The persistence and demonstration of the mosaic is seen by many Canadians to be central to their cultural survival. Therefore, the collection and study of the traditions viewed as necessary to maintain and demonstrate the mosaic are encouraged.

The Canadian populace, then, unconsciously accepts folklore as a very important voice for the nation's culture. However, except for some scholars (primarily of French Canada, Newfoundland, and various minority ethnic groups), Canadians do not attach intrinsic importance to folklore. Anglo Canadians have tended to view oral traditions as having only an instrumental significance. As indicated earlier, such material has primarily been considered important and worthy of attention when that attention seems to be of socio-political value. Consequently, academic folklore studies are somewhat retarded in the nation.

Ethnicity plays an important role in this situation. As previously mentioned, folklore is commonly associated by the larger society with ethnic groups. In fact, folklore functions as a primary means of making insider/outsider identifications in Canada and of maintaining the boundaries between the different minority cultural groups. Majority-group Canadians have been generally more concerned with such matters than with the paradigmatic development of Folklore Studies. It must be noted that the majority of discussions of oral traditions in Canada have been oriented towards description (rather than analysis) of the folklore and folklife of specific ethnic groups.

Through concerning themselves with the traditions of ethnic minorities, Anglo Canadians have been able to maintain their deeply ingrained belief that their country is one where people are freer than elsewhere to maintain their distinctiveness and where differences are not only tolerated but also encouraged. As the cultural minorities become more vocal, increasingly protest the prevailing representation of their tradition in the culture, and display their own tradition as they choose, the widespread Anglo-Canadian beliefs concerning cultural freedoms are challenged and the Anglo-Canadians' treasured conception of themselves as tolerant and beneficent is threatened. As a result of this threat, majority-group Canadians increasingly exhibit a tendency to respond favourably to ethnicity while minority-group Canadians, in the effort to attain full cultural status and recognition, increasingly display it.

Since the Royal Commission on Bilingualism and Biculturalism was established, and especially since the federal government adopted its cultural policy of multiculturalism within a bilingual framework,[25] minority groups and their traditions have been receiving considerably increased attention from governments, their departments and agencies, as well as from individual scholars. In part, this increased attention is a direct result of the availability of funds for multicultural research which is, in turn, a product of the society's — especially the majority group's — concern for ethnicity.

That availability and the application of the funds is, therefore, clearly associated with the current political and cultural expedience of such research. In effect, majority-group Canadians are now treating non-Native minority groups and their traditions in a manner akin to their long-standing treatment of the Native People and their traditions. In other words, the majority is more ready to use and/or abuse the minority traditions in order to maintain their position in the nation, to amuse or entertain themselves and to portray Canadian culture abroad.

This situation does not bode particularly well for the future of minority-group folklore research in Canada. When ethnicity and its display are no longer in fashion, and when the majority culture ceases to find socio-political applications for attending to minority-group traditions, then the current burgeoning of ethnic cultural studies will be no more, for the available funds will diminish as they are deployed elsewhere. Without the present governmental and cultural support, the only possibility of maintaining the currently developing academic tradition of minority-group folklore research rests with the minority-group members themselves. Ethnic folklore studies will evolve into an internationally recognized field of scholarship, supported by the groups concerned in the studies (as is already the case for the French-Canadian and Newfoundland work), only if the number of such studies continues to increase and its calibre to improve.

As more minority-group members undertake research on their own folklore, fewer outsiders are studying minority-group traditions, with the result that the materials are being viewed increasingly from the point of view of the insider. Increasingly then, the research exudes an awareness and understanding of meaningful cultural artifacts rather than the sense of exotica and ephemera which pervaded it when largely untrained Anglo Canadians dominated the activities concerning these traditions. This change is particularly noticeable in the recent publications concerning the Native Peoples' traditions.

Majority-group Canadians still do not consciously consider minority-group traditions to be particularly significant and worthy of serious concern. What is seen most in the general culture of such traditions are those that are decorative, interesting and easily accessible to the outsider, such as culinary customs, place names, folk dance, song and costume. Such traditions are useful and saleable to the general public, as discussed previously. However, Anglo Canadians have generally not come to realize the true importance of this folklore to the minority-group members themselves any more than they have recognized the existence of their own traditions. Even majority-group folklore scholars are guilty of treating Canadian ethnic folklore in a somewhat superficial manner, for they have failed to provide full data concerning the traditions, to do scholarly analyses, or to develop theoretical paradigms related to the materials. There has been no appreciable change in the popular attitudes over time despite the cultural support for ethnicity and the fact that in recent years more Canadians have received more training in folklore, resulting in more seriousness in their attitudes towards traditional materials.[26]

Considering the premise argued in this paper that ethnicity in Canada may commonly be interpreted as compensatory cultural articulation of suppressed or repressed people, it is conceivable, given the current socio-political circumstances, that Anglo Canadians may yet display intense ethnicity vis-à-vis their own traditions. Minority-group members may well increasingly exclude majority-group members from the collection, study and presentation of ethnic traditions, as the Native Peoples already have done to a certain extent. Since the majority group is tending more towards treating non-Native minority groups and their traditions in a fashion typical of the majority's longstanding treatment of the Native Peoples and their traditions, it is to be expected that the future reaction of other minority-group members might well be similar to that of some Native people today. Faced with such reactions from minority-group members, Anglo Canadians — particularly those interested in folklore — may be forced to consider their own traditions. The uncertainties associated with the sense of loss resulting from the denial of access to minority-group traditions could possibly activate the latent sense of cultural inferiority among the majority and intensify the present search for identity. Anglo Canadians might then become more actively engaged in the study and preservation of their own traditional materials, and thereby help to eradicate a serious lack in Canadian folkloristics.

Under the present circumstances, any analyses of minority-group traditions in Canada are necessarily limited by the lack of extensive collections and studies of the majority tradition, making significant comparative studies and discussions of inter-influences virtually impossible. For, in their desire to recognize, popularize and preserve minority-group traditions, many Anglo Canadian folklorists have failed to study their own group's traditions, leaving this folklore largely unknown and undervalued throughout the nation.

Just as the maintenance and display of traditions are related to the position of any minority group in Canadian society and culture, so, too, is the study of such traditions by members or outsiders related to socio-political factors. Anglo Canadians have been supreme in Canada. They have commonly displayed attitudes typical of the dominant group towards the dominated and their cultures. Paternalism, odious sentimentalization, considerable exploitation and haphazard preservation have characterized both scholarly and popular ethnic folkloristic endeavours undertaken by the majority group. Some good work has been done, nonetheless, such as Mary Weekes' collection of anecdotes, reminiscences and material items from Saskatchewan Indians;[27] Hugh Dempsey's work with the Blackfoot Indians around Calgary;[28] and Mark Mealing's research on the Doukhobors in British Columbia.[29]

Much remains undone, however, and the necessary research might never be undertaken or completed since most Canadians are unaware of the nature, value and purposes of Folklore Studies. Further, the populace seems unwilling to recognize the significant difference between the mosaic as it currently exists and a truly multicultural country. As a result, Anglo-Canadian supremacy and cultural domination, along with the popular misconceptions and general ignorance of folklore and its study, are likely to persist, generally undermining a full appreciation of the role of ethnic groups and their folk traditions in Canadian culture.

Carole H. Carpenter, 1975

Notes

"THE CUT-OFF HEAD FROZEN ON": SOME INTERNATIONAL VERSIONS OF A TALL TALE

1. I am indebted to Violetta M. Halpert for her firm editing of this article.

2. Antti Aarne and Stith Thompson, *The Types of the Folktale*, 2nd rev. (FF Communications No. 184; Helsinki, 1961); Stith Thompson, *Motif-Index of Folk-Literature*, rev. ed., 6 vols. (Bloomington, IN: Indiana Univ. Press, 1955-58).

3. Ernest W. Baughman, *Type and Motif-Index of the Folktales of England and North America* (Indiana Univ. Folklore Series, No. 20; The Hague: Mouton & Co., 1966), p. 579.

4. *The Newfoundland Journal of Aaron Thomas*, ed. Jean M. Murray ([London]: Longmans, 1968), pp. 157-58.

5. Rpt. in Karl Goedeke, *Schwänke des sechzehnten jahrhunderts (Deutsche Dichter des sechzehnten jahrhunderts*, XII; Leipzig, 1879), p. 63 (36. Lügengeschichten, No. 13. Kopf angefroren). I got the Goedeke reference from a manuscript "Catalog of Lying Tales," compiled by a Miss Bartelmex for Archer Taylor, and lent to me for copying.

6. My colleague, David S. Artiss, kindly revised my literal translation into idiomatic English.

7. Gerald Thomas, *The Tall Tale and Philippe d'Alcripe. An Analysis of the Tall Tale Genre with Particular Reference to Philippe d'Alcripe's "La Nouvelle Fabrique des Excellents Traits de Vérité, together with an Annotated Translation of the Work* (St. John's, Nfld.: The Department of Folklore, Memorial Univ. of Newfoundland, in association with The American Folklore Society, 1977), p. 144 (Tale 94).

8. Thomas, p. 3. See also Chapter 3.

9. Reprinted from *A Nest of Ninnies*, P. M. Zall, ed. (Lincoln, NB., c. 1970), p. 242, by permission of the University of Nebraska Press. Copyright 1970 by the University of Nebraska Press.

10. Zall, p. 237. For further discussion of Hicks (or Hickes), see Philip A. Shelley, "William Hicks, Native of Oxford," *Harvard Studies and Notes in Philology and Literature*, 20 (1938), 81-98.

11. Herbert Halpert, "Indiana Folktales," *Hoosier Folklore Bulletin*, 1 (1942), 22. The tale was contributed by Mira L. Glass, who secured it from Emma Robinson, of Bloomington, Indiana, in whose family the story was traditional.

12. The name of any Bloomington man that the storyteller thinks appropriate is used.

13. "Ones They Got Away With," *Tocher*, 2, No. 11 (Autumn 1973), 86, from David Work, Shapinsay, Orkney, 1971. Heard from an old Sanday man settled in Shapinsay. Reprinted with the permission of the collector-editor and the storyteller.

14. Isabel Cameron, *Folk of the Glen* (London: Lutterworth Press, 1937), p. 25.

15. Elsie Crane Blossom, "Fifty Below Zero," *The Potash Kettle*, 8, No. 3 (Spring 1960), p. 21 (from Rutland, Vermont). Reprinted with the permission of the Editor of *The Potash Kettle* and of the late writer's niece.

16. I am indebted to the Editor, Evelyn W. Stanley, for publishing a query about Elsie Crane Blossom in her publication, and for sending me the letter, dated August 12, 1978, which she received in reply from Marjorie R. Russell. The information in this paragraph is from that letter.

17. Letter dated August 31, 1978, from Sr. Catherine Jolicoeur, Centre universitaire SLM, Edmundston, N.B.

18. MUNFLA 74-103. In editing I have slightly re-arranged and condensed Mr. Genge's introductory comment. I have not tampered with the language of the story itself except to move one parenthetical sentence, and insert one word in parenthesis. I have, however, made some minor changes in punctuation.

19. The story has been edited for this paper by Violetta M. Halpert, from the careful detailed transcription made by Dr. John D. A. Widdowson from the tape recording. Nothing has been added except punctuation necessary for clarity. Omissions have been minimal, primarily repetitious or confusing words or phrases, and a number of the "pause" words and syllables which add so much to a storyteller's style but are distracting to a reader.

20. This paper had been completed when I discovered yet another version of the Cut-Off Head, in a small Newfoundland joke collection recently published. See Robert Sheppard and Edwin Noftle, *Newfie Laffs* (N.p. [Lewisport, Nfld.?] : The compilers, 1979), p. 4. Mr. Robert Sheppard, in his letter September 20, 1979, giving me permission to reprint the item, wrote: "This particular version of the story was told to me by a mate on one of the Canadian National ferries; he heard it at Goose Bay (Labrador)." Here is the Sheppard-Noftle version:
        Two boys were in the woods one winter cutting fire-

wood with their uncle. The axe, which was as sharp as a razor, slipped out of the boys' hands and cut their uncle's head completely off. The boys picked up their uncle's head and put it back on. Because it was a good frosty day, it stuck firmly and the uncle went on about his work. A few months later, someone who had heard about the accident asked the boys how their uncle was getting on.

"Uncle Garge drowned the other day," one of the boys informed him.

"Oh, what happened? Did he fall overboard?"

"No, no," the other boy said. "When we stuck his head back on last winter, we put it on upside down. We had that heavy rain the other day and the water ran up in his nose and drowned him!"

The first part of this story obviously belongs to the tradition I have presented in this paper. However, instead of retaining the suspense about when the head would thaw, this version explains the uncle's death with an ending from a different tall tale pattern.

THE MAN WHO PLUCKED THE GORBEY:
A MAINE WOODS LEGEND

1. Part of the material for this paper was gathered on field trips made possible by several generous grants from the Coe Research Fund of the University of Maine.

2. Phillips Barry, ed., *The Maine Woods Songster* (Cambridge, MA, 1939), p. 57.

3. The exception came from a man in Baie Comeau, Quebec, who said he had been an eyewitness to the event in a camp on Moccasin Lake near Whitney, Ontario.

4. (Portland, Maine, The Falmouth Book House, 1937), p. 147 f.

5. (Philadelphia and New York, 1948), pp. 115-29.

6. Ruth Ann Musick, "West Virginia Ghost Stories," *Midwest Folklore*, 8 (Spring 1958), 24-25.

7. Helen Creighton, *Bluenose Ghosts* (Toronto, 1957), p. 104.

8. *Bird-Lore*, IV (July-August, 1902), 109-14. This was the official Audubon magazine.

9. Ibid, p. 113.

10. Ibid, p. 113.

11. Edward Howe Forbush, *The Birds of Massachusetts and Other New England States* (Boston, 1929), II, 384; Ora W. Knight, *The Birds of Maine* (Bangor, 1908), p. 328; P. A. Taverner, *Birds of Canada* (Toronto, 1938), p. 304.

12. "Maine Birds," *Bulletin of the Museum of Comparative Zoology at Harvard College*, CII, 377-78.

13. There is one other hypothesis for the origin of this word that should be mentioned, though I feel that the derivation I have just given is the correct one. W. L. McAtee, in his monograph "Folk Names of New England Birds" (reprinted from *The Bulletin of the Massachusetts Audubon Society*, October 1955 to May 1956) suggests, although he does not insist upon it, that its derivation is "Apparently from 'corbie' — tracing to the Latin *corvus* — a name applied in Great Britain to several members of the crow family." I have found "corbie" reported for both crow and raven but for nothing else. And while the jay is a member of the crow family, there is very little obvious resemblance. That is, the two birds are of such different habits and appearance that they are not likely to be confused, especially by woodsmen. On the other hand, notice A. Richard's word "corberie" used above.

14.   For further support for this idea, see Horace P. Beck, "Folk-song Affiliations of Maine," *Midwest Folklore*, 6 (Fall 1956), 159-66. For another specific example of this homogeneity, see my article, " 'Ben Deane' and Joe Scott: a Ballad and its Probable Author," *JAF*, 72 (1959), 53-66.

IN DEFENCE OF PAUL BUNYAN

1.   This paper was originally presented at the American Folklore Society meeting in Portland, Oregon, October 31, 1974.

2.   Richard M. Dorson, "Folklore and Fake Lore," *American Mercury* 70 (1950), 335-48.

3.   Dorson, p. 336.

4.   Richard M. Dorson, *American Folklore* (Chicago: University of Chicago Press, 1959), p. 216.

5.   Jan Harold Brunvand, *The Study of American Folklore* (New York: Norton, 1968), p. 2.

6.   Brunvand, p. 92.

7.   Brunvand, p. 129.

8.   Daniel Hoffman, *Paul Bunyan: Last of the Frontier Demigods* (Philadelphia: University of Pennsylvania Press, 1952), p. 2.

9.   Hoffman, pp. 165-66.

10.   James MacGillivray, "The Round River Drive," *Detroit News Tribune* 24 June 1910; rpt. in *Legends of Paul Bunyan*, ed. Harold W. Felton (New York: Knopf, 1947), pp. 335-41.

11. Hoffman, p. 5.

12. Edward O. Tabor and Stith Thompson, "Paul Bunyan in 1910," *Journal of American Folklore*, 59 (1946), 134-35.

13. Bernice Stewart and Homer A. Watt, "Legends of Paul Bunyan, Lumberjack," *Transactions of the Wisconsin Academy of Sciences, Arts and Letters*, no. 18, pt. 2 (1916), 639-51.

14. Constance Rourke, "Paul Bunyon [sic]," *New Republic* 23 (7 July 1920), 176-79.

15. Rourke, p. 177.

16. J. D. Robins, "Paul Bunyan," *Canadian Forum*, 6 (February 1926), pp. 146-48; rpt. in *Our Sense of Identity*, ed. Malcolm Ross (Toronto: University of Toronto Press, 1954), pp. 130-35.

17. Robins, in *Our Sense of Identity*, p. 133.

18. Robins, p. 134.

19. Max Gartenberg, "Paul Bunyan and Little John," *Journal of American Folklore* 63 (1949), 416-22.

20. Letter from Kay Stone, 14 October 1974, quoting a letter from her father, 30 September 1974.

21. John Lee Brooks, "Paul Bunyan: American Folk Hero" (Master's Thesis, Southern Methodist University, Dallas, 1927), cited in Hoffman, pp. 51-52.

22. Earl Clifton Beck, *Lore of the Lumber Camps* (Ann Arbor: University of Michigan Press, 1948), pp. 328-42.

23. Dorson, *American Folklore*, pp. 222-23.

24. Herbert Halpert, "Tall Tales from Calgary, Alberta," *California Folklore Quarterly* 4 (1945), 38.

25. Helen Creighton, *Folklore of Lunenburg County, Nova Scotia* (Ottawa: National Museum, 1950), pp. 135-36.

26. Recorded from Joe Thibadeau, Bobcaygeon, Ontario, 11 October 1964. These and other tall tales from Mr. Thibadeau appear in my anthology, *Folklore of Canada* (Toronto: McClelland and Stewart, 1976), pp. 167-70.

27. Hoffman, pp. 83-84.

28. Hoffman, pp. 54-59.

DANCING IN CAPE BRETON ISLAND, NOVA SCOTIA

1. The bracketed numbers refer to the list of informants and bibliography appended.

2. In the Canadian census of 1941 there were approximately 10,000 people in Cape Breton Island who listed Gaelic as their mother tongue.

3. A typical eight-handed Reel of this more recent form is described on p. 216.

4. This form of stepping was employed even in the Fling and *Seann Truibhas*, but not in the Swords.

5. The Parisian Quadrilles consisted of the "head couple" figures of the First Set of Quadrilles. They were first introduced in England and Scotland, as a separate dance for two couples only, about the middle of the nineteenth century, and are

described in the ballroom guides published by the Glasgow teachers Willock and Wallace.

6.   The steps can also be adapted to jigs.

7.   These phrases occurred in various examples of stepping demonstrated to me by one or more of my informants.

8.   This corresponds to the Scottish "single treble."

9.   This corresponds to the Scottish "double treble."

LIST OF INFORMANTS AND REFERENCES

The following informants in Cape Breton Island were all visited in 1957:

(1)   Mr. John Gillis and Miss Margaret Gillis, Gillisdale, S. W. Margaree. Father and daughter; Mr. Gillis' grandfather came from Morar.

(2)   Mr. and Mrs. Archie Kennedy, Dunvegan. Mr. Kennedy is the son of Mr. Ronald Kennedy below; Mrs. Kennedy's great-grandparents came from Moidart.

(3)   Mr. Ronald Kennedy, Broad Cove. His grandfather came from Canna.

(4)   The Rev. Father McCormick, East Bay. His grandparents came from S. Uist.

(5)   Mrs. Mary Sarah MacDonald, Scotch Lake. A centenarian; her grandmother came from Barra.

(6)   The Rev. Father Stanley MacDonald, Big Pond. His grandparents came from Kinlochmoidart.

(7)   Mr. Dan E. MacDonald, Iona.

(8)   Mrs. MacDougal, East Bay.

(9)   Mr. Neil R. MacIsaac, Big Pond.

(10)   Mr. Hugh F. MacKenzie, Sydney. Brought up at Christmas
        Island; his family came from Barra.

(11)   Mrs. Christina MacLellan, Inverness.

(12)   Mr. Frank MacNeil, Big Pond. His grandfather came from
        Barra.

(13)   Mr. James C. MacNeil, Gillis Point, Iona.

(14)   Mr. Steve R. MacNeil, Iona.

(15)   Mrs. MacTigue, Inverness.

(16)   Mr. Peter Glen Moriston, Sydney.

(17)   Mrs. Donald Walker, Daliburgh, S. Uist, Scotland, 1956.

(18)   See Nos. 2, 3, 6, 7, 9, 11.

(19)   J. L. MacDougall, *History of Inverness County, Nova Scotia*,
        privately printed, 1922.

A SURVEY OF FOLK MEDICINE IN FRENCH CANADA
FROM EARLY TIMES TO THE PRESENT

1.   [Jacques Rousseau and Jean L. Launay], *Jacques Cartier et
        "La Grosse Maladie"* ("Reproduction photographique de son
        Brief Recit et Succincte Narration suivie d'une traduction en

langue anglaise du chapitre traitant des aventures de Cartier aux prises avec le scorbut et d'une nouvelle analyse du Mystère de l'Annedda'' [Montreal: XIXe Congrès International de Physiologie, 1953], p. [102]).

2. Sylvio Leblond, "Histoire de la médicine au Canada français," *Cahiers d histoire de la Société historique de Québec*, no. 2 (1970), p. 18.

3. Michel and Georges Ahern, *Notes pour servir à l'Histoire de la Médecine dans le Bas-Canada depuis la fondation de Québec jusqu'au commencement du XIXe siècle* (Quebec, 1923), pp. 435-41.

4. René Bélanger, "L'abbé Pierre-Joseph Compain, prêtre et médecin, 1740-1806," *Saguenayensia: Revue de la Société historique du Saguenay* (Chicoutimi), 13, no. 4(1971) 106-8.

5. *Traité élémentaire de matiére médicale et guide pratique des Soeurs de Charité de l'asile de la Providence* (Publié sous le patronage des Professeurs de l'Ecole de Médecine et de Chirurgie, Faculté de Médecine de l'Université Victoria" [Montreal, Sénécal, 1870], p. 376 and p. 587).

6. Marius Barbeau, "Boily le remancheur," *Liaison*, no. 13 (March 1948), 152-53.

7. *Il faut le mettre en prison* ("Le procès intenté à J.-A. Desfosses en Cour criminelle'' (Sherbrooke, 1939).

8. [Mgr. Jean-Baptiste de la Croix Chevrières de] Saint-Vallier, *Rituel du diocèse de Québec par l'ordre de Monseigneur de Saint-Valier, évêque de Québec* (Paris: Simon Langlois, 1703).

9. Luc Lacourcière, manuscript collection at the Archives de Folklore, nos. 190 to 193, collected at Saint-Hilarion, Charlevoix County, in September, 1946.

10. Nicolas Joseph Neris, "Recueil de remèdes, pour garentir les chevaux, des maladies et accidents, qui peuvent leurs survenir, augmente de plusieurs remèdes, pour le corps humain, fait par moy, Nicolas Joseph Neris, Maître maréchal a paris; y demeurant..." (Paris, 1780).

11. More than thirty lists of remedies, well localized and dated, have been published. Among those which have appeared in publications readily accessible, I would mention by way of example the following: E.-A. Massicrotte, "Les remèdes d'autrefois," *Journal of American Folklore*, 32(1919), 176-78; Horace Miner, *St. Denis, A French-Canadian Parish* (Chicago: University of Chicago Press, 1939), pp. 256-59; Soeur Marie-Ursule, *Civilisation traditionnelle des Lavalois (Les Archives de Folklore*, 5-6 [Quebec: Presses de l'Université Laval, 1951]), pp. 170-84; Carmen Roy, *Littérature orale en Gaspésie*, Musée National du Canada, Bulletin no. 134 (Ottawa, 1955), pp. 61-88; Anselme Chiasson, *Chéticamp* (Moncton, N.B., 1961), pp. 179-88; Catherine Jolicoeur, "Traditional Use of Herbs in Quebec," *The Potomac Herb Journal*, 7(Winter, 1971), 3-5.

12. Helen Creighton, *Bluenose Magic* (Toronto: Ryerson Press, 1968).

13. J. Frederick Doering, "Pennsylvania-German Folk Medicine in Waterloo, Ontario," *Journal of American Folklore*, 49(1936), 194-98.

THE MOTIF OF THE EXTERNAL SOUL
IN FRENCH-CANADIAN FOLKTALES

1. All type numbers are based on Antti Aarne and Stith Thompson. *The Types of the Folktale*. Second Revision. (Helsinki, 1961).

2.   Marius Barbeau, "Contes populaires canadiens," *Journal of American Folklore,* 29(1916), 110-111.

3.   Charles-Edmond Rouleau, "Légendes canadiennes," *Le Soleil,* Québec, 1901, pp. 151-64.

4.   Archives de Folklore, collection Luc Lacourcière, recording no. 3395. Told on July 29, 1957, by Mrs. Daniel Poirier of Egmont Bay, Prince county, P.E.I.

5.   Archives de Folklore, collection Jean-Claude Dupont, recording no. 282. *La bûche de bois qui conserve la vie.*

6.   Mary Frere, *Old Deccan Days* (John Murray, 1881), p. 12.

7.   Archives de Folklore, collection Luc Lacourcière, recording no. 783. Recorded in 1949, in Saint-Pascal des Eboulements, Charlevoix county, Québec, from Pierre Pilote.

8.   An analytical, comparative and anthological catalogue of French folktales in North America, *Le catalogue raisonné du conte populaire français en Amérique du Nord,* is presently being prepared at the Archives de Folklore with a grant from the Killam Foundation administered by the Canada Council. We have the great privilege of assisting Professor Luc Lacourcière in this important undertaking.

THE FUNCTION OF THREATS IN NEWFOUNDLAND FOLKLORE

1.   Ranke, F. "Kinderschrek, Popanz." In E. Hoffmann-Krayer and H. Bächtold-Staubli; eds. Handwörterbuch des deutschen Aberglaubens, IV (Berlin & Leipzig, 1931-32), cols. 1368-1369.

2.   Ibid., col. 1370.

3. In Newfoundland the word "stage" applies to the covered wooden structures at the edge of the harbour in which fish is split, gutted, salted and stored in salt bulk.

4. Some of these may also, of course, be dangerous places.

5. Szwed, John F. *Private Cultures and Public Imagery*: Interpersonal Relations in a Newfoundland Peasant Society (St. John's, 1966), p. 80.

6. Memorial University of Newfoundland Folklore and Language Archive.

A PARABLE IN CONTEXT: A SOCIAL INTERACTIONAL ANALYSIS OF STORYTELLING PERFORMANCE

* In the writing of this paper I greatly benefitted from the suggestions of Roger Abrahams, Dan Ben-Amos, Tom Burns, Alan Dundes, Robert Georges, Maxwell Gimblett, Marvin Herzog, Anthony Leeds, Elliott Oring and Ellen Stekert. The first draft of this study was written while on grants from the Canada Council and National Museum of Canada and was delivered at the November 1969 meeting of the American Folklore Society in Atlanta, Georgia.

1. Bronislaw Malinowski, *Myth in Primitive Psychology* (New York, 1926). Reprinted in *Magic, Science and Religion and Other Essays* (New York, 1948), 104.

2. Bronislaw Malinowski, *Coral Gardens and their Magic II* (London, 1935), 73, 45.

3. This general tendency is clearly seen in such major contributions to the study of folk narrative as Melville J. and Frances S. Herskovits, *Dahomean Narrative: A Cross-Cultural Analysis*

(Evanston, 1958); Ruth Benedict, *Zuni Mythology* (= *Columbia University Contributions to Anthropology* XXI) (New York, 1935); Jerome R. Mintz, *Legends of the Hasidim: An Introduction to Hasidic Culture and Oral Tradition in the New World* (Chicago, 1968); Melville Jacobs, comp., and John Greenway, ed., *The Anthropologist Looks at Myth* (= *Publications of the American Folklore Society, Bibliographical and Special Series* 17) (Austin and London, 1966).

4. Mintz, *Legends of the Hasidim*, 3. See pages 4-5 for a description of a typical tale session.

5. Among the Trobrianders, Limba, Bahamians, Hungarians and other European and African groups, the participants in this type of storytelling session are often interested in narration primarily as an act of sociability and in the tales as objects in themselves. And this interest is reflected in the competitive structure of joke swapping sessions where each raconteur may try to top the preceding narrator with a better or funnier anecdote and the participants may make special requests for their favourite tales.

   For detailed descriptions of such tale sessions, see Linda Dégh, *Folktales and Society: Storytelling in a Hungarian Peasant Community*, Emily Schossberger, trans. (Bloomington, 1969), 63-120. Dégh concludes her comprehensive discussion of the specialized type of tale occasion in Europe with a thorough analytical description of one storytelling event in particular. Ruth Finnegan, in *Limba Stories and Storytelling* (Oxford, 1967), 40-46, 64-69, also discusses in detail the tale occasions among the Limba and describes particular performances as cases in point. See also Daniel J. Crowley, *I Could Talk Old-Story Good: Creativity in Bahamian Folklore* (= *California Folklore Studies* 17) (Berkeley and Los Angeles, 1966) and Malinowski, *Myth*.

6. Erving Goffman, "On Facework: An Analysis of Ritual Elements in Social Interaction," *Psychiatry: Journal for the Study of Interpersonal Processes* (18 (1955), 213-31. Reprinted

in Goffman, *Interaction Ritual: Essays on Face to Face Behaviour* (New York, 1967), 5-45.

7.   The transcription of Yiddish words reflects the basic features of the speaker's dialect pronunciation. Dialect forms are placed in square brackets as are translations and glosses. Standard Yiddish forms are italicized. Translations and glosses of terms are based upon Uriel Weinreich's *Modern English-Yiddish Yiddish-English Dictionary* (New York, 1968). The Yiddish transliteration system used here is based on that used by the YIVO Institute for Jewish Research and the Library of Congress.

8.   See Archer Taylor, "A Classification of Formula Tales," *Journal of American Folklore* 46 (1933), 77-78.

9.   D. P. Rotunda, *Motif-Index of the Italian Novella in Prose* (Bloomington, 1942).

10. Haim Schwarzbaum provides detailed annotations for this tale in *Studies in Jewish and World Folklore* (Berlin, 1968), 326-28.

11. Analogues to this parable as a framed tale appear in Naftoli Gross, *Ma'aselech un Mesholim* (New York, 1955), 349; and in S. Y. Zevin, *Sippure Hassidim* I (Tel Aviv, 1956-57), 65-66.

12. Goffman, "On Facework," 35.

13. Peter Seitel, in "Proverbs: A Social Use of Metaphor," *Genre* 2:2 (1969), 143-61, distinguishes the occasion on which a proverb is used, the imaginary situation presented in the proverb, and the social situation to which the proverb refers. In the case of the parable analyzed in this paper, the occasion on which the parable is used is part of the situation to which the parable refers.

14. This story is AT 2040, "The Climax of Horrors," and this

particular version is taken from Y. M. Sokolov, *Russian Folklore* (Hatboro, Pennsylvania, 1966), 474.

15. Goffman, "On Facework."

16. Erving Goffman, in *Encounters: Two Studies in the Sociology of Interaction* (Indianapolis, 1963), 60 says: "When an alteration in official rules of irrelevance occurs, we can, perhaps, say, as Freud argued, that the 'energy' previously employed to 'bind' the suppressions can be set 'free.' Further, the new rules of irrelevance — the new frame of reference [the parable] — often provide a context in which it is especially difficult to maintain the previous suppressions. And so the participants flood out in regard to a definition of the situation that has just been displaced, it being safe to offend something no longer credited as reality."

    The laughter response, like open anger and crying, is a form of "flooding out" whereby individuals can no longer "sustain an appropriate expressive role in the current reaction" (*Ibid.*, 55). As soon as they start laughing, the actors cannot remain indignant or annoyed. "Flooding out" is one way of breaking the frame and this is precisely the strategy which Dvora adopts, referring to it as "breaking the ice" and "easing the tension with a little humour."

17. Theodore M. Mills, *The Sociology of Small Groups* (Englewood Cliffs, 1967), 74.

18. The narrator, Jack (Yankl) Starkman, was born in 1914 in Klimontow, Poland, and came to Canada in 1935. Mr. Heller told Jack this story in 1935. I recorded this text the evening of September 22, 1969, during an informal interview in my kitchen in Downsview, Ontario.

19. This proverb is from the Mishna, Avoth 4:2.

20. This saying appears in the Talmud, Berakoth 53b, "dirty hands

unfit one for grace." See p. 326 of the 1948 Soncino edition of the Babylonian Talmud. Technically, Torah is the Pentateuch. More broadly it is Jewish law and learning. The narrator is simply saying that his statements have an authoritative basis.

21. See Joshua A. Fishman, ed., *Readings in the Sociology of Language* (The Hague, 1968); A. Kimball Romney and Roy Goodwin D'Andrade, eds., *Transcultural Studies in Cognition* (= *American Anthropologist* 66:3) (1964); Dell Hymes, ed., *Language in Culture and Society: A Reader in Linguistics and Anthropology* (New York, Evanston and London, 1964); John J. Gumperz and Dell Hymes, eds., *The Ethnography of Communication* (= *American Anthropologist* 66:6) (1964); T. Gladwin and William C. Sturtevant, eds., *Anthropology and Human Behaviour* (Washington, 1962).

THE ETHNIC JOKE IN CANADA TODAY

1. An earlier version of this paper was delivered at the Annual Meeting of the American Folklore Society in Los Angeles, California, on November 12, 1970.

2. A brief survey of some relevant writings is found in Walter P. Zenner, "Joking and Ethnic Stereotyping," *Anthropological Quarterly*, 43 (1970), 93-113.

3. In contrast with other forms of oral lore in our contemporary, mainstream milieu, the ethnic joke functions not in accordance with social allocation but is at the service of all the layers of our social hierarchy.

4. "Polish Jokes Violation of Rights Act," *Ottawa Journal*, 9 April 1970, p. 4.

5. In this connection, see William M. Clements, *The Types of The*

Polack Joke, Folklore Forum, Bibliographic and Special Series No. 3 (Bloomington, Indiana, November 1969).

6. In this regard, it is interesting to note the apparent need for Julian Krzyzanowski to justify his attention to the "foreign origin" of Polish materials in his article on "Polish Antimasovian Anecdotes of Foreign Origins," *Fabula*, 8 (1966), 245: ". . .if it deprives them of this pretended 'Polishness,' it places them against the proper background of European folklore in the trails of our great cultural traditions. The gain achieved by this procedure is much greater than the apparent loss to the history of our culture."

7. In his discussion of "American Numskull Tales: The Polack Joke," *Western Folklore*, 26 (1967), 183-86, Roger L. Welsch divides his materials into two clear categories on p. 185. Very few of his examples belong outside the usual question-and-answer format which marks the centre of attention in the present paper.

8. It is interesting to note that most ethnic jokes tend to be circulated, delivered and noted down under circumstances that are sudden, unexpected, completely impromptu and outside the usual round of formal, interview sessions with informants.

9. See Donald C. Simmons on "universal donors" and the easy application of certain ethnic jokes to various groups in his "Anti-Italian-American Riddles in New England," *Journal of American Folklore*, 79 (1966), 476. Also, see William M. Clements, pp. 1, 8.

10. Q: Why are there only two pallbearers at a Polish funeral?
    A: Because garbage cans only have two handles.

11. For their help in assembling suitable, comparative materials for this paper, I wish to thank Paul Carpentier, Magnus E. Mullarky and Lucien Ouellet, all of the Canadian Centre for

Folk Culture Studies, National Museum of Man, Ottawa, Canada.

12. The joke underlines the popularity of pink plastic flamingoes as lawn ornaments in French Canada.

13. The joke refers to the popularity of family excursions into the bush to pick mushrooms, a favourite pastime of Ukrainians in Western Canada.

14. Like the Poles in the United States, so too the Newfie in Canada appears to have inherited much of the material which once characterized the moron joke cycles on this continent.

15. The implication here is that all Italians in Canada are supposedly associated with the construction industry.

16. Icelandic communities in the Province of Manitoba have long been associated with the fishing industry on Lake Winnipeg and adjacent lakes and waterways.

17. The expression appears in the title of a popular joke book, *It's Fun to Be a Polak*! (Glendale, California, 1965).

18. Simmons suggests that "the apparent recentness of these riddles is probably explicable by the rise in status of the third and fourth generation Italian-American, who is beginning to compete for, and to appear in, occupations formerly reserved for the traditional Yankee and, later, for the Irish-American. This competition is resented by the older groups. . .who give voice to their aggressive resentment by telling these riddles. . ." (p. 476).

19. Marshall McLuhan, *Understanding Media: The Extensions of Man* (New York, 1964), p. 323.

20. The term "dialect" was first introduced into the literature on the subject by Richard M. Dorson in "Dialect Stories of the Upper Peninsula: A New Form of American Folklore," *Journal*

of American Folklore, 61 (1948), 113-50.

21.   In this connection, it is interesting to note the observations of Americo Paredes on p. 114 of his article on "Folk Medicine and the Intercultural Jest," *Spanish-Speaking People in the United States, Proceedings of the 1968 Annual Spring Meeting of the American Ethnological Society*, ed. June Helm (University of Washington Press, 1968): "The jests help resolve these conflicts brought about by acculturation, involving not only a change from rural to urban values but from a basically Mexican culture to the generalized, English-speaking culture of the majority."

22.   These kinds of processes are implied by Americo Paredes when he notes that "there is a trend in the United States away from the uncompromising 100 per cent Americanism of earlier time. . . There is a tendency to admire the values of minorities and to recognize their role in the enrichment of the majority culture, especially in the contributions made to it from the folklore of diverse ethnic groups." ("Tributaries to the Mainstream: The Ethnic Groups," *Our Living Traditions: An Introduction to American Folklore*, ed. Tristram P. Coffin [New York, 1968], p. 71).

23.   The recent increase in the number of ethnic and/or regional folk festivals on this continent are, to a large extent, examples of such efforts at reformulation and rehabilitation.

LA VIE DE L'HABITANT: QUEBEC'S FOLK CULTURE OF SURVIVAL

1.   Northrop Frye, *The Bush Garden* (Toronto: House of Anansi, 1971), p. 133.

2.   Quoted in H. Gordon Green, *A Heritage of Canadian Handi-*

crafts (Montreal: McClelland and Stewart, 1967), p. 111. Trans. P. van Lent.

3. Quoted in Cyril Simard, *Artisanat Québécois* (Montreal: Les Editions de l'homme, 1975), p. 59. Trans. P. van Lent.

4. George Woodcock, *The Canadians* (Cambridge, Mass.: Harvard University Press, 1979), p. 119.

5. Ibid., p. 123.

6. In recent years many attractive and competent collections of French-Canadian folklore have been published. Two collections edited by Jean-Claude Dupont, *Le Légendaire de la Beauce* (Ottawa: Les Editions Leméac, 1978) and *Contes de bûcherons* (Montreal: Les Editions Quinze, 1976) are worthy of mention. Robert Lalonde's *Les Contes du portage* (Ottawa: Les Editions Leméac, 1973) presents both Quebec and Ojibwa folktales and several which show a blending of the two traditions. Luc Lacourcière has published the text and the cassette recordings of three popular folktales which he collected recently: *Trois Contes Populaires* (Montreal: Le Sono, 1975). Edith Fowke has translated a representative group of folk stories in her *Folktales of French Canada* (Toronto: NC Press, Ltd., 1979).

7. The reference is to the book by Pierre Vallières by the same title.

8. Alain Duhamel, *Woodenfolk* (St.-Jean-Port-Joli, Quebec: Editions Port-Joly, 1975), pp. 615.

9. Duhamel, *Woodenfolk*, pp. 14-15.

10. Quoted in Edith Fowke, *Folklore of Canada* (Toronto: McClelland and Stewart, 1976), p. 45, which is also the source of the information in the entire paragraph.

11. By personal transmission.

12. Henry Glassie, "Folk Art," in *Folklore and Folklife*, ed. Richard M. Dorson (Chicago: University of Chicago Press, 1972), p. 278.

13. For this term and throughout this part of the article, I am indebted to Nelson Graburn, *Ethnic and Tourist Arts* (Berkeley: University of California Press, 1976).

14. Graburn, *Ethnic and Tourist Arts*, p. 13.

15. Ibid., p. 5.

THE ETHNICITY FACTOR IN ANGLO-CANADIAN FOLKLORISTICS

1. Pierre E. Trudeau, as quoted by Hartwell Bowsfield on the title page of *Louis Riel: the rebel and the hero* (Toronto: Oxford University Press, 1971).

2. Unlike "history" or "English," the term folklore does not generally apply to the discipline of study as well as the materials studied. While "folkloristics" is not a totally acceptable term, it is widely used along with "Folklore Studies" to distinguish the materials, i.e., folklore, from the study, i.e., folkloristics.

3. This tendency was discussed in my paper "Folklore Scholarship and the Sociopolitical Milieu in Canada," *Journal of the Folklore Institute*, 10 (1973), 98-108.

4. George Grant notes this change in cultural orientation in his work, *Lament for a Nation* (Toronto: McClelland & Stewart, 1971).

5. This pattern was such as to encourage the formation of decidedly regional cultures, frequently ethnically oriented. See my

paper, *op. cit.*, for further discussion.

6. As discussed by Northrop Frye with reference to Canadian literature in "Conclusion" to Carl F. Klinck ed., *Literary History of Canada* (Toronto: University of Toronto Press, 1965), this mentality is one which cordons off areas of civilization surrounded by wilderness and focuses inwards on those areas. Many scholars maintain that such a garrison mentality is deeply ingrained in the Canadian psyche.

7. Many Canadian scholars have argued that Canadians are faced with a severe identity problem in that not only do they not know who they are but also they do not know where they are in the sense of not knowing this land. Margaret Atwood deals with this problem in her thematic study of Canadian literature, *Survival* (Toronto: Anansi, 1972).

8. Victoria Haywood, *Romantic Canada* (Toronto: Macmillan, 1922).

9. As indicated rather clearly by the title of a collection of Eastern-Canadian narratives by Eliza B. Chase, *In Quest of the Quaint* (Ferris, 1902).

10. This has resulted from feelings of superiority, leading to a common failure to recognize the Native Peoples' traditional lifestyle as a viable way of life, and to pressure from the general populace for the Native Peoples to assimilate.

11. See Norah Story ed., *The Oxford Companion to Canadian History and Literature* (Toronto: Oxford University Press, 1967), p. 377, for commentary on this misunderstanding.

12. I am indebted to my former colleague Dennis Martel for pointing out this dichotomy of attitudes. The same sort of mixture of attitudes exists today relative to non-Native, non-French, non-British minorities. Removal from such groups tends to idealism, while proximity often results in antagonism.

13. It has preserved their material cultural heritage which might otherwise have decayed and vanished. In recent years, some Native Peoples have been attempting (with some success) to repatriate some of their art treasures.

14. For discussion of the activities of this organization, see Morris Zaslow, *Reading the Rocks: The Story of the Geological Survey of Canada, 1842-1972* (Toronto: Macmillan of Canada in Association with the Department of Energy, Mines and Resources and Information Canada, 1975).

15. For example, Franz Boas' work among the Eskimo and the Pacific North Coast Indians.

16. Examples include Leonard Bloomfield, Paul Radin and Frank Speck.

17. An example of cultural defensive mechanisms as discussed by Anthony F. C. Wallace in *Culture and Personality*, 2nd ed. (New York: Random House, 1961), Chapter 5, "The Psychology of Cultural Change," pp. 165-206.

18. For example, George Clutesi, *Son of Raven Son of Deer* (Sidney, B.C.: Gray's Publishing, 1967); Indian Children of British Columbia, *Tales from the Longhouse* (Sidney, B.C.: Gray's Publishing, 1973); and Kenneth Harris, *Visitors Who Never Left* (Vancouver: University of B.C. Press, 1975).

19. For an extensive discussion of this characteristic of Canadian folklore activities, see my book *Many Voices: A Study of Canadian Folklore Activities and Their Role in Canadian Culture* (Ottawa: National Museum, CCFCS Mercury Series 26, 1979), Chapter 1, "The Pattern of Folklore Activities in Canada," pp. 21-87.

20. Between 1900 and 1914, nearly three million immigrants came to Canada, many of whom were of non-Anglo, non-French heritage.

21. For further discussion of these ideas and their influence on Canadian folkloristics, see my book, *op. cit.,* Chapter 4, "International Relations and National Distinctions," pp. 157-204.

22. It is noteworthy that this company should sponsor such events designed to unite Canada. The railway was originally built to accomplish the same purpose, and has, ever since, symbolized the union of the western provinces with the rest of Canada.

23. "Developing Canada's Immigrant Culture," *Edmonton Journal*, 15 December 1928.

24. A particularly noteworthy example of such events is "Caravan," a very popular and successful multicultural festival held annually in Toronto since 1969, and proudly cited as indicative of that city's cosmopolitan, tolerant nature.

25. Announced on October 8, 1971.

26. Most academically trained folklorists have taken their degrees in the United States or abroad since there are only two Folklore degree programs in Canada, at Université Laval and at Memorial University of Newfoundland. Attitudes of such academic folklorists are decidedly more serious than those of most amateurs or self-trained scholars.

27. Resulting in, among other things, one work used in Saskatchewan schools, *Great Chiefs and Mighty Hunters of the Western Plains* (Regina: School Aids and Text Book Publishing Co., n.d.).

28. His published work includes the important volume *Crowfoot, Chief of the Blackfoot* (Edmonton: Hurtig, 1972).

29. Undertaken first for his doctoral dissertation *Our People's Way: A Study in Doukhobor Hymnody and Folklife* (University of Pennsylvania, 1972).

Sources

I.   Early Accounts

Life Among the Haida
W. H. Collison, *In the Wake of the War Canoe* (Toronto: Musson, 1915), pp. 89-94, 101-103.

The Buffalo Hunt I
John Macoun, *Manitoba and The Great North-West* (London: Thomas & Jack, 1883), pp. 342-46.

The Buffalo Hunt II
Paul Kane, *Wanderings of an Artist Among the Indians of North America* (1859, rpt. Toronto: Radisson Society, 1925), pp. 56-60.

Notes on the Dialect of the People of Newfoundland
George Patterson, *Journal of American Folklore*, 8(1895), pp. 27-40.

String Figures of the Eskimo
Diamond Jenness, *Report of the Canadian Arctic Expedition, 1913-1918*, Vol. 13, Part B (Ottawa: King's Printer, 1924), pp. 171-83.

II. Personal Experience Accounts

A. *Participants*

Old-Time Customs
John B. Calkin, *Old-Time Customs, Memories and Traditions and Other Essays* (Halifax: MacKinley, 1918), pp. 26-35.

The Old-Order Mennonite Wedding and Highlights of Their Social Life
Allan M. Buehler, *The Pennsylvania German Dialect and the Life of an Old-Order Mennonite* (Cambridge, Ont.: Author, 1977), pp. 162-74.

A Heritage of Songs
Carrie Grover, *A Heritage of Songs* (Bethel, ME: n.p., rpt. Norwood, PA: Norwood, 1973), pp. 1-3.

B. *Collectors*

Ballad Singing in Nova Scotia
W. Roy Mackenzie, *Journal of American Folklore*, 22(1909), pp. 327-31.

Ballads from Devil's Island
Helen Creighton, *Dalhousie Review*, 12(1933), pp. 503-10.

Cruising for Ballads in Nova Scotia
W. M. Doerflinger, *Canadian Geographical Journal*, 16(Feb. 1938), pp. 91-100.

In Search of Inuit Music
Laura Boulton, *The Music Hunter* (New York: Doubleday, 1969), pp. 371-80.

D'Sonoqua
Emily Carr, *Klee Wyck* (Toronto: Clarke, Irwin, 1941), pp. 32-42.

III.   Surveys

The Cut-Off Head Frozen On: Some International Versions
of a Tall Tale
Herbert Halpert, *Canadian Folklore canadien*, 1(1979), pp. 13-23.

The Man Who Plucked the Gorbey: A Maine Woods Legend
Edward D. Ives, *Journal of American Folklore*, 74(1961), pp. 1-8.

In Defence of Paul Bunyan
Edith Fowke, *New York Folklore*, 5(Summer 1979), pp. 43-52.

Dancing in Cape Breton Island, Nova Scotia
Frank Rhodes, Appendix in *Traditional Dancing in Scotland* by J. R.
Fleet and T. M. Fleet (London: Routledge & Kegan Paul, 1961),
pp. 265-85.

Fiddle Music as a Manifestation of Canadian Regionalism
George A. Proctor, a paper delivered at the conference, "Regionalism
and National Identity," sponsored by the Australian and New
Zealand Association for Canadian Studies, University of Canterbury,
Christchurch, New Zealand, May 17-19, 1984. Dr. Proctor attended
the conference on an international travel grant from the Social
Sciences and Humanities Research Council of Canada.

A Survey of Folk Medicine in French Canada from Early Times
to the Present
Luc Lacourcière, in *American Folk Medicine*, ed. Wayland D. Hand
(Berkeley and Los Angeles: University of California Press, 1976),
pp. 203-14.

IV. Analyses

Buddhist Dirges on the North Pacific Coast
Marius Barbeau, *Journal of the International Folk Music Council*, 14(1962), pp. 16-21.

The Motif of the External Soul in French-Canadian Folktales
Margaret Low, *Laurentian University Review*, 8(Feb., 1976), 61-68.

The Function of Threats in Newfoundland Folklore
J. D. A. Widdowson, *If You Don't Be Good: Verbal Social Control in Newfoundland* (St. John's: Memorial University, 1977), pp. 80-92.

A Parable in Context: A Social Interactional Analysis
of Storytelling Performance
Condensed from Barbara Kirshenblatt-Gimblett, "A Parable in Context" in *Folklore: Performance and Communication*, ed. Kenneth S. Goldstein and Dan Ben-Amos (The Hague: Mouton, 1975), pp. 105-30.

The Ethnic Joke in Canada Today
Robert B. Klymasz, *Keystone Folklore Quarterly*, 15(1970), pp. 167-73.

La Vie de l'Habitant: Quebec's Folk Culture of Survival
Peter van Lent, *New York Folklore*, 7(Winter 1981), pp. 57-65.

The Ethnicity Factor in Anglo-Canadian Folkloristics
Carole Henderson Carpenter, *Canadian Ethnic Studies*, 7:2(1975), pp. 7-18.

Selected References

The following list includes major periodicals, a selection of the most important books on Canadian folklore in English, and works cited or directly relevant to the articles in this collection. The sources for these articles appear in the preceding section and are not repeated here. The many works on Indian and Inuit oral traditions and the wide range of publications on folklife and material culture are not covered. (Those interested in these areas will find listings up to 1979 in Fowke and Carpenter, *A Bibliography of Canadian Folklore in English*.)

Les Archives de folklore, Université de Laval, Québec, 1946.

Barbeau, C. Marius. "Asiatic Survivals in Indian Songs." *Queen's Quarterly*, 47(1940), 67-76.

Barbeau, C. Marius. *Jongleur Songs of Old Quebec*. Toronto: Ryerson, 1962.

Barbeau, Marius, and Edward Sapir. *Folk Songs of French Canada*. New Haven, CN: Yale Univ. Press, 1925.

Boulton, Laura, coll. *The Eskimos of Hudson Bay and Alaska*. Folkways FE 4444, 1954.

Canadian Ethnic Studies, Special Issue: Ethnic Folklore in Canada, 7:2, 1975.

Canadian Folk Music Bulletin, 1981—

Canadian Folk Music Journal, 1973–

Canadian Folklore canadien, 1979–

Carpenter, Carole H. *Many Voices: A Study of Folklore Activities in Canada and Their Role in Canadian Culture*. Ottawa: National Museum, CCFCS Mercury Series 26, 1979.

Cazden, Norman. "Regional and Occupational Orientations of American Traditional Song." *Journal of American Folklore*, 72(1979), 310-44.

Creighton, Helen. *Bluenose Ghosts*. 1957; rpt. Toronto: McGraw-Hill Ryerson, 1976.

Creighton, Helen. *Bluenose Magic*. Toronto: Ryerson, 1968.

Creighton, Helen. *Folklore of Lunenburg County, Nova Scotia*. 1950; rpt. Toronto: McGraw-Hill Ryerson, 1976.

Creighton, Helen. *Folksongs from Southern New Brunswick*. Ottawa: National Museum, 1971.

Creighton, Helen. *A Life in Folklore*. Toronto: McGraw-Hill Ryerson, 1975.

Creighton, Helen. *Maritime Folk Songs*. Toronto: Ryerson, 1962; rpt. St. John's: Breakwater, 1979.

Creighton, Helen. *Songs and Ballads from Nova Scotia*. Toronto: Dent, 1932; rpt. New York: Dover, 1966.

Creighton, Helen, and Doreen H. Senior. *Traditional Songs from Nova Scotia*. Toronto: Ryerson, 1950.

Culture and Tradition, Memorial University, and Université de Laval, 1976–.

Doerflinger, William M. *Shantymen and Shantyboys: Songs of the Sailor and Lumberman*. 1951; rpt. as *Songs of the Sailor and Lumberman*. New York: Macmillan, 1972.

Ethnomusicology, Canadian Issue, 16:3, Sept. 1972.

Fauset, Arthur Huff. *Folklore from Nova Scotia*. Philadelphia: American Folklore Society, 1931.

Fowke, Edith. *Folklore of Canada*. Toronto: McClelland & Stewart, 1976.

Fowke, Edith. *Folktales of French Canada*. Toronto: NC Press, 1979.

Fowke, Edith. *Lumbering Songs from the Northern Woods*. Austin: Univ. of Texas Press, 1970.

Fowke, Edith. *The Penguin Book of Canadian Folk Songs*. Harmondsworth: Penguin, 1973.

Fowke, Edith. *Sally Go Round the Sun*. Toronto: McClelland & Stewart, 1969.

Fowke, Edith. *Traditional Singers and Songs from Ontario*. Hatboro, PA: Folklore Associates, 1965.

Fowke, Edith, and Carole Henderson Carpenter. *A Bibliography of Canadian Folklore in English*. Toronto: Univ. of Toronto Press, 1981.

Fraser, Mary L. *Folklore of Nova Scotia*. 1931; rpt. Antigonish: Formac, 1975.

From the Heart: Folk Art in Canada. Toronto: McClelland & Stewart in cooperation with the National Museum of Man, 1983.

Goldstein, Kenneth S., ed. *Canadian Folklore Perspectives*. St. John's: Memorial University, 1978.

Goldstein, Kenneth S., and Neil V. Rosenberg. *Folklore Studies in Honour of Herbert Halpert*. St. John's: Memorial University, 1980.

Greenleaf, Elisabeth B., and Grace Y. Mansfield. *Ballads and Sea Songs of Newfoundland*. Cambridge: Harvard Univ. Press, 1922; rpt. Hatboro, PA: Folklore Associates, 1968.

Grysky, Camella. *Cat's Cradle, Owl's Eyes. A Book of String Games*. Toronto: Kids Can Press, 1983.

Halpert, Herbert. *Maritime Sampler*. St. John's: Memorial University, 1982.

Halpert, Herbert. "Tall Tales and Other Yarns from Calgary, Alberta." *California Folklore Quarterly*, 4(1945), 29-49. Rpt. in *Folklore of Canada*. Ed. Edith Fowke. Toronto: McClelland & Stewart, 1976; pp. 171-89.

Halpert, Herbert, and George M. Story, eds. *Christmas Mumming in Newfoundland*. Toronto: Univ. of Toronto Press, 1969.

Hogan, Dorothy, and Homer Hogan. "Canadian Fiddle Culture." *Communique: Canadian Studies*, 3(Aug. 1970), 72-88.

Ives, Edward D. *Joe Scott, The Woodsman-Songmaker*. Urbana: Univ. of Illinois Press, 1979.

Ives, Edward D. *Larry Gorman: The Man Who Made the Songs*. Bloomington: Indiana Univ. Press, 1964.

Ives, Edward D. *Lawrence Doyle: The Farmer Poet of Prince Edward Island*. Orono: Univ. of Maine, 1971.

Jenness, Diamond. *The Indians of Canada*. 1931; rpt. Toronto: Univ. of Toronto Press, 1977.

Journal of American Folklore, vols. 29:1; 30:1; 31:1 and 2; 32:1; 33:3 and 4; 36:3; 39:4; 44:3; 53:2; 63:2; and 67:2.

Karpeles, Maud. *Folk Songs from Newfoundland*. London: Faber & Faber, 1971.

Klymasz, Robert B. *Folk Narrative among Canadians in Western Canada*. Ottawa: National Museum, CCFCS Mercury Series 4, 1973.

Klymasz, Robert B. *The Ukrainian Immigrant Folksong Cycle*. Ottawa: National Museum, Bulletin 234, 1970.

Laurentian Review, Special Issue: Folklore and Oral Tradition in Canada, 8:2(1976).

Leach, MacEdward. *Folk Ballads and Songs of the Lower Labrador Coast*. Ottawa: National Museum, Bulletin 201, 1965.

Mackenzie, W. Roy. *Ballads and Sea Songs from Nova Scotia*. Cambridge: Harvard Univ. Press, 1928; rpt. Hatboro, PA: Folklore Associates, 1963.

Mackenzie, W. Roy. *The Quest of the Ballad*. Princeton: Princeton Univ. Press, 1919.

Manny, Louise, and J. Reginald Wilson. *Songs of Miramichi*. Fredericton: Brunswick, 1968.

Mercer, Paul. *Newfoundland Songs and Ballads in Print 1841-1974. A title and first-line index*. St. John's: Memorial University, 1979.

Northeast Folklore, Orono: Univ. of Maine, 1958—

Peacock, Kenneth. *Songs of the Newfoundland Outports*. 3 vols. Ottawa: National Museum, Bulletin No. 197, 1965.

Proctor, George. "Old-Time Fiddling in Ontario." Ottawa: *National Museum Bulletin* 190, 1960, pp. 193-208.

Rahn, Jay. "Canadian Folk Music Holdings at Columbia University," *Canadian Folk Music Journal*, 5(1977), 46-69.

Rosenberg, Neil V., ed. *Folklore and Oral History*. St. John's: Memorial University, 1978.

Taft, Michael. *A Regional Discography of Newfoundland and Labrador 1904-1972*. St. John's: Memorial University, 1975.

Thomas, Philip J. *Songs of the Pacific Northwest*. North Vancouver: Hancock, 1979.

Wells, Evelyn. *The Ballad Tree*. New York: Ronald, 1950.

Wintemberg, W. J. *Folk-Lore of Waterloo County, Ontario*. Ottawa: National Museum, Bulletin 116, 1950.

Index

400